D1414956

אֲנִי מַאֲמִין

Beyond Never Again: How the Holocaust Speaks to Us Today

JEWISH LEARNING INSTITUTE

Printed in the United States
© Published and Copyrighted 2010 by
The Rohr Jewish Learning Institute
822 Eastern Parkway, Brooklyn, NY 11213

(888) YOUR-JLI/718-221-6900
www.myJLI.com

The **Rohr Jewish Learning Institute**
gratefully acknowledges
the pioneering support of

George and Pamela Rohr

SINCE ITS INCEPTION
the **Rohr JLI** has been
a beneficiary of the vision, generosity,
care and concern
of the **Rohr family**

In the merit of
the tens of thousands of hours of Torah study
by **JLI** students worldwide,
may they be blessed with health,
Yiddishe Nachas from all their loved ones,
and extraordinary success
in all their endeavors ఎ

אלה אזכרה ונפשי עלי אשפכה

These I remember;
Within, my heart pours with tears.
YOM KIPPUR MUSAF PRAYER

לזכרון הקדושים

ר׳ יקותיאל יהודה ב״ר צבי הירש הי״ד
מרת לאה בת ר׳ דובער הי״ד

תנצב״ה

In loving memory of our grandparents
who perished at Auschwitz.

May the study of Torah be an everlasting tribute to their names.

Dedicated by **George Rohr**

Table of Contents

Prologue

Remember the days of old, understand the years of generation after generation.

(Deuteronomy 32:7)

A key value of Judaism is to remember the past and learn its lessons. A central requirement of the Passover seder, the event that celebrates our freedom and birth as a people, is to recount the past. This past includes the Jewish people's years of slavery and suffering as well as its glorious redemption. History provides us with perspective, a way to live more appropriately in the present and to plan a better future. But the price of neglecting to remember is steep. In the words of George Santayana, "Those who cannot remember the past are condemned to repeat it."

The Holocaust is the singular event of the last century that has most marked the face of contemporary Jewish life. It devastated our people, destroying the structure of the European Jewish community. As world Jewry struggled to rebuild from the rubble, it forced each Jew to confront his or her deepest beliefs about what it means to continue to live as a Jew.

Those who reflect on the Holocaust often summarize their response with the phrase "never again." Never again may genocide be permitted to occur while the world turns its head away from the travesty occurring in its presence.

As we commemorate the sixty-fifth anniversary of the liberation of the concentration camps, we strive to remember this universal message, and also to go even further. What does the Holocaust continue to teach us about G-d and humanity? What message does the Holocaust convey about the search for meaning and values? How will our memories of the past help to chart a life course for us and for future generations?

Lesson 1

Wrestling with G-d
Can We Understand Human Suffering?

Introduction

Our world is not perfect. There is pain and suffering, death and disease. The Jewish nation, throughout its long and bitter exile, has been subjected to the worst trials and tribulations that have ever faced any nation or people. And within our own age, the Jewish nation has been subjected to the horrors of the Holocaust. Does Jewish tradition have insights for us concerning the intense suffering that we undergo as individuals and as a nation?

In the first lesson, we will explore some of the ideas found in Jewish thought that deal with the question of an omnipotent, omniscient, benevolent G-d and the suffering that surrounds us.

Who is Bothered by Suffering?
The Outcry

TEXT 1

אמר לפניו: רבונו של עולם
מפני מה יש צדיק וטוב לו ויש צדיק ורע לו
יש רשע וטוב לו ויש רשע ורע לו

תלמוד בבלי ברכות ז,א

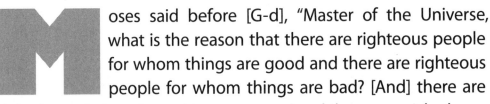

oses said before [G-d], "Master of the Universe, what is the reason that there are righteous people for whom things are good and there are righteous people for whom things are bad? [And] there are wicked people for whom things are good and there are wicked people for whom things are bad?"

TALMUD, BERACHOT 7A

TEXT 2

עַד אָנָה ה' שִׁוַּעְתִּי וְלֹא תִשְׁמָע אֶזְעַק אֵלֶיךָ חָמָס וְלֹא תוֹשִׁיעַ

לָמָּה תַרְאֵנִי אָוֶן וְעָמָל תַּבִּיט וְשֹׁד וְחָמָס לְנֶגְדִּי וַיְהִי רִיב וּמָדוֹן יִשָּׂא

עַל כֵּן תָּפוּג תּוֹרָה וְלֹא יֵצֵא לָנֶצַח מִשְׁפָּט

כִּי רָשָׁע מַכְתִּיר אֶת הַצַּדִּיק עַל כֵּן יֵצֵא מִשְׁפָּט מְעֻקָּל . . .

לָמָּה תַבִּיט בּוֹגְדִים תַּחֲרִישׁ בְּבַלַּע רָשָׁע צַדִּיק מִמֶּנּוּ

חבקוק א,ב–יג

Lord! How long will I cry and You will not hear! I cry out
to You of violence, and You will not save! Why do You
show me iniquity and look upon mischief; and plunder
and violence are before me; and the one who bears
quarrel and strife endures.

Therefore Torah is slackened, and justice does not go out forever, for
a wicked man surrounds the righteous; therefore, justice emerges
perverted. . . .

Why should You gaze upon traitors, be silent when a wicked man
swallows up one more righteous than he?

Habakkuk 1:2–13

Who Asks This Question?

Text 3

אף שכל הנזכר לעיל כתוב בתור מענה על מכתבך

אבל העיקר הוא

לא רק שאני לא מאמין לזה שאת כותבת

שאינך מאמינה באלקים חס ושלום

אלא ברור לי שגם את לא מאמינה לזה

וההוכחה היא, שמדי ראותך העדר הצדק והיושר בסביבתך

או מדי העלותך על זכרונך ענין השואה בעקבות היטלר ימח שמו

כמו שמזכירה את במכתבך

הרי זה מבלבל מנוחתך

ואילו היתה המציאות שאין מנהיג ומתכנן

מהו הפלא כשיש מאורעות היפך הצדק והיושר

והגדול מחברו חיים בולעו וכו'?

והשאלה היא לא רק במממדים גדולים כמו השואה הנזכר לעיל

כי גם במסלול החיים הנקראים "חיים אפורים" של כל יום ויום

רואים במוחש שכל תופעה שהיא היפך הצדק והיושר

מבלבלת מנוחת הנפש

ומביטים על זה כמאורע שלא צריך הי' להיות כן

והרי בודאי שחומר הדומם ואפילו בעלי חיים שבסביבתנו

אין הם מצווים על הצדק והיושר

ובודאי שחוסר מנוחה הנגרמת על ידי תופעות אלו

מקושר במשהו שהוא למעלה מהדומם צומח וחי

ואפילו למעלה מן האדם

ו"משהו" זה נמצא בלב כל אדם פנימה

ומזה הודאות בעיני כל אחד ואחת שהצדק צריך להיות השולט בעולם

וההנהגה בסביבתו צריכה להיות דווקא על פי יושר

שלכן אם נראה לעין משהו שלא בסדר
מחפש הוא בכל המרץ והדרכים
למצוא את הגורם שגרם ההיפך ממה שצריך הי' להיות
לקוטי שיחות לג 254

have written all of the above in reply to your letter. In truth, however, not only do I not believe you when you say that you do not believe in G-d (G-d forbid), but it is also clear to me that you do not believe so either.

My proof of this is that on every occasion that you witness injustice in your surroundings or when you think of the Holocaust perpetrated by Hitler (may his name be blotted out), as you mention in your letter, you are outraged. But if it were the case that the world has no Ruler and Planner, why should it surprise you that there transpire unjust things and that whoever is bigger and more powerful than his fellow swallows him alive?

This applies not only to events on the scale of the Holocaust, but also to the routine flow of our daily lives, in which every time we perceive something that is wrong and unjust, this disturbs our tranquility, since we are convinced that things should not be this way. [But why shouldn't they be?] The physical substance of the universe is not supposed to be moral and neither are the animals. Obviously, our outrage over the injustice we see derives from the conviction in something higher than all physical beings, including human beings. This conviction is embedded in the heart of every human being, which is why all concur [that there is right and wrong and] that the world ought to conform to what is right. Thus, when we witness a wrong, we immediately seek an explanation: Why is it so? What has caused something to be other than what it ought to be?

RABBI MENACHEM MENDEL SCHNEERSON, LIKUTEI SICHOT, VOL. 33 P. 254

Rabbi Menachem Mendel Schneerson (1902–1994). Known as "the Lubavitcher Rebbe," or simply as "the Rebbe." Born in southern Ukraine. Rabbi Schneerson escaped from the Nazis, and arrived in the U.S. in June 1941. The towering Jewish leader of the twentieth century, the Rebbe inspired and guided the revival of traditional Judaism after the European devastation, and often emphasized that the performance of just one additional good deed could usher in the era of Mashiach.

Why Do Bad Things Happen to Good People?

TEXT 4

n its classical formulation, the problem of evil is a problem of logical consistency. The opponent of theism alleges that a triad of properties traditionally held to belong to God's nature—omniscience, omnipotence, and omnibenevolence—are not jointly consistent with the existence of evil in the world.

HUGH J. McCANN, "DIVINE PROVIDENCE," THE STANFORD ENCYCLOPEDIA OF PHILOSOPHY (SPRING 2009 EDITION), EDWARD N. ZALTA (ED.)

Table 1.1
Examining the Three Foundations

Nature of deity	Omnipotent, Benevolent, but not Omniscient	Omniscient, Benevolent, but not Omnipotent	Omniscient Omnipotent, but not Benevolent
Do children suffer?			
Does prayer work?			
Is this a "good" world?			
Does this resolve the contradiction between G-d and suffering?			

How to View
the Suffering of Others

TEXT 5

וַה' אָמָר הַמֲכַסֶּה אֲנִי מֵאַבְרָהָם אֲשֶׁר אֲנִי עֹשֶׂה

וְאַבְרָהָם הָיוֹ יִהְיֶה לְגוֹי גָּדוֹל וְעָצוּם וְנִבְרְכוּ בוֹ כֹּל גּוֹיֵי הָאָרֶץ

כִּי יְדַעְתִּיו לְמַעַן אֲשֶׁר יְצַוֶּה אֶת בָּנָיו וְאֶת בֵּיתוֹ אַחֲרָיו

וְשָׁמְרוּ דֶּרֶךְ ה' לַעֲשׂוֹת צְדָקָה וּמִשְׁפָּט

לְמַעַן הָבִיא ה' עַל אַבְרָהָם אֶת אֲשֶׁר דִּבֶּר עָלָיו

וַיֹּאמֶר ה' זַעֲקַת סְדֹם וַעֲמֹרָה כִּי רָבָּה וְחַטָּאתָם כִּי כָבְדָה מְאֹד

אֵרֲדָה נָּא וְאֶרְאֶה הַכְּצַעֲקָתָהּ הַבָּאָה אֵלַי עָשׂוּ כָּלָה וְאִם לֹא אֵדָעָה

וַיִּפְנוּ מִשָּׁם הָאֲנָשִׁים וַיֵּלְכוּ סְדֹמָה וְאַבְרָהָם עוֹדֶנּוּ עֹמֵד לִפְנֵי ה'

וַיִּגַּשׁ אַבְרָהָם וַיֹּאמַר הַאַף תִּסְפֶּה צַדִּיק עִם רָשָׁע

אוּלַי יֵשׁ חֲמִשִּׁים צַדִּיקִם בְּתוֹךְ הָעִיר

הַאַף תִּסְפֶּה וְלֹא תִשָּׂא לַמָּקוֹם לְמַעַן חֲמִשִּׁים הַצַּדִּיקִם אֲשֶׁר בְּקִרְבָּה

חָלִלָה לְּךָ מֵעֲשֹׂת כַּדָּבָר הַזֶּה לְהָמִית צַדִּיק עִם רָשָׁע וְהָיָה כַצַּדִּיק כָּרָשָׁע

חָלִלָה לָּךְ הֲשֹׁפֵט כָּל הָאָרֶץ לֹא יַעֲשֶׂה מִשְׁפָּט

וַיֹּאמֶר ה' אִם אֶמְצָא בִסְדֹם חֲמִשִּׁים צַדִּיקִם בְּתוֹךְ הָעִיר

וְנָשָׂאתִי לְכָל הַמָּקוֹם בַּעֲבוּרָם

בראשית יח,יז–כו

God said, "Shall I hide from Abraham what I am going to do? Abraham is about to become a great and mighty nation, and through him all the nations of the world will be blessed. I have given him special attention so that he will command his children and his household after him, and they will keep God's way, doing charity and justice. God will then bring about for Abraham everything He promised."

God [then] said, "The outcry against Sodom is so great, and their sin is so very grave. I will descend and see. Have they done everything implied by the outcry that is coming before Me? If not, I will know."

The men turned from where they were, and headed toward Sodom. Abraham was still standing before God.

He came forward and said, "Will You actually wipe out the innocent together with the guilty? Suppose there are fifty innocent people in the city. Would You still destroy it, and not spare the place for the sake of the fifty good people inside it? It would be sacrilege even to ascribe such an act to You—to kill the innocent with the guilty, letting the righteous and the wicked fare alike. It would be sacrilege to ascribe this to You! Shall the whole world's Judge not act justly?"

God said, "If I find fifty innocent people in Sodom, I will spare the entire area for their sake."

BEREISHIT/GENESIS 18:17–26

Text 6

וַיְדַבֵּר ה' אֶל מֹשֶׁה לֶךְ רֵד כִּי שִׁחֵת עַמְּךָ אֲשֶׁר הֶעֱלֵיתָ מֵאֶרֶץ מִצְרָיִם

סָרוּ מַהֵר מִן הַדֶּרֶךְ אֲשֶׁר צִוִּיתִם עָשׂוּ לָהֶם עֵגֶל מַסֵּכָה

וַיִּשְׁתַּחֲווּ לוֹ וַיִּזְבְּחוּ לוֹ

וַיֹּאמְרוּ אֵלֶּה אֱלֹהֶיךָ יִשְׂרָאֵל אֲשֶׁר הֶעֱלוּךָ מֵאֶרֶץ מִצְרָיִם

וַיֹּאמֶר ה' אֶל מֹשֶׁה רָאִיתִי אֶת הָעָם הַזֶּה וְהִנֵּה עַם קְשֵׁה עֹרֶף הוּא

וְעַתָּה הַנִּיחָה לִּי וְיִחַר אַפִּי בָהֶם וַאֲכַלֵּם וְאֶעֱשֶׂה אוֹתְךָ לְגוֹי גָּדוֹל

וַיְחַל מֹשֶׁה אֶת פְּנֵי ה' אֱלֹקָיו וַיֹּאמֶר לָמָה ה' יֶחֱרֶה אַפְּךָ בְּעַמֶּךָ

אֲשֶׁר הוֹצֵאתָ מֵאֶרֶץ מִצְרַיִם בְּכֹחַ גָּדוֹל וּבְיָד חֲזָקָה

לָמָּה יֹאמְרוּ מִצְרַיִם לֵאמֹר

בְּרָעָה הוֹצִיאָם לַהֲרֹג אֹתָם בֶּהָרִים

וּלְכַלֹּתָם מֵעַל פְּנֵי הָאֲדָמָה

שׁוּב מֵחֲרוֹן אַפֶּךָ וְהִנָּחֵם עַל הָרָעָה לְעַמֶּךָ

זְכֹר לְאַבְרָהָם לְיִצְחָק וּלְיִשְׂרָאֵל עֲבָדֶיךָ אֲשֶׁר נִשְׁבַּעְתָּ לָהֶם בָּךְ

וַתְּדַבֵּר אֲלֵהֶם אַרְבֶּה אֶת זַרְעֲכֶם כְּכוֹכְבֵי הַשָּׁמָיִם

וְכָל הָאָרֶץ הַזֹּאת אֲשֶׁר אָמַרְתִּי אֶתֵּן לְזַרְעֲכֶם וְנָחֲלוּ לְעֹלָם . . .

וַיָּשָׁב מֹשֶׁה אֶל ה' וַיֹּאמַר

אָנָּא חָטָא הָעָם הַזֶּה חֲטָאָה גְדֹלָה וַיַּעֲשׂוּ לָהֶם אֱלֹהֵי זָהָב

וְעַתָּה אִם תִּשָּׂא חַטָּאתָם וְאִם אַיִן מְחֵנִי נָא מִסִּפְרְךָ אֲשֶׁר כָּתַבְתָּ

שמות לב,ז–לב

od declared to Moses, "Go down, for the people whom you brought out of Egypt have become corrupt. They have been quick to leave the way that I ordered them to follow, and they have made themselves a cast-metal calf. They have bowed down and offered sacrifice to it, exclaiming, 'This, Israel, is your god, who brought you out of Egypt.'"

God then said to Moses, "I have observed the people, and they are an unbending group. Now do not try to stop Me when I unleash my wrath against them to destroy them. I will then make you into a great nation."

Moses began to plead before God his Lord. He said, "O God, why unleash Your wrath against Your people, whom you brought out of Egypt with great power and a show of force? Why should Egypt be able to say that You took them out with evil intentions, to kill them in the hill country and wipe them out from the face of the earth? Withdraw Your display of anger, and refrain from doing evil to Your people.

"Remember Your servants, Abraham, Isaac, and Jacob. You swore to them by Your very essence, and declared that You would make their descendants as numerous as the stars of the sky, giving their descendants the land You promised, so that they would be able to occupy it forever." . . .

Moses went back up to God, and he said, "The people have committed a terrible sin by making a golden idol. Now, if You would, please forgive their sin. If not, You can blot me out from the book that You have written."

SHEMOT/EXODUS 32:7–32

Optional Exercise: A Letter To Sam

Sam Goldberg is beloved by everyone who knows him. He is regarded as an exemplary human being. He is hard-working and scrupulously honest. He has a beautiful family, a wonderful marriage, and has raised well-adjusted children who are moral and upstanding people. He is deeply committed to Judaism and practices *mitzvot* in his daily life. In short, Sam Goldberg is a real *mensch.*

When Sam turns fifty, his life begins to fall apart. First, he is fired from his job. Then Sam receives a call from his doctor informing him that he had developed an incurable form of cancer which usually results in death within six months.

Sam has e-mailed you asking for a response to the following question: "Why are such bad things happening to me when I have always tried to be a good person?"

It is your turn to write a one-paragraph letter to Sam.

What will you say?

Send   Save Now   Discard

To: Sam

Subject: Dear Sam

Dear Sam

Send   Save Now   Discard

How Could the Holocaust Happen in G-d's World?

Refusing to Embrace Easy Answers

Text 7

ויש דברים ימצא האדם תשוקתו להשגתם עצומה

והתגברות השכל לבקש אמתם ולחפשה

נמצא בכל אומה כת מעיינת מבני אדם ובכל זמן

ובדברים ההם ירבו הדעות

ותפול המחלוקת בין המעיינים ויתחדשו הספקות

מפני התלות השכל בהשגת הדברים ההם, כלומר התשוקה אליהם

והיות כל אחד חושב שהוא מצא דרך ידע בה אמתת הדבר

מורה הנבוכים א,לא

There are things for which man will find that he has a great longing to apprehend. The sway of the intellect endeavoring to seek for and to investigate their true reality exists in every group of men engaged in speculation, in every age. With regard to such things there is a multiplicity of opinions, disagreement arises between the men engaged in speculation and doubts crop up; all this because the intellect is attached to an apprehension of these things, I mean to say because of its longing for them, and also because everyone thinks that he has found a way by means of which he will know the true reality of the matter.

MAIMONIDES, GUIDE FOR THE PERPLEXED 1:31

Rabbi Moshe ben Maimon (1135–1204). Better known as Maimonides or by the acronym Rambam. Born in Córdoba, Spain. After the conquest of Córdoba by the Almohads, he fled Spain and eventually settled in Cairo, Egypt. There, he became the leader of the Jewish community and served as court physician to the vizier of Egypt. His rulings on Jewish law are considered integral to the formation of halachic consensus. He is most noted for authoring the *Mishneh Torah*, an encyclopedic arrangement of Jewish law, and for his philosophical work, *Guide for the Perplexed*.

An Answer That Is in Principle Unknowable

TEXT 8

וַיַּעַן ה' אֶת אִיּוֹב מִן הַסְּעָרָה וַיֹּאמַר

מִי זֶה מַחְשִׁיךְ עֵצָה בְמִלִּין בְּלִי דָעַת

אֱזָר נָא כְגֶבֶר חֲלָצֶיךָ וְאֶשְׁאָלְךָ וְהוֹדִיעֵנִי

אֵיפֹה הָיִיתָ בְּיָסְדִי אָרֶץ הַגֵּד אִם יָדַעְתָּ בִינָה . . .

הֲבָאתָ עַד נִבְכֵי יָם וּבְחֵקֶר תְּהוֹם הִתְהַלָּכְתָּ

הֲנִגְלוּ לְךָ שַׁעֲרֵי מָוֶת וְשַׁעֲרֵי צַלְמָוֶת תִּרְאֶה

הִתְבֹּנַנְתָּ עַד רַחֲבֵי אָרֶץ הַגֵּד אִם יָדַעְתָּ כֻלָּהּ

איוב לח,א–יח

Then the Lord answered Job from the tempest and said, "Who is this who gives dark counsel, with words, without knowledge? Now gird your loins like a man and I will ask you and [you] tell Me. Where were you when I founded the earth? Tell if you know understanding. . . .

"Have you come until the locks of the sea and have you walked in the searching out of the deep? Have the gates of death been revealed to you and do you see the gates of the shadow of death? Do you understand [everything] until the breadths of the earth? Tell if you know it all."

JOB 38:1–18

TEXT 9

כִּי לֹא מַחְשְׁבוֹתַי מַחְשְׁבוֹתֵיכֶם וְלֹא דַרְכֵיכֶם דְּרָכָי נְאֻם ה'
כִּי גָבְהוּ שָׁמַיִם מֵאָרֶץ
כֵּן גָּבְהוּ דְרָכַי מִדַּרְכֵיכֶם וּמַחְשְׁבֹתַי מִמַּחְשְׁבֹתֵיכֶם

ישעיהו נה,ח–ט

or My thoughts are not your thoughts, neither are your ways My ways," says the Lord. "As the heavens are higher than the earth, so are My ways higher than your ways and My thoughts [higher] than your thoughts."

ISAIAH 55:8–9

Knowing Why We Cannot Know

TEXT 10

דע אתה המעיין במאמרי זה
שהנה יקרה בהשגות השכליות . . . דבר ידמה למה שיקרה להשגות החושיות
והוא שאתה כשתעיין בעיניך תשיג מה שבכח ראותך שתשיגהו
וכשתכריח עיניך ותפליג בעיון
ותטרח לעיין על רוחק גדול יותר ארוך ממה שבכחך לעיין ברוחקו
או תסתכל בכתיבה דקה או פתוח דק שאין בכחך להשיגו
ותכריח ראותך לאמתו
לא יחלש ראותך על זה אשר לא תוכל עליו לבד
אבל יחלש גם כן על מה שבכחך שתשיגהו, ויחלש ראותך

ולא תראה מה שהיית יכול להשיג קודם הפלגת ההבטה וההטרחה . . .
ובזה העניין נאמר: דבש מצאת אכול דייך פן תשבענו והקאתו (משלי כה,טז) . . .
ומה נפלא זה המשל . . . וזכר הערב שבמזונות והוא הדבש

והדבש בטבעו כשירבו ממנו יעורר האיסטומכא ויבא הקיא

וכאלו אמר, שטבע זאת ההשגה עם גדולתה ועצמתה ומה שבה מן השלמות

אם לא יעמדו בה אצל גבולה וילכו בה בשמירה, יהפך לחסרון

כאוכל הדבש, אשר אם יאכל בשעור יזון ויערב לו, ואם יוסיף יאבד הכל . . .

ואין הרצון באלו הכתובים אשר אמרום הנביאים והחכמים ז"ל

לסתום שער העיון לגמרי, ולבטל השכל מהשיג מה שאפשר להשיגו

כמו שיחשבו הפתאים והמתרשלים

אשר ייטב להם שישימו חסרונם ופתיותם שלמות וחכמה . . .

אבל כוונת כולם להגיד שיש לשכל האנושי גבול יעמוד אצלו

מורה הנבוכים א,לב

You must consider, when reading this treatise, that mental perception . . . is subject to conditions similar to those to which physical perception is subject. That is to say, if your eye looks around, you can perceive all that is within the range of your vision; if, however, you overstrain your eye, exerting it too much by attempting to see an object which is too distant for your eye, or to examine writings or engravings too small for your sight, and forcing it to obtain a correct perception of them, you will not only weaken your sight with regard to that special object, but also for those things which you otherwise are able to perceive; your eye will have become too weak to perceive what you were able to see before you exerted yourself and exceeded the limits of your vision. . . .

Respecting this it has been said, "Have you found honey? Eat so much as is sufficient for you, lest you be filled with it and vomit it" (Proverbs 25:16) . . .

How excellent is this simile! . . . [In comparing knowledge to food, the author of Proverbs] mentions the sweetest food, namely, honey, which has the further property of irritating the stomach and of causing sickness if one consumes too much of it. He thus fully describes the nature of knowledge. Though great, excellent, noble, and perfect, it is injurious if not kept within bounds or not guarded properly; it is like honey which gives nourishment and is pleasant when eaten in moderation, but is totally thrown away when eaten immoderately. . . .

It was not the object of the prophets and our sages in these utterances to close the gate of investigation entirely and to prevent the mind from comprehending what is within its reach, as is imagined by simple and idle people, whom it suits better to put forth their ignorance and incapacity as wisdom and perfection . . . The whole object of the prophets and the sages was to make it known that the intellects of human beings have a limit at which they stop.

MAIMONIDES, GUIDE FOR THE PERPLEXED 1:32

A Question Not Meant to Be Answered

TEXT 11

The religious question is, therefore, not, "Why did this happen?" But "What then shall we do?" That is why . . . along with our prayers for the injured and the bereaved, we will be asking people to donate money to assist the work of relief. The religious response is not to seek to understand, thereby to accept. We are not God. Instead we are the people He has called on to be his "partners in the work of creation." The only adequate religious response is to say, "God, I do not know why this terrifying disaster has happened, but I do know what You want of us: to help

Rabbi Dr. Jonathan Sacks (1948–). Born in London, chief rabbi of the United Hebrew Congregations of the Commonwealth. Attended Cambridge University and received his doctorate from King's College, London. A prolific and influential author, his books include *Will We Have Jewish Grandchildren?* and *The Dignity of Difference.* Recipient of the Jerusalem Prize in 1995 for his contributions to enhancing Jewish life in the diaspora. Knighted in 2005.

the afflicted, comfort the bereaved, send healing to the injured, and aid those who have lost their livelihoods and homes."

RABBI JONATHAN SACKS, "WHY DOES GOD ALLOW TERRIBLE THINGS TO HAPPEN TO HIS PEOPLE?" THE TIMES OF LONDON, JANUARY 1, 2005

TEXT 12

בִּלַּע הַמָּוֶת לָנֶצַח

וּמָחָה ה' אֱלֹקים דִּמְעָה מֵעַל כָּל פָּנִים

וְחֶרְפַּת עַמּוֹ יָסִיר מֵעַל כָּל הָאָרֶץ כִּי ה' דִּבֵּר

ישעיהו כה,ח

e has concealed death forever and the Lord God shall wipe the tears off every face and the shame of His people He shall remove from upon the entire earth, for the Lord has spoken.

ISAIAH 25:8

Key Points

1. Human beings in the twenty-first century are not the first ones to notice that it is often the righteous who suffer and the wicked who prosper. Jews have been questioning this fact for over 3,000 years.

2. The questioning of suffering should not be condemned as a sign of lack of faith. Moses and other great Jewish leaders asked these questions.

3. It is ultimately the believer in G-d who questions suffering. To the non-believer, the answer is painfully clear—the world is a jungle.

4. Jewish tradition affirms that G-d is omnipotent, omniscient, and good. This leads to a seeming contradiction between what one would expect the world to look like and the real suffering that exists within the world.

5. The Jewish response to suffering divides the issue into two parts. The suffering that others are enduring must not be viewed in the same way that one might view his or her own experiences.

6. In the tradition of Abraham and Moses, a person can and should turn to G-d and demand that the suffering of others should cease.

7. One approach to "why the Holocaust happened" is a subtle and sophisticated recognition that we cannot know, because to understand the reason for suffering might lessen our sensitivity to it.

8. The ultimate answer to the question concerning the suffering around us is that no answer is acceptable. The goal is to get the suffering to stop. The suffering of others should be alleviated, not rationalized.

9. Judaism does not glorify suffering; it is a temporary aberration with which we should never make peace. Jewish tradition firmly believes in a time when suffering will end, and and "G-d shall wipe the tears off every face."

Supplementary Texts

TEXT A

מִשָּׁמַיִם הִבִּיט ה' רָאָה אֶת כָּל בְּנֵי הָאָדָם
מִמְּכוֹן שִׁבְתּוֹ הִשְׁגִּיחַ אֶל כָּל יֹשְׁבֵי הָאָרֶץ
הַיֹּצֵר יַחַד לִבָּם הַמֵּבִין אֶל כָּל מַעֲשֵׂיהֶם
אֵין הַמֶּלֶךְ נוֹשָׁע בְּרָב חָיִל גִּבּוֹר לֹא יִנָּצֵל בְּרָב כֹּחַ
שֶׁקֶר הַסּוּס לִתְשׁוּעָה וּבְרֹב חֵילוֹ לֹא יְמַלֵּט
הִנֵּה עֵין ה' אֶל יְרֵאָיו לַמְיַחֲלִים לְחַסְדּוֹ
לְהַצִּיל מִמָּוֶת נַפְשָׁם וּלְחַיּוֹתָם בָּרָעָב
נַפְשֵׁנוּ חִכְּתָה לַה' עֶזְרֵנוּ וּמָגִנֵּנוּ הוּא

תהלים לג,יג–כ

The Lord looked from heaven; He saw all the sons of men. From His dwelling place He oversees all the inhabitants of the earth. He Who forms their hearts together, Who understands all their deeds. The king is not saved with a vast army; a mighty man will not be rescued with great strength. A horse is a false hope for victory and with his power, he will not escape. Behold the eye of the Lord is to those who fear Him, to those who hope for His kindness, to rescue their soul from death and to sustain them in famine. Our soul waits for the Lord; He is our help and our shield.

TEHILIM/PSALMS 33:13–20

וַיְהִי כִּי זָעֲקוּ בְנֵי יִשְׂרָאֵל אֶל ה' עַל אֹדוֹת מִדְיָן

וַיִּשְׁלַח ה' אִישׁ נָבִיא אֶל בְּנֵי יִשְׂרָאֵל

וַיֹּאמֶר לָהֶם כֹּה אָמַר ה' אֱלֹקֵי יִשְׂרָאֵל

אָנֹכִי הֶעֱלֵיתִי אֶתְכֶם מִמִּצְרַיִם וָאֹצִיא אֶתְכֶם מִבֵּית עֲבָדִים

וָאַצִּל אֶתְכֶם מִיַּד מִצְרַיִם וּמִיַּד כָּל לֹחֲצֵיכֶם

וָאֲגָרֵשׁ אוֹתָם מִפְּנֵיכֶם וָאֶתְּנָה לָכֶם אֶת אַרְצָם

וָאֹמְרָה לָכֶם אֲנִי ה' אֱלֹקֵיכֶם

לֹא תִירְאוּ אֶת אֱלֹהֵי הָאֱמֹרִי אֲשֶׁר אַתֶּם יוֹשְׁבִים בְּאַרְצָם

וְלֹא שְׁמַעְתֶּם בְּקוֹלִי

וַיָּבֹא מַלְאַךְ ה' וַיֵּשֶׁב תַּחַת הָאֵלָה אֲשֶׁר בְּעָפְרָה אֲשֶׁר לְיוֹאָשׁ אֲבִי הָעֶזְרִי

וְגִדְעוֹן בְּנוֹ חֹבֵט חִטִּים בַּגַּת לְהָנִיס מִפְּנֵי מִדְיָן

וַיֵּרָא אֵלָיו מַלְאַךְ ה' וַיֹּאמֶר אֵלָיו ה' עִמְּךָ גִּבּוֹר הֶחָיִל

וַיֹּאמֶר אֵלָיו גִּדְעוֹן בִּי אֲדֹנִי וְיֵשׁ ה' עִמָּנוּ וְלָמָּה מְצָאַתְנוּ כָּל זֹאת

וְאַיֵּה כָל נִפְלְאֹתָיו אֲשֶׁר סִפְּרוּ לָנוּ אֲבוֹתֵינוּ לֵאמֹר

הֲלֹא מִמִּצְרַיִם הֶעֱלָנוּ ה' וְעַתָּה נְטָשָׁנוּ ה' וַיִּתְּנֵנוּ בְּכַף מִדְיָן

וַיִּפֶן אֵלָיו ה' וַיֹּאמֶר לֵךְ בְּכֹחֲךָ זֶה וְהוֹשַׁעְתָּ אֶת יִשְׂרָאֵל מִכַּף מִדְיָן הֲלֹא שְׁלַחְתִּיךָ

שופטים ו, ז–יד

![N] ow it was when the children of Israel cried to the Lord concerning Midian, that the Lord sent a prophet to the children of Israel, and he said to them, "Thus says the Lord, God of Israel; I brought you up from Egypt and I brought you out of the house of bondage. And I saved you from the hand of Egypt and from the hand of all your oppressors; and I drove them out from before you and I have given you their land. And I said to you, 'I am the Lord your God, you shall not fear the gods of the Amorites in whose land you dwell.' But you have not obeyed me."

And the angel of the Lord came and sat under the oak which was in Ophra, that belonged to Joash the Abiezrite; and his son Gideon was beating out wheat in the winepress, to be enabled to flee from Midian.

And the angel of the Lord appeared and said to him, "The Lord is with you, mighty man of valor."

And Gideon said to him, "Please my lord, if the Lord be with us, why then has all this befallen us? And where are all His wonders which our forefathers told us, saying, 'Did not the Lord bring us up from Egypt?' But now the Lord has forsaken us and He has delivered us into the hand of Midian."

And the Lord turned toward him and said, "Go, with this your strength, and save Israel from the hand of Midian. Have I not sent you?"

SHOFTIM/JUDGES 6:7–14

TEXT C

. . . הטענה והתביעה היא (לא לבני ישראל, אלא) להקב"ה

וכדברי גדעון: למה מצאתנו כל זאת

ואי' כל נפלאותיו אשר ספרו לנו אבותינו הלא ממצרים העלנו ה' וגו'

ואדרבא בגלל זה:

ויפן אליו ה' ויאמר לך בכחך זה (בכח זכות שלמדת על בני)

והושעת את ישראל

ועל אחת כמה וכמה לאחרי כל הגזירות והשמדות

שעברו כל בני ישראל במשך כל הדורות

ובפרט בדור האחרון

בודאי ובודאי שצריכים לבקש ולצעוק להקב"ה על אריכות הגלות:

"עד מתי"

ספר השיחות תנש"א 251

ur complaints and demands should be directed toward G-d . . . similar to the [complaint in the] words of Gideon, "Why then has all this befallen us? And where are all His wonders which our forefathers told us, saying, 'Did not the Lord bring us up from Egypt?'" And because of this [demand], "the Lord turned toward him and said, "Go, with this your strength [with the strength of your positive statements about the merit of the Jewish nation] and save Israel.'"

How much more so, after all of the harsh decrees and persecutions that the Jewish people have endured throughout so many generations and specifically [the suffering of the Holocaust experienced] in the last generation, with certainty and conviction we must implore and cry out to G-d over the length of the exile, *Ad matai*!" [Until when!]

RABBI MENACHEM MENDEL SCHNEERSON, SEFER HASICHOT 5751, P. 251

TEXT D

וַיְהִי אַחַר דִּבֶּר ה' אֶת הַדְּבָרִים הָאֵלֶּה אֶל אִיּוֹב

וַיֹּאמֶר ה' אֶל אֱלִיפַז הַתֵּימָנִי

חָרָה אַפִּי בְךָ וּבִשְׁנֵי רֵעֶיךָ כִּי לֹא דִבַּרְתֶּם אֵלַי נְכוֹנָה כְּעַבְדִּי אִיּוֹב

וְעַתָּה קְחוּ לָכֶם שִׁבְעָה פָרִים וְשִׁבְעָה אֵילִים

וּלְכוּ אֶל עַבְדִּי אִיּוֹב וְהַעֲלִיתֶם עוֹלָה בַּעַדְכֶם

וְאִיּוֹב עַבְדִּי יִתְפַּלֵּל עֲלֵיכֶם

כִּי אִם פָּנָיו אֶשָּׂא לְבִלְתִּי עֲשׂוֹת עִמָּכֶם נְבָלָה

כִּי לֹא דִבַּרְתֶּם אֵלַי נְכוֹנָה כְּעַבְדִּי אִיּוֹב

איוב מב,ז-ח

Now it came to pass after the Lord had spoken these words to Job, that the Lord said to Eliphaz the Temanite, "My wrath is kindled against you and your two companions because you did not speak correctly, as did My servant Job. And now, take to yourselves seven bulls and seven rams and go to My servant Job and offer up a burnt offering for yourselves and Job, My servant, will pray for you, for I will favor him not to do anything unseemly to you, for you did not speak to Me correctly, as did My servant Job."

JOB 42:7-8

TEXT E

אם היו יסורין באין עליו
אם היו חלאים באין עליו, או שהיה מקבר את בניו
אל יאמר לו כדרך שאמרו לו חביריו לאיוב:
הלא יראתך כסלתך תקותך ותם דרכיך
זכר נא מי הוא נקי אבד (איוב ד,ו–ז)
תלמוד בבלי בבא מציעא נח,ב

If someone had suffering visited upon him [or] if someone had diseases visited upon him or if someone buried his children, one should not say to him in the way that the colleagues of Job said to him, "Surely, your fear was your foolishness, your hope, and the sincerity of your ways. Remember now, who was innocent that perished, and where were the upright destroyed?" (Job 4:6–7).

TALMUD, BAVA METSIA 58B

Additional Readings

Judaism, Justice and Tragedy: Confronting the Problem of Evil

Transcript of a lecture by **Rabbi Jonathan Sacks**

Friends, first of all I want to say thank you. I think it is absolutely fantastic of every one of you to turn out on such a revolting day. If there is any greater testimony to your faith, I hope it will be justified. I can't think of one. You know, thirteen years ago, in 1987, we had this wonderful moment Shmini Atzeret. On Shmini Atzeret we say for the first time in the year, "*mashiv haruakh umored hagashem.*" We pray to God "Who makes the wind blow." That night there was a hurricane. If you remember, it was that night which blew down half the trees in southeast England. Next morning I came into shul, Simchat Torah morning, and the first person I met said, "Rabbi, next time could you pray a little less hard?!"

This year we have had the sedra of Noah and the flood and I think maybe that next year we will leyn it a little less hard. But thank you very much for coming.

Let me begin, if I may, with a story just to relax you. Or, if you don't need relaxing, I do. Of course it is one of my favorites. It is the story that is told about a Rosh Yeshivah who was approached one day by a young man who wanted to come to the yeshivah to learn. The Rosh Yeshivah really did not particularly want to admit this young man. He thought he did not know enough to be able to learn. But the young man was very, very insistent so the Rosh Yeshivah said, "All right, I am going to ask you a question to see if you can learn Gemara, if you can understand the rabbinic mind. If you can answer the question, I'll let you in."

So the young man said, "Fine."

The Rosh Yeshivah said, "Here is the question. If two men come down a chimney and one comes down dirty and one comes down clean, which one has a wash?"

The young man thinks for a moment and says, "The dirty one."

"Wrong!" says the Rosh Yeshivah, "Obviously the dirty one looks at the clean one and sees he is clean so he thinks 'I must be clean.' The clean one looks at the dirty one and sees he is dirty and thinks 'I must be dirty.' The clean one has a wash!"

"Aagh!" says the young man and goes away in dismay.

The next day he comes again. "Reb Rosh Yeshivah, I have been thinking and I really feel I now understand Gemara. Please let me in!"

The Rosh Yeshivah says, "Alright. I will ask you one question and if you get it right I will admit you to the yeshivah but if you get it wrong you're really not up to it."

So the young man says "Fine," and the Rosh Yeshivah asks the following question:

"If two men come down a chimney and one comes down dirty and one comes down clean, which one has a wash?"

"The clean one!" says the young man.

"Wrong!" says the Rosh Yeshivah. "Obviously the clean one looks at his hands, sees they are clean and he knows he is clean. The dirty one looks at his hands, sees they are dirty and the dirty one has a wash."

"Ok. Aagh," says the young man and goes out in total dismay.

The next day, he knocks again on the door of the Rosh Yeshivah and says, "Rebbe, please, you know, I really think now I'm beginning to master talmudic logic."

The Rosh Yeshivah says, "All right. But this is the last time. I will ask you one question and, one way and another, if you don't get it right, you do not enter the yeshivah.

The young man says, "Yes," and the Rosh Yeshivah asks him the following question:

"If two men come down a chimney, one comes down dirty, one comes down clean: who has a wash?" The young man thinks—the dirty one, the clean one, the dirty one, the clean one?

Finally he gives up but says, "Tell me, Rosh Yeshivah, which one has a wash?"

The Rosh Yeshivah looks at the young man and says, "Tell me, young man, how can two men come down a chimney and one came out dirty and one came out clean?"

Friends, I was trying to explain in my first lecture that Judaism, as you will understand from that story, is a religion of multiple perspectives, of many ways of looking at the truth. Some of you who followed that lecture—did any of you follow that lecture? [Laughter]. It was a bit tough going but some of you followed that lecture and understood absolutely correctly that it was nothing whatsoever with the title of that lecture which was "Faith." Listen, I'm sorry. What can I do? The truth is: I will come to faith, I promise you, probably in the third lecture, possibly in the last. One way or another, we'll get there. But first of all I really have to take you with me on a journey to see Judaism as different, as less familiar, as more radical than we ever imagined. If we can do that, we will be able to take things we have known about for ages and see in them something new. We will undergo what I call a "paradigm shift."

My thesis in the first lecture, the story so far for those of you who missed it, as far as I can summarize it, is this: that Judaism as I portrayed it was and is a radical alternative not only to the ancient world of myth but to the central paradigm of western civilization, namely to Greek thought whose characteristic mode is philosophy, at least Platonic, and Cartesian philosophy, whose master discipline is logic. As I said, the unspoken assumptions of western thought—and of course I am being crude here but you don't want a lecture with footnotes as well—are the following:

That knowledge is cognitive.

The metaphor of cognition is sight. It's a visual matter; truth is something we see. And, in particular truth is something we see from a particular perspective. That perspective which is God's eye point of view, the point of view of the detached spectator—what Thomas Nagel calls "the view from nowhere."

That is represented in Greek myth by the figure of Zeus; in Greek culture, by Greek art and by Greek drama at which the spectator and the audience are outside the world of reality in the painting or in the theatre, and in Greek thought, as I say, in Plato seeing reality as he emerges from the cave. In other words, the detached spectator theory or as the (here's evidence of a mis-spent youth) as they put it in a graffito in one of the loos (excuse me) of the Cambridge University library and they wrote: "God exists. It's just that He doesn't want to get involved." That is the paradigm of western thought.

In Judaism, by contrast, God does get involved but He also makes space for humanity to get involved. He does this by conferring integrity, legitimacy, and dignity on the point of view of man. That means that in Judaism at the very least—at the very least—there are two viewpoints, never less than two: ultimately, the viewpoint of how things appear to God and how they appear to us. And in Judaism both of those are legitimate: truth as it is in heaven; truth as it is on earth.

Those of you familiar with the world of rabbinic midrash will know there is a very famous midrash on this. You know that we have the story of Genesis Chapter 1. It unfolds in that beautiful way, "And God said, 'Let there be'—and there was and God saw that it was good." In only one of the creations, God has a kind of fore-thought. He kind of discusses it in advance. Which one is that? [No reply from audience.] The case of man where, instead of God saying "yehi,"—"let there be," God as it were reflectively says, "*Na'aseh adam betzalmainu kidmutainu*" – "Let us make man in Our image and Our likeness." And, you know, the rabbis obviously wanted to know who is the "us." Who is keeping God company? It is lonely being the God of monotheism! You don't have a lot of friends around for dinner! So who was He talking to? Of course the sages, in their way, which is both deceptively simple but ultimately very profound, said that God discussed this with the angels. That is their way of representing moral dilemmas or internal conflict. He discussed it with four angels. The angel of *chesed* said, "Let man be created because he is *oseh chasadim*—human beings do kind deeds." The angel of truth said, "Let him not be created *ki kulo shekarim*— because human beings are full of lies." The angel of tzedek said, "Let man be created *ki oseh tzedakot*." It is a bit untranslatable in English but it roughly means, "We give to charity." (Now how come this is a Jewish event and we haven't asked anyone to give to charity yet? Are you thinking up something?) Anyway, the angel of peace said, "Let man not be created *ki kulo ketatah*— because he is full of strife." And the midrash says, very opaquely, "*Ma asa Hakodesh barechu*?—What did God do? *Lakach emet vehishlich ota artza*. He took Truth and threw it to the ground." And the angel said, "*Mipnei ma ata mevazeh et hatachsis shelcha*?—Truth, Almighty, is your signature, your seal. Why are you throwing it down to the ground?" And God replied, "*Emet mi'eretz titzmach*—Let truth grow up from the ground."

Now, what this midrash is telling us is that there is indeed a challenge against human existence. As T. S. Eliot said, "Humankind cannot bear very much reality"— that is, too much truth. But God replies, "I don't ask of man that he or she understand truth as it is in heaven." It's sufficient if we understand truth as it exists down here on earth. The midrash has many more depths than that but at the simplest level the midrash is saying: There is truth as it is in heaven; truth as it is on earth—and God wants us to aspire to truth as it is on earth. That is terribly important.

So, in Judaism, truth is always a truth from somewhere. And because that somewhere can be distributed some place either in space or in time, they generate multiple perspectives and in Judaism, in other words, there is not a single dimension in which all truths coexist because not all truths do coexist. If they are separated in space, there can be conversation between x and y—somebody who is here and somebody who is there—ultimately God and humanity, and I call that the "dialogical imagination," the truth by conversation. Or it can be distributed in time: one truth which we see now and another truth which we live or embody at another time—and I call that the "chronological imagination."

So, as opposed to the logical imagination of the Greeks and western philosophy, which I do not denigrate in any shape or form, Judaism though operated on a different system: the chronological and the dialogical imagination. In other words, if I can put it as simply as I can: in Judaism truth is not impersonal; truth is inter-personal. It is the truth that exists when two beings separated in space or time relate to one another. Well, *ad kan hakafah rishonah* - up to there is what I tried to say last time. Does it now make sense to any of you? No, no, no, all right! Read the book! Well—I haven't written it yet, so—[laughter] . . .

Anyway, now I want to take that lecture, that framework and see whether it will help us understand. It won't help us solve, for heaven's sake! It will not help us solve —but see if we can understand in a new way that most difficult of all problems in religious thought, perhaps in human thought as a totality, namely the problem of evil or the problem of injustice, the thing which we describe when we talk about 'when bad things happen to good people' or what the rabbis said in terms of *tzadik vera lo*, which is the rabbinic equivalent.

That problem is so deep that it has given rise to a whole theological discipline, primarily a Christian one, a very distinguished discipline. And I please pray of you, all of you, that whenever I contrast Judaism and something else, I am never trying to denigrate that something else. I really mean that. To be a Jew is to make space for "otherness." If I were to sum up the whole of these six lectures, it would be in that phrase: "To be a Jew is to make space for otherness." But that means we do our thing and we respect those who do other things. Therefore, Christianity developed a whole theological discipline, which so too did the Jewish philosophers of the Middle Ages, which is called theodicy. It is the whole attempt to understand how if God exists, evil exists.

What I want to argue tonight is that any attempt to deal with this subject as it is conventionally dealt with in western thought, in classic western theology, through the discipline logic, any such attempt must fail! Not because it is false but because it is just too simple. It fails to do justice to the complexity of the issue: and that failure is not just intellectual; it is also moral and existential. Here we will see—I hope in tonight's lecture—very clearly, what is at stake in terms of the difference between the logical imagination and the dialogical imagination.

Now, let me begin by saying that it is here, above all, that you will find the most passionate expressions of dialogue in the whole of the Jewish literature. Not only are they the most passionate, I think they are virtually unique. I challenge, as I am sure many of you here tonight know more about this than I do, but the conversations, the dialogues that I am going to mention are very famous. I do not know of analogues to them in any other religion, in any other religious literature. Here they are.

The first, of course, hits us between the eyes: Abraham's challenge to God. When he hears from God about the prospective fate of the cities of the plain of Sodom and Gomorrah, Abraham says to God in words that are still stunning—I mean, they send a shiver down my spine whenever I read them—*"Halilah lecha mei'asot kadavar hazeh."* Says Abraham, "God forbid that You should do such a thing—*lehamit tzadik im rasha*—to kill the righteous with the wicked--*vehaya katzadik karasha halilah lach*—so that the righteous should have the same fate as the wicked, God forbid!—*hashofet kol ha'aretz lo ya'aseh mishpat*?—Shall the Judge of all the earth not do justice?"

How can a human being who says, as Abraham says, "I am but dust and ash," how can human finitude say such words to God? In any other faith, it seems to me, those words would be close to, maybe even tantamount to, blasphemy! And yet there they are at the core of Jewish faith, one of the great prophetic utterances in our literature. Abraham is not alone.

Moshe Rabainu says, as you know, to God, very early on in the history of his mission to Egypt—(You know why Moshe Rabainu was the greatest of the prophets? My theory is because when God offered him to be Chief Rabbi of the Jewish people he said "No" five times. There was a man who could foresee the future! [Laughter])--Anyway, Moshe Rabainu, as you know, begins his mission. The immediate result is that Pharaoh actually makes the work harder and more difficult and Moshe Rabainu turns to God and says (listen to this!), *"Lamah harai'ota le'am hazeh?*—Why have You done evil to this people?—*Lamah zeh shelachtani?*—Why did You ever send me?"

Or Jeremiah. Listen to Jeremiah. Here is Jeremiah, the first Jewish barrister if you like, summoning God to a court case. Jeremiah, Chapter 12.

"You are always right, O Lord, when I bring a case before You. Whenever I bring You to court, You always win. Yet I want to speak to You about justice. Why does the way of the wicked prosper? Why are the evil people always at ease?"

I mean, this is explicit language of a court case. Stunning words of Jeremiah, Chapter 12.

And, of course, the most astonishing of all, by far the most astonishing book in any religious literature known to me, the book of Job. Job, as you know, suffers a series of mishaps. His friends, three of them and then a fourth later in the course of the book, try to comfort him and they do so in the classic terms of theodicy. They say to Job that since God is just and he has suffered, he must have done something to deserve it--and they argue their case throughout this very long and powerful book. Job refuses to accept their arguments and insists not that he is innocent but he insists that he has a right to a hearing directly in the presence of God.

He wants to bring God to court and argue his innocence in front of Him—and of course he does. As you know, what is the answer God gives him? Well, as you know, the Jewish custom is that you answer a question with another question. Job has questions. God answers Job with four chapters of questions of His own. There is not a single statement, just questions.

I always said, when the Sunday Times first brought to light the "cash for questions" scandal, I said, "You know, this is the difference between the Jewish people and minhag Anglia—the English way of doing things. In England you have to pay somebody to ask questions. In Judaism you have to pay somebody not to ask questions!"

But there it is—this extraordinary book, which again, teeters on the very brink of heresy by any conventional standards. Then, at this denouement, we receive this extraordinary proposition: Job, after being battered by four chapters of questions from the Almighty says, "You are right, Almighty. I should never have said such a thing," and we think the story has a happy ending. God is right. Job is wrong. Job's comforters were right all along. But the book still has a surprise for us—and it is the biggest surprise of the lot! God says that he should go and tell his friends, Elifaz the Temanite and so on, "I am angry with you and your two friends [Job's comforters] because you have not spoken of me what is right: my servant Job did."

Unbelievable! The whole story has been leading up to the fact that Job is wrong and he is going to accept that he is wrong. Finally, the twist is that Job was right and his comforters were wrong. The conventional approach of theodicy, that Job must have done something to deserve his fate, is torn up by God Himself. This is unbelievable.

So we have here an extraordinary situation, a situation which the book of Job embodies, is structured around what looks to us like a contradiction. The book of Job is a contradiction. Logic fails.

What I want to say about these passages is, number one, to repeat: I don't know of any analogue in any other faith. Number two, the obvious point that all four of these passages are dialogues. They really are. Man speaks. God replies. There is an interchange between them.

However, the third fact is much more important. Does anyone know what happens just prior to the first of these conversations? You know, when Abraham has his dialogue. Do you know what immediately precedes that in the Torah? Anyone know? [Inaudible answer from audience.] Ah, the angel visits Sarah. Yes, and when that visit is over, listen to the words: "*Hamechaseh ani mei'Avraham asher ani oseh*?" God says, "Shall I hide from Abraham that which I am about to do?"

In other words, God invites Abraham's challenge! If God had not spoken out loud—that He was going to destroy the cities, that He had heard of the evil from the cities and it was very grievous, and so on—if He had not spoken it out loud in the presence of Abraham, Abraham would never have known! God invites the dialogue. He says it explicitly. "Shall I hide from Abraham that which I am about to do?" In other words, God knew that Abraham would challenge him. He invited him to challenge Him.

Let me say further that it is more than this. If you know the concept—I am sure you are familiar with this—Buber and Rosenzweig: the idea of a motif word. You know what in Ivrit is called *mila mancheh*. Yes? A certain word functions in the Torah as a motif. Now listen very carefully. God goes on to say, "Shall I hide from Abraham that which I am about to do? ... *Ki yedativ*—for I have known him, for I have chosen him—*lema'an asher yetzaveh et banav ve'et baito acharav*—so that he will instruct his children and his household after him—*veshamru derech Hashem*—that they may keep the way of the Lord—*la'asot tzedakah umishpat*—I have chosen Abraham so that he will teach his children to do *tzedakah umishpat*—righteousness and justice."

If you recall what I said to you just before, those are the key words of Abraham's speech. (Are you with me?) "*Halilah lecha mei'asot kadavar hazeh*—God forbid that You should do this—*lehamit tzadik im rasha vehaya katzadik karasha . . . hashofet kol ha'aretz lo ya'aseh mishpat*?"

The key words in Abraham's challenge to God are *tzedek* and *mishpat*. God has given those to Abraham before Abraham has spoken: Abraham, this is what you are all about! *Tzedek umishpat*. And Abraham takes the cue and immediately says to God—What about the *tzedek*? What about the *mishpat*? God teaches Abraham how to challenge God.

Now that is incredible—and he gives him the language in which to do so. And don't think that is the only case. Let me give you an example which the rabbis themselves in the Gemara are stunned by. You remember when Moses is up the mountain and the Israelites make the golden calf. Listen to what God says. "*Ve'ata hanichah li*—now, leave Me alone—*vayichar api bahem va'achalaim*—so that I can get angry with them and destroy them." And the rabbis want to know: what was Moses doing? He never even heard of it before. "Leave me alone so that I can get angry with them . . ." If that isn't a tacit invitation, if "leave me alone" isn't a way of saying, "Please don't leave!" It is a paradoxical intention for those familiar with this odd school of psychotherapy. But that is what it is. God is inviting Moses to play exactly as he invited Abraham to play.

So these passages plunge us into an awareness that in Jewish thought the problem of evil—which was what Abraham, Moses, Jeremiah and Job all raise with God—is fraught with drama, with dialogue, with tension and with conflict. I have to tell you very bluntly: these passages are fraught with contradiction—and let me explain why. Let us just take that first case of Abraham. Was God right or wrong to destroy the cities of the plain? Right or wrong? [Shout from audience: "Wrong!"]

Well, listen, listen, listen! If He was right, why did He invite Abraham to challenge Him? And if He was wrong, why did He think of doing it in the first place? (Are you with me?) If God was right—I mean God knows everything. OK? He knows all the stuff. He's got files on every member of Sodom and Gomorrah. He's done all the research. If, therefore, there are not 50 or 45—or Abraham leaves it off with 10—how many righteous people were there in Sodom, incidentally? ["Four?"—from audience.] There were absolutely zero because, as you know, in the very next chapter there is a little controlled experiment. Two visitors come to Lot. "Everyone surrounds the house--Nasabu . . . kol ha'am." The Bible says, "everyone in the town—mina'ar ve'ad zakain—from the young to the old, surrounded the house and said, 'Bring us out these men that we may know them.'" An act of, as you know, homosexual rape which made Sodom synonymous with something or other. Anyway, one way or another, there is a controlled experiment to show that Lot and his family, who were "kacha"[so-so]—you know, I don't know whether they were great or not so great—but they were mishpachah [family] of Abraham so they got saved.

But there is a controlled experiment in the Bible in Genesis, Chapter 19, to make us aware that actually no one was righteous. God knew that in advance; otherwise he would never have thought of destroying the city. So if God was right, why did He invite Abraham to challenge Him? If He was wrong, how could He have conceived of destroying the cities in the first place? So, please understand that we are dealing here with stuff that does not fit the template of logic. By any standards we are dealing here with a contradiction that can only be solved by mapping it on a different way of seeing the universe.

And now I am going to begin the answer. I want to begin with the opening words of Jewish history, the opening words of this week's sidra, the first words of God to Abraham, the words that set the history of the people of the covenant in motion, "Lech lecha mi'artzecha umimoladetecha umibait avicha el ha'aretz asher are'eka—Get thee out from your land, your birthplace and your father's house to a land which I will show you."

Those are the first words that set Jewish history in motion and I want to ask, right at the outset: Why did God choose Abraham? This is not a trick question. It is an open question. Why did God choose Abraham? [Inaudible answer from audience.] I don't know. It doesn't say that He did. All of a sudden, out of nowhere, these words, Vayomer hashem el-Avram lech-lecha. There's no preamble to those words.

Now please be aware that if the Torah does not give us a reason why God chose Abraham, we have a lacuna here. It is a glaring absence. Why did God choose Adam? Nobody else to choose from! There wasn't a whole lot of choice! Why did God choose Noah? It says so at the beginning of Noah, last week's sidra. "Noach ish tzadik tamim hayah bedorotav et-ho'elokim hithalech Noach. Noah was a righteous man, perfect in his generations. He walked with God."

None of which are ever said about Abraham. Why did God choose Moses? Well, look, if you read the beginning of the book of Exodus you will see there three scenes: Egyptian hitting a Jew—Moses intervenes on the side of justice; Jew hitting a Jew--Moses intervenes on the side of justice. He escapes for his life and then meets the daughters of Midian who are being driven away from the well by some other Midianite shepherds, non-Jew against non-Jew—Moses intervenes on the grounds of justice. So Moses has passed his three ordeals. Number one, when injustice is being committed, he does not stand still. Number two, this is not chauvinism: he doesn't care. If it is a Jew persecuting a non-Jew, he'll defend the non-Jew. Justice in Judaism is impartial. Moses is a man of character. So we know why God chose Moses. In general, either the Torah tells us something very remarkable about the character of the individual or in some cases there is a story of a miraculous birth.

Who is obviously singled from birth because they have a miraculous birth? [Responses from audience.] Samuel. Samson. Moses, yes. A sort of miraculous birth. Isaac. Jacob. You know that Rivka was infertile—*vaye'atair Yitzhak lashem lenochakh ishto ki akarah hi*—she was infertile—another miraculous birth. Who else was infertile? Rachel was infertile. So we have here: Isaac, Jacob, Joseph, question mark, Moses, Samson, Samuel. There is a miraculous birth, or there is some story of their biography that tells us why they were singled out.

None of this applies to Abraham. There is no miraculous birth. There is no preamble. (Are you with me?) This is a glaring silence. And let me tell you that this is a particularly glaring silence because not only is this the first moment of Jewish history, it is also the defining moment at which the entire biblical world shifts on its axis. Until the beginning of Genesis, Chapter 12, the first words of this week's sidrah, the Torah has been concerned with what? With the universe. With everyone—culminating with Noah. Adam and Eve. Cain and Abel. Noah and the Flood. The Tower of Babel. All of these are about universals. About humanity as a whole.

Then, all of a sudden, the Torah switches into a different key and with Abraham we suddenly deal with the particular people: an individual and his family. A nation. An *am segulah*. This is the point at which the Torah shifts on its axis and here it is: total silence. And if nature abhors a vacuum, Judaism abhors silence.

We are a noisy bunch, aren't we? Years ago, many more years than I care to remember, there was (I think on BBC television) a documentary series, a six-part series, about the world's great faiths. When the presenter of this program (I've completely forgotten who it was) came to Judaism, he was obviously shell-shocked by this difference between the terribly pious other faiths that he went to and this rabble called Judaism. He wanted a title for the program. He called it "The Holy Argument" and I will never forget this wonderful interchange he had with Elie Wiesel. He said, "Professor Wiesel, Judaism seems to be a very noisy religion. Is there such a thing as a silence in Judaism?" And Wiesel replied in these words: "Judaism is full of silences. But we don't talk about them." [Laughter]

So this is a glaring silence. Why Abraham? Now I repeat: Judaism doesn't like silences and, therefore, the Jewish tradition filled in the gap. You know the famous story 'Number One'? Abraham was the first iconoclast. He took the idols that his father sold or that Nimrod sold and, quietly one night, he smashed the lot of them and left the hammer in the hands of the biggest idol. The next morning, when everyone wanted to know who broke the idols, he said, "Look, this big idol"—you know the story. You learned it in *cheder*. Abraham, the first iconoclast.

According to Maimonides, Hilhot Avoda Zara, Chapter 1, Abraham was the first philosopher. There he sees the universe, the stars wheeling in their axes, and he says to himself: How can the stars move if nobody moves them? How can the universe exist if nobody created them?—Abraham was, in other words, proto-Aristotle or Rambam—whatever it was. The first philosopher. The first person to think of what Aristotle calls "God as the prime mover." You know those stories.

I now want to tell you a third story, which is very enigmatic. This one is going to hold the key to everything I have to say. Here it is. Midrash Raba says, "God said to Abraham Lech lecha." Says the Midrash, "*Mashal le'ehad shehaya over mimakom lemakom vera'ah birah ehad doleket*. What is this like? God has called to Abraham. It is like somebody who is on a journey and in the middle of a place he sees a palace in flames. He says to himself, '*Tomar shebirah hazu belo manhig*? How can this palace be in flames? Surely a palace has an owner? If it has an owner, somebody is looking after it, somebody should be putting out the fire!' At that moment the owner of the palace appears on the battlements and says, 'I am the owner of the palace.'"

So Abraham was saying to himself: Is it possible that the world doesn't have a *manhig*, a ruler? *Hitzitz shelo beKodesh barechu ve'amar lo*—God looked down on him and said: *Ani hu ba'al ha'olam*. I am the owner of the universe.

That is the passage: Midrash Raba on Lech Lecha. This is a very enigmatic passage. So enigmatic that it was subject to beautiful misinterpretations by 20th century theologians—one of them, a wonderful man, the late A. J. Heschel. I don't know if you have read A. J. Heschel's work. A. J. Heschel was a Jewish mystic, grandson of one of the great hasidic leaders after whom he was named, the Apter Rav. Heschel translated *birah doleket* - which I have translated as 'a palace in flames'—Heschel translated it as 'he saw a palace full of light.'

According to this, Abraham was a mystic, a kind of Wordsworth, wandering "lonely as a cloud," seeing the whole world full of the glory of God.

"I have felt
A presence that disturbs me with the joy
Of elevated thoughts; a sense sublime
Of something far more deeply interfused,
Whose dwelling is the light of setting suns . . ."

Anyway, there it is—the radiance of the Creator. He saw a palace full of light. Unfortunately, *birah doleket* means "a palace in flames." It does not mean "a palace full of light."

Louis Jacobs in one of his books gives it a different theme. Abraham is a philosopher, a rationalist. Somebody who has reason to believe, and he says the following thing. He says that this is like the cosmological argument. You know: the argument from design. The famous argument put forward by Paley that if you are wandering along in a desert and you see a rock or a hill, you don't ask who created that. But if you are wandering along a desert and you see a watch, you say: Listen, somebody made that. The bits are too intricate. They fit together too carefully. They were obviously designed with a function in mind and therefore, since they have design, they must have had a designer.

So, says Abraham, according to Louis Jacobs, even though the world sometimes appears to us as if it is on fire, nonetheless, underneath it all there is a palace. It looks as if it has architecture. The universe looks as if it has structure: the human genome. Whatever. I will talk about that some other time. Anyway, that is the second explanation. However, I think both of those are beautiful interpretations: only they do not mean what the passage means!

Here it is. And I repeat: this is radical stuff but bear with me.

Abraham sees a palace. That means that he sees the world has order. Therefore, it has a Creator. But the palace is in flames—which means the world is full of disorder. It is full of evil, violence, injustice. Now nobody builds a building and then goes away and deserts it. Therefore, if there is a fire, there must be somebody in charge to put it out. The building must have an owner. Where is he? And that is Abraham's question. Where is God in this world?

That is the question that gives Abraham no peace. Here, if I am right, that is the starting point of Jewish faith. In Judaism, faith does not begin with an answer. It begins with a question. It doesn't begin in harmony. It begins in dissonance. Here it is: if God created the world then God created man. Why then does God allow man to destroy the world? How can we reconcile the order of the world with the disorder of human society? Can God have made the world only to desert it? That is Abraham's question. *"Efshar sheha'olam beli manhig*?—Can it be the world has no one in charge, no owner?" That is his question.

I now want to outline to you the two logical possibilities which are the only possible answers to that question. Here they are—and these have been the two defining possibilities throughout most of human culture. There are two ways of seeing the world.

Way one—and this one, as you know, prevailed at certain times in the past and certainly prevails today in many quarters. According to this view, there is no God. There are only contending forces: there is chance and there is necessity. There is genetic mutation and natural selection. The strong, the well adapted survive; the weak, the maladapted die. The evolution of the universe is governed by forces which are inexorable and blind. There is no justice because there is no judge. Therefore, there is no question. We can only ever ask "How?" that is, the scientific question. We can never ask the question, "Why?" because there is no "Why?" There is no palace. There are only flames. That is the logical possibility: one.

Logical possibility: two. This is the opposite of the first. God exists. Therefore, everything that is, is because He made it. Everything that happens, happens because He willed it, in which case all injustice must be an illusion. We think it is evil because we don't really understand. When people suffer, either it is they are being punished because they did wrong or, if they are innocent, it is to purge them, to purify them, to teach them sympathy or compassion or serenity. Somehow God organizes the soul's perfection through the body's torments. All evil is good in disguise. If we could only see things through God's perspective, we would have no question because everything, being from God, is good. There are no flames: there is only the palace.

Those are the two—and only two—logical possibilities. The faith of Abraham begins in a refusal to accept either answer. Because both contain an element of truth and between them there is a contradiction. Either God exists, in which case there is no evil. Or evil exists, in which case there is no God. But supposing both exist? Supposing there are both God and evil? Supposing there are both the palace and the flames?

Now if that is so, if my interpretation is right, then Judaism begins not in the conventional place where faith is thought to begin, namely in wonder that the world is. Judaism begins in the opposite, in the protest against a world that is not as it ought to be. At the very heart of reality, by which I mean reality as we see it, from our point of view, there is a contradiction between order and chaos: the order of creation and the chaos we make.

Now the question is: how do we resolve that contradiction? And the answer is that that contradiction between the palace and the flames, between the world that is and the world that ought to be, cannot be resolved at the level of thought. It doesn't exist! You cannot resolve it! Logically, philosophically, in terms of theology or theodicy, you cannot do it! The only way you can resolve that tension is by action; by making the world better than it is.

That is the only way you can lessen the tension between the palace and the flames. When things are as they ought to be, when there is only a palace and no flames—then we have resolved the tension. Then we have reached our destination. But that is not yet. It was not yet for Abraham and it is not yet for us. And from this initial contradiction, from this cognitive dissonance, are born the following four fundamental features of Judaism.

Feature one: the primary thing in Judaism is "doing," is action, is deed, is mitzvah. Because only the mitzvah

makes the world a little less dissonant between what it is and what it ought to be.

Secondly: the whole program of Judaism, the project of the Torah, is *tikkun olam* in the precise sense "mending a fragmented, fractured, world."

Thirdly: (and I'm telling you a whole book in an hour here) we have the revolutionary concept in Judaism of linear time. There is an American writer called Thomas Cahill who wrote a bestseller in America a year or two back called "The Gifts of the Jews." He is actually Catholic. His whole book is on this idea, linear time. He says that if only for this alone, Jews would have changed the course of western civilization. Namely, that as time goes by, we lessen the dissonance between the world as it is, and the world as it ought to be. In which case, not everything in the world stays the same. In which case time is not just like time on the clock that goes round and round and round. The cyclical time of myth: day, night, summer, autumn, winter, spring, etc. etc. The cyclical time of mythical thought, of Greek thought, of Nietzschean thought, eternal occurrences—Judaism crashes through that and says: No, time also has a linear dimension. It is a journey towards a destination. It has a beginning and an end, an endpoint very distant from here. It is like a story, a narrative that has a beginning, middle and end because the world changes. Because we see that there is something wrong with the world. That is linear time which, according to most people, originated in Judaism.

Fourthly: obviously, already we can see here the very beginning of the story, the concept of the destination which is called *yemot haMeshiach*—the Messianic Age, which makes Judaism, alone of all the great faiths and all the great cultures, the one culture (with, of course, the exception of Marxism) which sees the Golden Age not as something in the past but as something in the future. Which gave the world the concept of hope. Here's my plug for my new book which just came out today, called "The Politics of Hope" on the concept of hope, which is the basic concept of the Messianic age.

In other words, faced with conflicting evidence between order and chaos, between God and evil, it would have been so easy to deny the reality of one or the other. Either we deny God, in which case we have despair:

or we deny evil, in which case we have consolation. Judaism refuses the premature and easy options: despair on the one hand; consolation on the other. If either of those logical alternatives were true—either there is no justice or everything in the world is just—then we could live at peace with the world. But to be a Jew is to refuse those easy answers and to live within the tension which sees evil as real and therefore rejects premature consolation, acceptance of the world. And it is also to say that God is real and therefore hope is not an illusion.

If God exists then life has a purpose. If evil exists then we have not yet achieved that purpose. Until then we must travel: *lech lecha*—like Abraham and Sarah traveled and as Jews have traveled ever since—*el ha'aretz asher are'eka*—to the land which I will show you—which is always just over the horizon which is always not quite yet.

What is haunting about this midrash is not only Abraham's question but also God's reply. What He does is that He stands there and He says, *"Ani hu ba'al habirah.*—I am the Owner of the palace. I am the Ruler of the world. In effect, all He says is, "I am here." That's all He says. Abraham asks God, *"Ribono shel olam*—the world is on fire: where are You?" And God replies with the first words He said to Adam and Eve as they were about to leave the Garden—*"Ayeka*?—Where are you?"

Abraham says: "God, why did you abandon the world?" God says to Abraham: "Why did you abandon Me?"

And there then begins that dialogue between Heaven and Earth which has not ceased in 4,000 years—that dialogue in which God and Man find one another—whose resolution is not an answer—a solution whose resolution is an action. Because God says to Man: Only you can put out the flames and I will show you how.

Now look: I find this an extraordinary analysis. But only thus can we understand the great dialogues between God and Abraham and Moses and Jeremiah and Job—dialogues which, I repeat, are unique to Judaism—dialogues which never ended in the Bible! I don't know if you know, but those dialogues between the prophets and God, the mood of those dialogues was a never-ending feature in Judaism.

They were even accentuated in the midrashic and aggadic literature. They exist if you read it carefully in the literature of lament of the mediaeval period, the things we call *kinot* and *slichot*. They exist in hassidic stories, especially for those of you familiar with hassidic stories about the great hassidic Rebbe, Levi Yitzhak of Berdichev. Many of his stories are that kind of dialogue with God. And they exist of course in the Holocaust literature, the most famous example the recently republished dialogue or monologue, whatever, called "Yossel Rakover speaks to God."

In other words, that dialogue over the existence of evil has been a non-stop feature of Judaism from biblical times to the present and that is what I call the dialogical imagination as opposed to the logical imagination.

Now I want to show you something. Here it is. I want to show you how this feature of biblical Judaism got carried over to rabbinic thought. I want to show you just one simple example that I find fascinating. Here it is. For those of you who want to look them up, the sources from which I am quoting are the Mishnah in Brachot, Chapter 9—you will find it in the Talmud Bavli on page 54a, and the commentary of the Babylonian Talmud which you will find on Brachot page 60a and 60b. To understand this little drama that unfolds on the pages of the Talmud, you just have to understand one distinction. The Torah has two kinds of literature, right? The five Mosaic books—on the one hand there is narrative; on the other hand there is law.

Now what are the rabbinic equivalents of narrative and law? What do we call those? Law is halachah; and narrative etc. is aggadah. So aggadah is all the stuff that isn't law. It is biblical interpretation. It is theological speculation. It is stories and so on. Or to put it in a more focused way: what question does halachah answer?—How shall I act? What question does aggadah answer?—Why did this happen? Those are the two questions.

Now I want to tell you about the Mishnah in the last chapter of Brachot. The Mishnah contains three—well, it contains lots of statements but I am going to focus only on three. Here they are.

No. 1: If you get good news, you need to make a brachah. If you get bad news, you also need to make a brachah, a different brachah. What is the brachah for good news? *Hatov vehamaitiv.* Brachah over bad news (you shouldn't know of such things) - *Dayan ha'emet.* Ok? That is number one.

Number two is a very obscure passage. I don't know what it means. It says *mevareich al hara'a m'ain al hatovah; mevareich al hatovah mi'ain al hara'a.* You make a blessing over the bad that contains a bit of good and over the good that contains a bit of bad. We'll explain that in a moment.

Then the third statement: *hayav adam levareich al hara keshem shemevareich al tovah.* You have to make a blessing over bad news as well as over good news.

Ok. That is the third statement. Let's take the third statement first. Here it goes. What does it mean when the Gemara says you need to make a blessing over the bad news as well as good? The Gemara says the following. Reb Huna said in the name of Rav in the name of Rabbi Meir and Rabbi Akiva also said: A person should always say *kol de'avid rahmanah letovah avid.* Whatever God does is for the best. Whatever the Almighty does is for the good. Here it is. Rabbi Akiva was once on a journey and he came to a town and he wanted a room. Everyone refused to give him a room. Can you imagine such a thing? A Jewish town without *hachnasat orchim*? So Rabbi Akiva, instead of getting upset, said, *kol de'avid rahmanah letovah avid.* Or, as we probably say, *gam zu letovah.* This too is for good. He didn't know how, but he assumed that the Almighty meant it for good.

Then, of course, Rabbi Akiva had with him a cockerel, an ass and a lamp. During the night, the wind came and blew out the lamp. A fox came and ate the cock. A lion came and ate the ass. So he wakes up and there is nothing there. Rabbi Akiva says: *Gam zu letovah.* This also is for good.

So the Gemara says, Well, when he came back into the town the next morning, he discovered that some bandits had entered the town and taken all the inhabitants off as captives. So Rabbi Akiva said: "Wasn't I right to say *gam zu letovah*? All this is for the good. You see, if I had got a room in the town, I would have been taken captive. If the light had been burning, they would have known I was there. If the cock had been there it would have crowed and they would have known I was there. If the ass had been there, it would have brayed and they would have known I was there. So, obviously, whatever the Almighty does is for good, baruch Hashem."

You ask a Jew how things are: he says "Baruch Hashem," and you say, "Gevalt, that bad?"

So that is the aggadah. Whatever God does is for the best. The Gemara doesn't ask what the inhabitants of the town thought about Rabbi Akiva's sunny view of things. But there it is. The view that whatever God does is for the best, which we associate philosophically with Gottfried Leibniz: "All is for the best in the best of possible worlds" which, as you rightly say, was pilloried or satirized in Voltaire's *Candide* in the figure of Dr. Pangloss. That is an aggadah. Ok?

However, now I want to show you something surprising. If whatever God does is for the best, then what should you say over bad news? Baruch Hashem. *Hatov vehamaitiv.* But the halachah isn't like that. The halachah says that over good news one says *hatov vehamaitiv;* over bad news one says *baruch Dayan emet.*

So the halachah recognizes the reality of evil, which Rabbi Akiva's aggadah did not recognize. And now I come to the third statement which is, what is *mevareich al hara'a mi'ain al hatovah; mevareich al hatovah mi'ain al hara'a*? And here is the Gemara. The Gemara asks the following question—and it must be being asked in several towns in England at the moment.

Your field is flooded. This is bad news now. On the other hand, I don't know. Do floods improve the quality of fields? They did in the Middle East because they brought alluvial deposits and all fresh earth. So, when all the bad is over it is going to be good. You know this at the time you see the flood. You know it is bad now but it is good in the future. What bracha do you make? [Inaudible response from audience.] Is that good news or bad news? The answer is: not both. On this one, Judaism is unequivocal. You make a bracha - *Dayan emet.* The halachah is interested in now. It is not interested in the future. It is interested in now. In general, the halachah is interested in now. So if you have got bad news, which is one day going to be good news, you still make *Dayan emet*. Now you understand that that Gemara which is in Brachot 60A directly contradicts the brachah on the next page, 60B, in which Rabbi Akiva says: "Whatever God does is for the best—because even though it is bad now, as I discovered, by the next morning it is good."

There is a fat contradiction between Aggada, the world in which everything is good, and halachah in which not everything is good: in which evil is real and recognized as such by the halachah. And, of course, how do you resolve that contradiction? I said to you before, you can resolve a contradiction either by saying that it represents two different viewpoints in space, or two different viewpoints in time—chronological or dialogical. In this case the answer lies in time.

If we look back at the past, we can ask the aggadic question: Why did this happen? And we can try and find explanations, consolations that actually it happened for the best. But when we look towards the future: What then shall I do? When we look towards the future, halachah insists in living in a world in which evil is real and not to be confused with good! If you make the brachah *"hatov vehamaitiv"* over bad news, even though one day it is going to be good, you have made a blessing in vain. You have broken the third commandment.

I want you to see how halachah and aggadah are two different perspectives on the universe. When we reflect on the past, we can find consolation. When we look to the future, we must refuse to be consoled. In aggadah you can ask--God forbid we should ask, but in aggadah you can ask: Why did that child die? Why did that innocent person get caught up in the bomb blast? Why, if x was such a good human being, did he suffer so many things in this life? You can ask those in aggadah. But in halachah you can never accept a situation which maybe you can change as a fait accompli to be accepted. You may not! Because evil is evil and halachah does not allow you to confuse it with good—even if maybe it will bring about good. That which can be changed is not sacred. If you can cure an illness, if you can remedy an injustice, if you right a wrong—then halachah says you must! Because you cannot be at ease with it because God does everything for the best.

Looking back on the past, maybe you can. Last summer, Elaine and I were in the University of Stirling where Mel Gibson fought the battle against the British in "Braveheart"—it's a great place, a lovely place—twenty-seven countries—Maccabi European Olympics—great stuff—lots of kids; 1500 Jewish kids. We went there; we spent Shabbos with them. We were there for the opening of the games. We spent Shabbos with 1500 Jewish kids from 27 different countries.

It was beautiful; one of the loveliest experiences I ever went through. I said to them as Shabbos came in that I wanted to tell them a little story: For most of you, this is the first time you have ever been here in Stirling University. For me, it is the second time. (A true story—I tell it in "Celebrating Life.") I said, I was here in this room 30 years ago, almost exactly. I will tell you that 30 years ago I had just finished Cambridge and I applied for my first job: lecturer in philosophy at Stirling University. I didn't get it. I've got to tell you that I got turned down for every job I ever applied for. (Laughter) Yes!

So there I was. I was 21 years old. I had just been turned down after the first job application I ever made. For 30 years that has rankled. Then I said to them: Supposing I had got the job? I would never have become a rabbi. I would never have become a Chief Rabbi and I would never be here to welcome 1500 Jews celebrating Shabbos together because the University is on holiday and all the academics are away. Now—now I understand—after 30 years, that *gam zu letovah*! And I am sure all of you must have had some experience when you look back on your life and you saw that thing which seemed so painful or bad or wrong at the time—it turned out to be a necessary stage in a journey which brought you to where you are today.

Once in a while we can look back and say *gam zu letovah*. But when we look forward, we can not. And now I hope we are able to understand this incredible complex duality at the heart of Judaism which explains halachah and aggadah. Which explains the dialogues of Abraham, Moses, Jeremiah and Job, because there are two points of view: there is God's point of view and there is Man's point of view. From God's point of view, sub specie æternitates—if you can see everything, then doubtless everything has an explanation. We don't doubt this! If only we could see the totality of things! If only we could see the long run. If we could only see the next world as well as this world, I am sure we would understand why everything that happened, happened.

You know the famous analogy, the one that Rav Soloveitchik brings: you are looking at the underside of a Persian carpet. You are looking underneath and there are all these strings and threads of different colors in apparent chaos and you don't know what they are doing. If only you could go round to see it from the top, not from the underneath, you would see that every one of them was necessary to make this brilliant and beautiful and intricate pattern. That is how things look from God's point of view and that is a point of view we sometimes glimpse from Tenach and, as I say, we sometimes glimpse in life. That is the tone of voice you find in aggadah. That is the tone of voice you sometimes get when God answers the prophets.

However, that is God's point of view. What is crucial to Judaism is that God's point of view is not the only point of view. When God empowered us, when God asked us to be his partner in the work of creation, when God said: Let not only Me be creative, let this human being that I have made also be creative—then God made space for us and, in order to make space for us, He had to confer legitimacy on the world as it appears to us. So although God knew that all the inhabitants of Sodom and Gomorra were evil, Abraham didn't know. Abraham didn't know! Therefore God empowers Abraham to make the speech in their defense. Although God knew He was going to redeem the Israelites, Moses didn't know! Therefore God empowers Moses to protest *lama hari'osa le'am hazeh*. Although God knew the reasons for Job's suffering, Job didn't know and therefore God empowers Job to protest his innocence. And where do you see this obviously? In the case of Noah, for heaven's sake!

Let me ask you a simple question. We read Noah on Shabbos. Tell me, what did Noah say to God while the flood was going on?—Not a word. Not a word. I told you he wasn't Jewish! [Laughter] Not a word—not a word. Just three times: Noah did everything that God commanded. Noah was obedient. Noah didn't protest. Believe it or not, that thing which surely in every religious system is the highest virtue—that you are obedient, that

you accept God's decree—in Judaism is not the highest. In fact, that is why Noah fails and that is why Abraham succeeds. Because Noah accepts but Abraham protests.

Only somebody who protests, who sees the reality of evil from a human perspective; only somebody who sees not only the palace but also the flames—only that person understands the fundamental proposition of Judaism that we are here not to accept the world but to change the world. And, yes—we agree that in the fullness of time or in the world to come, or if we could understand how it is that the butterfly's wings fluttering in China will give George W. Bush victory in the United States [Laughter]—we would understand why bad things happen—not that I mean for one moment that that might be a bad thing—but our very humanity means that we cannot see the fullness of time! We cannot envisage the world to come! We cannot understand the interconnectedness of things. We haven't got that infinity to wait. As the Yiddish prayer goes—it's my favorite prayer of all—*"Ribono shel olam,* I know You're going to help me, but please could You help me until You help me?!"

Our perspective is very fragmentary, fragile and short-term and, therefore, we do not understand. Therefore, evil seems to us real and it is real for us. And God affirms our humanity.

Now I come back to where I began, with those two logical alternatives—and I want to state them, as clearly as I can in a post-Holocaust context. On the one hand, maybe Nietzsche was right, maybe there is no justice. Maybe there is no Judge. Maybe there is no God and no meaning to life. Maybe there is no palace—only the flames. In which case, any attempt to find moral meaning in the universe is destined to fail. All we have is the struggle for existence and what Nietzsche called "the will to power." The strong crush the weak. The clever outwit the simple. The powerful dominate the powerless. And in such a world there is no reason not to expect a holocaust.

On the other hand, maybe Leibniz is right. Maybe the devout believer is right. Maybe all evil is an illusion. Maybe everything that happens happens in the world because God willed it so. In which case we may not know why the Holocaust happened. But there is a reason for it: God's reason. And we must accept it. We must accept the fact of the Holocaust as God's unfathomable will.

I tell you that I as a Jew refuse to accept either alternative. I refuse to accept them because either of them would allow me to live at peace with the world and I believe it is morally impossible to live at peace in a world that contained an Auschwitz. Therefore, I hope I have shown you how this faith of multiple perspectives, of cognitive dissonance, which is lived out in time through the conversation between Earth and Heaven and lived out in dialogue, is the energizing tension at the heart of Judaism. It is what drives us to act and try to change the world. If we see the dissonance between our world and God's world, between the flames and the palace, between the "is" and the "ought," then we know that that tension can be resolved only by action which is inspired by revelation, which moves us closer to redemption.

That is what happens when we see the palace and we see the flames. We call out to God and we find Him calling out to us saying, "You must fight the fire. You, human beings, must put out the flames and I will show you how."

Friends, let me sum up what I have tried to say "rabbonishly." I am sorry I have been a bit philosophical and intellectual. Let me sum it up in another way, in the form of a dvar Torah. You know that there is a famous and very moving moment in the Torah when the brothers return to Jacob with the bloodstained cloak of Joseph whom they have sold into slavery, and they have faked this coat dipped in goat's blood. They ask Jacob if he recognized it as the coat of his son, Joseph. An evil beast has devoured him. And Jacob recognizes it and he says that well, an evil beast must have devoured him. And he weeps and the brothers try to comfort him. The Torah uses two extraordinarily powerful and strange words. "*Vayema'ain lehitnakhaim*—He refused to be comforted."

Now you know and I know that in Judaism there is a fundamental principle—*yesh gvul le'availut*—there is a limit to mourning. There is shiva. There is shloshim. For

a parent, there is a year. And when that time has passed, Judaism forbids us to mourn any longer. The Gemara says "*Hamitkasheh al maito yoter midai*"—someone who mourns for too long—God says to him, "Are you more compassionate than I am?"

It is forbidden in Jewish law to refuse to be comforted. Why then did Jacob refuse to be comforted? The answer is very simple—and it is given by an ancient midrash and here it is.

When is it that we can be comforted? The answer is: only when we are sure that somebody is dead. When we have given up hope of ever seeing them alive again, then we can be comforted. Jacob was not sure that Joseph was dead. He was not convinced that the bloodstained coat was telling him the truth. He did not give up hope that one day he would see his son Joseph alive again. And, in fact, he did see Joseph alive again. When do you refuse to be comforted? When you refuse to give up hope.

Many faiths, many philosophers, give us—as Alain de Botton puts it, quoting that interpolated palimpsest . . . "The Consolations of Philosophy." Many philosophies, many faiths give us consolations—nekhamah, comfort. They reconcile us to the work. Judaism is *Vayema'ain lehitnakhaim*. We refuse to be comforted. We refuse to be comforted when the world still contains violence and oppression and evil. And the reason we refuse to be comforted is that we refuse to give up hope. Because if we can change ourselves, we can change the world. And if we can change the world, we can put out the fire so that the palace, God's palace, is no longer in flames.

Thank you very much. [Applause]

Reprinted with permission from chiefrabbi.org.

Lesson 2

The Voice of Your Brother's Blood Cries Out
How the Holocaust Impacts Us as Jews

Introduction

The word "Holocaust" refers to the murder and destruction of much of European Jewry. But who can understand the Holocaust? As Elie Wiesel relates:

> The stories that I want to tell, that I feel I must tell, I most often keep to myself. Because I feel nobody would comprehend. I know people read and explain. Some people are moved. But I do know that no one will know what I know. No one will know what we who were there know. That knowledge cannot be communicated. And it pains me, it haunts me, because this is exactly what the killers wanted to attain. They pushed their brutality, their cruelty, beyond the limits of language, so that when we tell the tale, nobody knows what we are talking about. And yet . . . we try. Maybe five hundred years from now, someone will sit here or anywhere and pick up a book that . . . I have written and that person will feel more than the person today does.

(*CONVERSATIONS WITH ELI WIESEL,* p. 124)

And so we too, will try. We will try to explore some of the individual experiences of the Holocaust so that we can feel just a little bit more and so that we can understand just a little bit more.

Six Million Individuals

TEXT 1

The more we come to know about the Holocaust, how it came about, how it was carried out, etc., the greater the possibility that we will become sensitized to inhumanity and suffering whenever they occur. If we take shortcuts, we are in danger of losing all distinctions, of what [Professor] Yosef Yerushalmi calls the "debasement of our vocabulary." We may soon have simply one more word which for a short time was a new and powerful symbol, but which quickly became emptied of all meaning.

EVA FLEISCHNER, ED.
AUSCHWITZ: BEGINNING OF A NEW ERA? PP. 228–229

Eva Fleischner (1925–). Professor emerita of religion from Montclair State University. Born in Vienna to Catholic parents, she fled to England after the *Anschluss* because of her father's Jewish roots. She is the editor of the influential book *Auschwitz: Beginning of a New Era?*

TEXT 2A

קוֹל דְּמֵי אָחִיךָ צֹעֲקִים אֵלַי מִן הָאֲדָמָה

בראשית ד,י

The voice of the bloods [*sic*] of your brother are crying out to Me from the ground.

BEREISHIT/GENESIS 4:10

Text 2B

שכן מצינו בקין כשהרג את הבל

נאמר בו: קול דמי אחיך צועקים אלי מן האדמה

אינו אומר דם אחיך אלא דמי אחיך, דמו ודם זרעיותיו . . .

לפיכך נברא אדם יחידי בעולם

ללמד: שכל המאבד נפש אחת מעלין עליו כאילו איבד עולם מלא

וכל המקיים נפש אחת מעלין עליו כאילו קיים עולם מלא

משנה, תלמוד ירושלמי ד,ט

So do we find in the case of Cain, who slew [his brother] Abel. It states, "The voice of the 'bloods' of your brother are crying out to Me from the ground." It does not read "blood of your brother," but "bloods of your brother," [which means] his blood and the blood of his descendants. . . . Therefore, the [first] human being was created singly in the world, to teach you that one who destroys a single human being is considered [by the Torah] as if he had destroyed a whole world, and one who saves a single human being is considered [by the Torah] as if he saved a whole world.

MISHNAH, JERUSALEM TALMUD, SANHEDRIN 4:9

קוֹל דְּמֵי אָחִיךָ צֹעֲקִים אֵלַי
מִן הָאֲדָמָה

Universal Suffering and Particular Pain

TEXT 3

Anne Frank (1929–1945). A German-Jewish teenager who spent over two years with her family in hiding during World War II before being arrested by the Nazis and deported to a concentration camp. Frank died of typhus at Bergen-Belsen at the age of fifteen. Her diary, first published in 1947, has been translated into sixty-seven languages, and is one of the most widely-read books about the Holocaust.

Who has inflicted this on us? Who has set us apart from all the rest? Who has put us through such suffering? It's God who has made us the way we are, but it's also God who will lift us up again. In the eyes of the world, we're doomed, but if, after all this suffering, there are still Jews left, the Jewish people will be held up as an example. Who knows, maybe our religion will teach the world and all the people in it about goodness, and that's the reason, the only reason, we have to suffer. We can never be just Dutch or just English or whatever, we will always be Jews as well. And we have to keep on being Jews, but then, we'll want to be.

ANNE FRANK, THE DIARY OF ANNE FRANK, ENTRY, APRIL 11, 1944

TEXT 4

I also believe that although the event was a Jewish event, a Jewish tragedy, it had universal implications and applications. . . .

Don't give up your Jewishness in order to become universal. The only way for me to become universal is through my Jewishness. I do fight for other causes; I always have. My life is testimony to that, and I am still fighting . . .

But I cannot allow my Jewishness to be wiped out in exchange for something I would do for others. I don't want to do that. If I were to kill the Jew in me, what would I do? I would actually do what Hitler did, on a different scale . . .

I repeat: a Jew can attain universality through his or her Jewishness, and that the aim, really, is to attain universality through that consciousness.

ELIE WIESEL, CONVERSATIONS WITH ELIE WIESEL, PP. 166–169

Elie Wiesel (1928–). Professor of the Humanities at Boston University. Born in Sighet, Transylvania, he was deported by the Nazis to Auschwitz at the age of fifteen. Wiesel is the author of more than forty books of fiction and non-fiction, including the acclaimed memoir *Night*, which has appeared in more than thirty languages. In 1986, Wiesel won the Nobel Prize for Peace. Soon after, Wiesel and his wife established The Elie Wiesel Foundation for Humanity. For his literary and human rights activities he has received numerous awards including the Presidential Medal of Freedom and the U.S. Congressional Gold Medal.

A War Against Jews

TEXT 5

Saul P. Friedlander (1933–). Renowned author and Holocaust historian; Professor of Jewish History at UCLA. Born in Prague. Shortly before his parents were sent to the Nazi death camps, Friedlander was left by his parents in a monastery where he was raised. Friedlander grew up Catholic, but in 1947 discovered his Jewish roots, reclaimed his Jewish identity, and emigrated to Israel. In 1983 he was awarded the Israel Prize for his scholarship. In 2008 he won the Pulitzer Prize in the general nonfiction category for his book *The Years of Extermination: Nazi Germany and the Jews, 1939-1945.*

Whereas ordinary racial anti-Semitism is one element within a wider racist worldview, in redemptive anti-Semitism, the struggle against the Jews is the dominant aspect of a worldview in which other racist themes are but secondary appendages.

Redemptive anti-Semitism was born from the fear of racial degeneration and the religious belief in redemption. The main cause of degeneration was the penetration of the Jews into the German body politic, into German society, and into the German bloodstream. Germanhood and the Aryan world were on the path to perdition if the struggle against the Jews was not joined; this was to be a struggle to the death. Redemption would come as liberation from the Jews—as their expulsion, possibly their annihilation . . .

What drove Hitler was his anti-Jewish hatred . . . For Hitler, the struggle against the Jews was the immutable basis and obsessional core of his understanding of history, politics, and political action.

SAUL FRIEDLANDER, NAZI GERMANY AND THE JEWS, P. 102

A mother and her young boy are gathering mushrooms in the German forest. The boy finds some poisonous ones. The mother explains that there are good mushrooms and poisonous ones, and, as they go home, says, "Look, Franz, human beings in this world are like the mushrooms in the forest. There are good mushrooms and there are good people. There are poisonous, bad mushrooms and there are bad people. And we have to be on our guard against bad people just as we have to be on guard against poisonous mushrooms. Do you understand that?"

"Yes, mother," Franz replies. "I understand that in dealing with bad people trouble may arise, just as when one eats a poisonous mushroom. One may even die!"

"And do you know, too, who these bad men are, these poisonous mushrooms of mankind?" the mother continued.

Franz slaps his chest in pride, "Of course I know, mother! They are the Jews! Our teacher has often told us about them."

The mother praises her boy for his intelligence, and goes on to explain the different kinds of "poisonous" Jews: the Jewish peddler, the Jewish cattle-dealer, the Kosher butcher, the Jewish doctor, the baptized Jew, and so on.

"However they disguise themselves or however friendly they try to be, affirming a thousand times their good intentions to us, one must not believe them. Jews they are and Jews they remain. For our Volk they are poison."

"Like the poisonous mushroom!" says Franz.

"Yes, my child! Just as a single poisonous mushroom can kill a whole family, so a solitary Jew can destroy a whole village, a whole city, even an entire Volk."

Franz has understood.

"Tell me, mother, do all non-Jews know that the Jew is as dangerous as a poisonous mushroom?"

Mother shakes her head.

"Unfortunately not, my child. There are millions of non-Jews who do not yet know the Jews. So we have to enlighten people and warn them against the Jews. Our young people, too, must be warned. Our boys and girls must learn to know the Jew. They must learn that the Jew is the most dangerous poison-mushroom in existence. Just as poisonous mushrooms spring up everywhere, so the Jew is found in every country in the world. Just as poisonous mushrooms often lead to the most dreadful calamity, so the Jew is the cause of misery and distress, illness and death."

German youth must learn to recognize the Jewish poison-mushroom. They must learn what a danger the Jew is for the German Volk and for the whole world. They must learn that the Jewish problem involves the destiny of us all.

The following tales tell the truth about the Jewish poison-mushroom. They show the many shapes the Jew assumes. They show the depravity and baseness of the Jewish race. They show the Jew for what he really is: the devil in human form.

THE POISONOUS MUSHROOM, PUBLISHED BY JULIUS STREICHER

Questions for Discussion

1. According to the story, what threat did Jews hold for German society?

2. Why is no distinction made between the baptized Jew, who left Jewish principles behind, and other Jews?

3. Why does the story characterize the Jews as the "devil"?

TEXT 7

The founders of Nazism and the party leaders created a scientific ideology on deeper foundations. They have a complete doctrine which analyzes the Jewish spirit inside and out. Judaism and Nazism are two world outlooks, neither of which is compatible with the other, and for this reason they cannot live together. For two thousand years Judaism has left its imprint, culturally and spiritually, on the nations of the world. It stood like a rock, blocking the spread of German paganism. . . . Two kings cannot use one crown. Either humanity would be Judaic or it would be idolatrous-German. Up until now it was Judaic. . . . The new world which Nazism will fashion is directed toward primitive idolatry with all of its attitudes. It is therefore ready to fight Judaism to the finish.

CHAIM A. KAPLAN, DIARY ENTRY, MARCH, 10, 1940, SCROLL OF AGONY P. 130

Chaim Aron Kaplan (1880–1943). Born in Horodyszcze in 1880, then part of the Russian Empire, today in Belarus. He received a Talmudic education at the famous Yeshiva of Mir. In about 1902 he settled in Warsaw and he founded an elementary Hebrew school of which he was principal for the next forty years. He began his first diary in 1933, and continued writing until he was deported to Treblinka in August, 1942, where he is believed to have perished a few months later.

Spiritual Resistance

TEXT 8A

Lucy S. Dawidowicz (1915–1990). Scholar of Jewish life and history. Born in New York in 1915, she traveled to Vilna, Poland, and was there during the years 1938–1939 when she witnessed the rising European anti-Semitism. Her most famous work is *The War Against the Jews,* widely regarded as a pioneering study of the Nazi genocide.

The Germans deliberately chose observant Jews to force them to desecrate and destroy the sacred articles of Judaism, even to set fire to synagogues. In some places, the Germans piled the Torah scrolls in the marketplace, compelling the Jews to set fire to the pile. . . .

Another German pleasure was "feeding" pork to pious Jews, usually in the presence of an invited audience. The most popular German game, played in countless variations, was "beards." In its simplest versions, Germans seized bearded Jews and beat them. . . . In some places the Jews were assembled in the town square and shorn in a ceremony of mass mockery; elsewhere, beards were set afire.

LUCY S. DAWIDOWICZ, THE WAR AGAINST THE JEWS, PP. 201–202

TEXT 8B

The Germans, denying that the Jews were a religious group, had rendered the entire public existence of the observant community illegal. Not only were observant Jews singled out for German sport and persecution, not only were most synagogues destroyed or desecrated, but all functions pertaining to the observance of Judaism were outlawed: public and/or private worship, religious study and religious teachings, *shehita.* . . .

Like Kashrut, the Sabbath was nearly impossible to observe . . . for the most part, the Germans, with deliberate sadism, forced the Jews to work on Saturdays and the High Holy Days.

LUCY S. DAWIDOWICZ, THE WAR AGAINST THE JEWS, PP. 250–251

TEXT 9

The Holocaust was an unprecedented occurrence that combined a war on Judaism with a war on the Jews. The elements of the war against the Jewish spirit (e.g., abuse of rabbis, violence on Jewish holidays, desecration of synagogues and sacred objects, destruction of religious books) were not only a means of spiritual oppression. They were an end just as the killing was an end.

This unique aspect was rooted in anti-Semitic ideology and especially in Nazi beliefs. For the first time in history, biological race was linked with the human spirit, culture, and morality. The "Jewish germ" was not only the blood that had intermingled with that of the other nations, but the principles of morality, the spirit of liberalism, and the civilization that Judaism had introduced into Europe— everything that represented the antitheses of Nazism. Hitler, as the successor to the nineteenth-century anti-Semites, preached against Judaism no less than against the Jew.

Esther Farbstein. Director of the Holocaust Education Center at Jerusalem's *Michlala* Women's College, and author of *Hidden in Thunder.* The book focuses on the acts of spiritual heroism and documents adherence to Torah practice under the most difficult circumstances imaginable.

Hence, the Nazis had two aims and they furthered each other. The physical extermination was also meant to bring about spiritual annihilation, and the spiritual annihilation was intended to lessen the Jews' physical strength to survive.

ESTHER FARBSTEIN, HIDDEN IN THUNDER, PP. 162–163

TEXT 10

To be a Jew then meant to fight both the complacency of the neutral and the hate of the killers. And to resist—in any way, with any means. And not only with weapons. The Jew who refused death, who refused to believe in death, who chose to marry in the ghetto, to circumcise his son, to teach him the sacred language, to bind him to the threatened and weakened lineage of Israel—that Jew was resisting. The professor or shopkeeper who disregarded facts and warnings and clung to illusion, refusing to admit that people could so succumb to degradation—he, too, was resisting. There was no essential difference between the Warsaw ghetto fighters and the old men getting off the train in Treblinka: because they were Jewish, they were all doomed to hate and death.

In those days, more than ever, to be Jewish signified *refusal*. Above all, it was a refusal to see reality and life through the enemy's eyes—a refusal to resemble him, to grant him that victory, too.

ELIE WIESEL, A JEW TODAY, PP. 8–9

Yaffa Eliach. Professor of Judaic Studies at Brooklyn College, pioneer scholar in Holocaust Studies, and creator of the acclaimed "Tower of Life" at the United States Holocaust Memorial Museum in Washington. Born in Eishyshok in what is now Lithuania, she survived the Holocaust, and immigrated to Palestine with her aunt and uncle in 1946. Her more famous publications include *Hasidic Tales of the Holocaust* and *There Once Was a World*.

TEXT 11

Together with Rabbi Israel Spira [the Rabbi of Bluzhov] in Janowska were twin brothers. . . . One day all the inmates were taken out to work. Three people were left behind to sweep up the barracks: one of the twins, Rabbi Israel Spira, and a third Jew. The German guard ordered the young boy to bring him water. In no time, the boy returned with the water. . . . The German walked over and emptied his revolver into the child's body. "Take him away!" the guard now roared at the rabbi. Rabbi Spira took the boy into his arms and carried him to the pile of bodies while his tears washed the lifeless boy's face.

How would he tell the other twin about his brother's death? Rabbi Spira began to ponder. How would he break the terrible news to one of two souls that were so close to each other? "Tell him that his twin brother is very sick," the other Jew advised the Rabbi.

Evening came. The inmates returned to camp. "Chaim, your brother is very sick, his life is in danger. It is quite possible that he is no longer alive," said the Rabbi of Bluzhov, trying to avoid the boy's eyes.

The brother began to cry, "Woe unto me! What am I going to do now?" The rabbi tried to comfort the boy, but he refused to be comforted.

"Today was his turn to watch over the bread. I left all the bread with him, now I don't have a single piece of bread left," lamented Chaim.

The rabbi was shocked but continued his ruse, saying that the other twin had sent Chaim's share. With a trembling hand, he took from under his jacket a small piece of bread which was his ration for the day and gave it to the boy. Chaim glanced at the stale piece of bread and said, "It's missing a few grams. The piece I left with him was a much larger one."

[The Rabbi replied,] "I was hungry and ate some of it. Tomorrow, I will give you the rest of the bread."

YAFFA ELIACH, HASIDIC TALES OF THE HOLOCAUST, PP. 153–154

Questions for Discussion

1. Of all the caring acts that the rabbi performs in this story, which seems most significant to you?

2. Could the rabbi's actions be characterized as "resistance" against the Nazis? Why or why not?

TEXT 12

Hanukkah came to Bergen Belsen. It was time to kindle the Hanukkah lights. A jug of oil was not to be found, no candle was in sight, and a hanukkiah belonged to the distant past. Instead, a wooden clog, the shoe of one of the inmates, became a hanukkiah; strings pulled from a concentration camp uniform, a wick; and the black camp shoe polish, pure oil. . . .

The Rabbi of Bluzhov [Rabbi Israel Spira] lit the first light and chanted the first two blessings, in his pleasant voice, and the festive melody was filled with sorrow and pain. When he was about to recite the third blessing, he stopped, turned his head, and looked around as if he were searching for something.

But immediately, he turned his face back to the quivering small lights and in a strong, reassuring, comforting voice, chanted the third blessing: "Blessed art Thou, O Lord our God, King of the Universe, who has kept us alive, and hast preserved us, and enabled us to reach this season."

Among the people present at the kindling of the lights was a Mr. Zamietchkowski, one of the leaders of the Warsaw Bund. . . . As soon as the Rabbi of Bluzhov had finished the ceremony of kindling the lights, Zamietchkowski elbowed his way to the rabbi and said, "Spira, you are a clever and honest person. . . . But the fact that you recited the third blessing is beyond me. How could you thank God and say, 'Blessed art Thou, O Lord our God, King of the Universe, who has kept us alive, and hast preserved us, and enabled us to reach this season'? How could you say it when hundreds of dead Jewish bodies are literally lying within the shadows of the Hanukkah lights, when thousands of living Jewish skeletons are walking around in camp, and millions more are being massacred? For this you are thankful to God? For this you praise the Lord? This you call 'keeping us alive'?"

"Zamietchkowski, you are a hundred percent right," answered the rabbi. "When I reached the third blessing, I also hesitated and asked myself, what should I do with this blessing? I turned my head in order to ask the Rabbi of Zaner and other distinguished rabbis who were standing near me, if indeed I might recite the blessing. But just as I was turning my head, I noticed that behind me a throng was standing, a large crowd of living Jews, their faces expressing faith, devotion, and concentration as they were listening to the rite of the kindling of the Hanukkah lights. I said to myself, if God blessed be He, has such a nation that at times like these, when during the lighting of the Hanukkah lights they see in front of them the heaps of bodies of their beloved fathers, brothers, and sons, and death is looking from every corner, if despite all that, they stand in throngs and with devotion listening to the Hanukkah blessing 'who wrought miracles for our fathers in days of old, at this season'; if, indeed, I was blessed to see such a people with so much faith and fervor, then I am under a special obligation to recite the third blessing."

YAFFA ELIACH, HASIDIC TALES OF THE HOLOCAUST, PP. 13–15

Questions for Discussion

1. Why was the rabbi himself in doubt about whether the *shehechiyanu* blessing should be recited? Isn't it part of the traditional liturgy?

2. Upon what was the rabbi's *shehechiyanu* recited? Was it upon being able to light the Chanukah candles or upon the people who had come to participate in the holiday lighting?

3. What do you think the lighting of a Chanukah menorah symbolized to Jews in Bergen-Belsen?

Key Points

1. To save one life is to save an entire universe; to destroy one life is to destroy an entire universe.

2. The most important Jewish number is one. When it comes to suffering, we feel the pain of each individual.

3. The Holocaust was the murder of one Jew. It happened six million times.

4. A Jew can attain universality through his or her Jewishness. The aim is to reach universality through that consciousness.

5. Understanding Jewish suffering is a window into responding to suffering in the world-at-large.

6. Nazism waged a war against the Jews and attempted to dehumanize them.

7. Jews who refused to adopt Nazi values were engaging in a form of spiritual resistance that was as difficult and courageous as armed resistance.

8. There were Jews who were able to wrestle with issues of meaning, faith, and life from a position of spiritual freedom amidst the horror of their physical surroundings.

Supplementary Texts

Text A

f, with the help of his Marxist creed, the Jew is victorious over the other peoples of the world, his crown will be the funeral wreath of humanity and this planet will, as it did thousands of years ago, move through [the] ether devoid of human beings.

b. Today I believe that I am acting in accordance with the will of the Almighty Creator: by defending myself against the Jew, I am fighting for the work of the Lord.

c. If at the beginning of the War [WWI] and during the War, twelve or fifteen thousand of these Hebrew corrupters of the people had been held under poison gas, as happened to hundreds of thousands of our very best German workers in the field, the sacrifice of millions at the front would not have been in vain.

d. Anti-Semitism as a political movement cannot and should not be determined by emotional factors, but on the contrary, by an understanding of the facts. [The facts are] in the first instance, Jewry is without question a race and not a fellowship. . . . The effect of Jewry will be racial tuberculosis of nations.

e. Rational anti-Semitism, however, must lead to a systematic legal opposition and elimination of the special privileges which Jews hold in contrast to the other aliens living among us (alien's legislation). Its final objective must unswervingly be the removal of the Jews altogether.

f. The racial question gives the key not only to world history, but to all human culture. . . In the blood alone resides the strength as well as the weakness of man.

g. What we must fight for is to safeguard the existence and reproduction of our race and our people, the sustenance of our children and the purity of our blood, the freedom and independence of the fatherland, so that our people may mature for the fulfillment of the mission allotted to it by the Creator of the universe.

ADOLF HITLER, SELECTIONS FROM MEIN KAMPF

TEXT B

As a child, [I] remember always asking the question you asked me in the letter—everyone in his language. Lachego . . . Pourquoi . . . Why . . . What did I do? What was my crime? Why did you beat me? Why did you make me starving and freezing? Why did you murder my parents? A brother of thirteen years—yesterday sixty-six years ago he went to Treblinka and never came back. Thirteen years old. Why? Is there any reason, any logic? Was I your enemy? [The] National Socialist Party was afraid of me? Did I threaten them?

No answer. Seventy years later we, human beings, have no answer. We can try to explain anti-Semitism. Not only you cannot justify it, you cannot really explain it.

When we were in Warsaw, people—some people used to say—they hate the Jews because they are so strange. Look at their appearance, their language; they don't speak Polish, they speak Yiddish. Their mentality! Look at them—their clothes, their beards, their hats. If they were equal—we would give them all the rights.

One kilometer from Poland is Germany. The Jews in Germany didn't wear beards, or black long coats, and they spoke German beautifully. And they were involved in all fields of society—musicians, authors, philosophers, industrialists, commerce, literature, science. So how can you explain this logic—this un-logic: when you are different, we hate you. When you are too close to us, equal to us—we hate you as well.

RABBI YISRAEL MEIR LAU, SPEECH TO EUROPEAN PARLIAMENT, BRUSSELS, NOVEMBER 10, 2008

Rabbi Yisrael Meir Lau (1937–). Chief rabbi of Tel Aviv-Jaffa, and former chief rabbi of the State of Israel. Born in Piotrków Trybunalski, Poland to Rabbi Moshe Chaim Lau, who was rabbi of the town. At the age of eight he was liberated in Buchenwald by American forces. His writings include *Do Not Raise Your Hand Against the Boy*, his best-selling autobiographical account of his Holocaust experiences. In 2005 Rabbi Lau received the Israel Prize for Lifetime Achievement.

TEXT C

The second episode took place inside the kingdom of night. In one of the barracks several hundred Jews gathered to celebrate Simhath Torah. In the shadow of shadows? Yes—even there. On the threshold of the death chambers? Yes—even there. But since there was no *Sefer Torah*, how could they organize the traditional procession with the sacred scrolls? As they were trying to solve the problem, an old man . . . noticed a young boy—who was so old, so old—standing there looking on and dreaming.

"Do you remember what you learned in heder?" asked the man.

"Yes, I do," replied the boy.

"Really?" said the man, "you really remember *Sh'ma Yisrael*?"

"I remember much more," said the boy.

"*Sh'ma Yisrael* is enough," said the man. And he lifted the boy, clasped him in his arms and began dancing with him—as though *he* were the Torah. And all joined in. They all sang and danced and cried. They wept, but they sang with fervor—never before had Jews celebrated Simhath Torah with such fervor. . . .

Never mind that our enemies are powerful—we shall fight them nonetheless. Never mind that they seek our destruction—we shall resist them in our own Jewish way, which means that we will not allow them to tell us when to be joyous and when to mourn, when to sing and when to be silent! I, for one, will not allow them to decide whether I should or should not celebrate Simhath Torah! These decisions are ours to make—and we make them as free and sovereign Jews. That was why we *had* to celebrate Simhath Torah. Sure, it wasn't easy to rejoice with a heavy heart. Yet in spite of the tears, in spite of the pain and agony, we had to rejoice—and let the world know that Jews can sublimate pain and agony! And that Jews are able to draw new reasons for hope from their despair. We did so one generation ago when our reasons to despair were infinite. Those who emerged from that ordeal were the stronger for it. They were the strongest Jews in history, and their strength, paradoxically, had its source in the Holocaust.

Thus Judaism teaches us to turn every experience into a dynamic force. We must not let the enemy impose his laws. Our strength is in our freedom. Ultimately, we alone must decide what to do—what to be. Whenever the enemy wants to arouse our anger, hoping thus to distort the image we have of ourselves, we will not let him. Whenever the enemy wants us to open ourselves to hate and despair, we will not listen.

Elie Wiesel, A Jew Today, pp. 162–165

Additional Readings

Death in Tehran
A Holocaust Experience

By **Viktor Frankl**

In Auschwitz, I had laid down a rule for myself which proved to be a good one and which most of my comrades later followed. I generally answered all kinds of questions truthfully. But I was silent about anything that was not expressly asked for. If I were asked my age, I gave it. If asked about my profession, I said "doctor" but did not elaborate. The first morning in Auschwitz an SS officer came to the parade ground. We had to fall into separate groups of prisoners: over forty years, under forty years, metal workers, mechanics, and so forth. Then we were examined for ruptures and some prisoners had to form a new group. The group that I was in was driven to another hut, where we lined up again. After being sorted out once more and having answered questions as to my age and profession, I was sent to another small group. Once more we were driven to another hut and grouped differently. This continued for some time, and I became quite unhappy, finding myself among strangers who spoke unintelligible foreign languages. Then came the last selection, and I found myself back in the group that had been with me in the first hut. They had barely noticed that I had been sent from hut to hut in the meantime. But I was aware that in those few minutes fate had passed me in many different turns.

When the transport of sick patients for the "rest camp" was organized, my name (that is, my number) was put on the list, since a few doctors were needed. But no one was convinced that the destination was really a rest camp. A few weeks previously the same transport had been prepared. Then, too, everyone had thought that it was destined for the gas ovens. When it was announced that anyone who volunteered for the dreaded night shift would be taken off the transport list, eighty-two prisoners volunteered immediately. A quarter of an hour later the transport was canceled, but the eighty-two stayed on the list for the night shift. For the majority of them, this meant death within the next fortnight.

Now the transport for the rest camp was arranged for the second time. Again, no one knew whether this was a ruse to obtain the last bit of work from the sick—if only for fourteen days—or whether it would go to the gas ovens or to a genuine rest camp. The chief doctor, who had taken a liking to me, told me furtively one evening at a quarter to ten, "I have made it known in the orderly room that you can still have your name crossed off the list; you may do so up till ten o'clock."

I told him that this was not my way; that I had learned to let fate take its course. "I might as well stay with my friends," I said. There was a look of pity in his eyes, as if he knew. . . . He shook my hand silently, as though it were a farewell, not for life, but from life. Slowly, I walked back to my hut. There I found a good friend waiting for me.

"You really want to go with them?" he asked sadly.

"Yes, I am going."

Tears came to his eyes, and I tried to comfort him. Then there was something else to do—to make my will:

"Listen, Otto, if I don't get back home to my wife, and if you should see her again, then tell her that I talked of her daily, hourly. You remember. Secondly, I have loved her more than anyone. Thirdly, the short time I have been married to her outweighs everything, even all we have gone through here."

Otto, where are you now? Are you alive? What has happened to you since our last hour together? Did you find your wife again? And do you remember how I made you learn my will by heart—word for word—in spite of your childlike tears?

The next morning I departed with the transport. This time it was not a ruse. We were not heading for the gas chambers, and we actually did go to a rest camp. Those who had pitied me remained in a camp where famine was to rage even more fiercely than in our new camp. They tried to save themselves, but they only sealed their own fates. Months later, after liberation, I met a friend from the old camp. He related to me how he, as camp policeman, had searched for a piece of human flesh that was missing from a pile of corpses. He confiscated it from a pot in which he found it cooking. Cannibalism had broken out. I had left just in time.

Does this not bring to mind the story of Death in Teheran? A rich and mighty Persian once walked in his garden with one of his servants. The servant cried that he had just encountered Death, who had threatened him. He begged his master to give him his fastest horse so that he could make haste and flee to Teheran, which he could reach that same evening. The master consented and the servant galloped off on the horse. On returning to his house, the master himself met Death, and questioned him, "Why did you terrify and threaten my servant?" "I did not threaten him; I only showed surprise in still finding him here when I planned to meet him tonight in Teheran," said Death.

The camp inmate was frightened of making decisions and of taking any sort of initiative whatsoever. This was the result of a strong feeling that fate was one's master, and that one must not try to influence it in any way, but instead let it take its own course. In addition, there was a great apathy, which contributed in no small part to the feelings of the prisoner. At times, lightning decisions had to be made, decisions which spelled life or death. The prisoner would have preferred to let fate make the choice for him. This escape from commitment was most apparent when a prisoner had to make the decision for or against an escape attempt. In those minutes in which he had to make up his mind—and it was always a question of minutes—he suffered the tortures of Hell. Should he make the attempt to flee? Should he take the risk?

I, too, experienced this torment. As the battle-front drew nearer, I had the opportunity to escape. A colleague of mine who had to visit huts outside the camp in the course of his medical duties wanted to escape and take me with him. Under the pretense of holding a consultation about a patient whose illness required a specialist's advice, he smuggled me out. Outside the camp, a member of a foreign resistance movement was to supply us with uniforms and documents. At the last moment, there were some technical difficulties and we had to return to camp once more. We used this opportunity to provide ourselves with provisions—a few rotten potatoes—and to look for a rucksack.

We broke into an empty hut of the women's camp, which was vacant, as the women had been sent to another camp. The hut was in great disorder; it was obvious that many women had acquired supplies and fled. There were rags, straw, rotting food, and broken crockery. Some bowls were still in good condition and would have been very valuable to us but we decided not to take them. We knew that lately, as conditions had become desperate, they had been used not only for food, but also as washbasins and chamber pots. (There was a strictly enforced rule against having any kind of utensil in the hut. However, some people were forced to break this rule, especially the typhus patients, who were much to weak to go outside even with help.) While I acted as a screen, my friend broke into the hut and returned shortly with a rucksack which he hid under his coat. He had seen another one inside which I was to take. So we changed places and I went in. As I searched in the rubbish, finding the rucksack and even a toothbrush, I suddenly saw, among all the other things that had been left behind, the body of a woman.

I ran back to my hut to collect all my possessions: my food bowl, a pair of torn mittens "inherited" from a dead typhus patient, and a few scraps of paper covered with shorthand notes (on which, as I mentioned before, I had started to reconstruct the manuscript which I lost at Auschwitz). I made a quick last round of my patients, who were lying huddled on the rotten planks of wood on either side of the huts. I came to my only countryman who was almost dying, and whose life it had been my ambition to save in spite of his condition. I had to keep my intention to escape to myself, but my comrade seemed to guess that something was wrong (perhaps I showed a little nervousness). In a tired voice he asked me, "You, too, are getting out?" I denied it, but I found it difficult to avoid his sad look. After my round I returned to him. Again, a hopeless look greeted me and somehow I felt it to be an accusation. The unpleasant feeling that had gripped me as soon as I had told my friend I would escape with him became more intense. Suddenly I decided to take fate into my own hands for once. I ran out of the hut and told my friend that I could not go with him. As soon as I told him with finality that I had made up my mind to stay with my patients, the unhappy feeling left me. I did not know what the following days would bring, but I had gained an inward peace that I had never experienced before. I returned to the hut, sat down on the boards at my countryman's feet and tried to comfort him; then I chatted with the others, trying to quiet them in their delirium.

Our last day in camp arrived. As the battle-front came nearer, mass transports had taken nearly all the prisoners to other camps. The camp authorities, the Capos and the cooks had fled. On this day an order was given that the camp must be evacuated completely by sunset. Even the few remaining prisoners (the sick, a few doctors, and some "nurses") would have to leave. At night, the camp was to be set on fire. In the afternoon the trucks which were to collect the sick had not yet appeared. Instead the camp gates were suddenly closed and the barbed wire closely watched, so that no one could attempt an escape. The remaining prisoners seemed to be destined to burn with the camp. For the second time my friend and I decided to escape.

We had been given an order to bury three men outside the barbed wire fence. We were the only two in camp who had strength enough to do the job. Nearly all the others lay in the few huts which were still in use, prostrate with fever and delirium. We now made our plans: along with the first body we would smuggle out my friend's rucksack, hiding it in the old laundry tub which served as a coffin. When we took out the second body we would also carry out my rucksack, and on the third trip, we intended to make our escape. The first two trips went according to plan. After we returned, we waited while my friend tried to find a piece of bread so that we would have something to eat during the next few days in the woods. I waited. Minutes passed. I became more and more impatient as he did not return. After three years of imprisonment, I was picturing freedom

joyously, imagining how wonderful it would be to run toward the battlefront. But we did not get that far.

The very moment when my friend came back, the camp gate was thrown open. A splendid, aluminum-colored car on which were painted giant red crosses slowly rolled on to the parade ground. A delegate from the International Red Cross in Geneva had arrived, and the camp and its inmates were under his protection. The delegate billeted himself in a farmhouse in the vicinity, in order to be near the camp at all times in case of emergency. Who worried about escape now? Boxes with medicines were unloaded from the car, cigarettes were distributed, and we were photographed and joy reigned supreme. Now there was no need for us to risk running toward the fighting line.

In our excitement we had forgotten the third body, so we carried it outside and dropped it into the narrow grave we had dug for the three corpses. The guard who accompanied us—a relatively inoffensive man—suddenly became quite gentle. He saw that the tables might be turned and tried to win our goodwill. He joined in the short prayers that we offered for the dead men before throwing soil over them. After the tension and excitement of the past days and hours, those last days in our race with death, the words of our prayer asking for peace were as fervent as any offered by the human voice.

And so the last day in camp passed in anticipation of freedom. But we had rejoiced too early. The Red Cross delegate had assured us that an agreement had been signed, and that the camp must not be evacuated. But that night the SS arrived with trucks and brought an order to clear the camp. The last remaining prisoners were to be taken to a central camp, from which they would be sent to Switzerland within forty-eight hours—to be exchanged for some prisoners of war. We scarcely recognized the SS. They were so friendly, trying to persuade us to get in the trucks without fear, telling us that we should be grateful for our good luck. Those who were strong enough crowded into the trucks and the seriously ill and feeble were lifted up with difficulty. My friend and I—we did not hide our rucksacks now—stood in the last group, from which thirteen would be chosen for the next to last truck. The chief doctor counted out the requisite number, but he omitted two of us. The thirteen were loaded into the truck and we had to stay behind. Surprised, very annoyed and disappointed, we blamed the chief doctor, who excused himself by saying that he had been tired and distracted. He said that he had thought we still intended to escape. Impatiently, we sat down, keeping our rucksacks on our backs, and waited with the few remaining visitors for the last truck. We had to wait a long time. Finally we lay down on the mattress of the deserted guard-room, exhausted by the excitement of the last few hours and days, during which we had fluctuated continuously between hope and despair. We slept in our clothes and shoes, ready for the journey.

The noise of rifles and cannons woke us; the flashes of tracer bullets and gun shots entered the hut. The chief doctor dashed in and ordered us to take cover on the floor. One prisoner jumped on my stomach from the bed above me and with his shoes on. That awakened me all right! Then we grasped what was happening; the battle-front had reached us! The shooting decreased and morning dawned. Outside on the pole at the camp gate a white flag floated in the wind.

Many weeks later we found out that even in those last hours fate had toyed with us few remaining prisoners. We found out jut how uncertain human decisions are, especially in matters of life and death. I was confronted with photographs which had been taken in a small camp not far from ours. Our friends who had thought they were traveling to freedom that night had been taken in the trucks to this camp, and there they were locked in the huts and burned to death. Their partially charred bodies were recognizable on the photograph. I thought again of Death in Teheran.

From *Man's Search for Meaning*.
Reprinted by permission of the publisher.

Two Candles

By **Simon Wiesenthal**

When I was a young student, I often spent a few weeks in the Polish mountain resort of Zakopane in the Carpathians. In summertime there were the woods, sunshine, peace. In winter there was good skiing. Today, Zakopane is again a popular place for skiers. Not far away is the small town of Rabka. And there once lived a little Jewish boy named Sammy Rosenbaum. I first heard of Sammy Rosenbaum one morning in September 1965, when a Mrs. Rawicz from Rabka came into my office in Vienna. I was looking for witnesses who might testify at a trial that was to be held in Germany in connection with Nazi crimes at Rabka.

Mrs. Rawicz had known Sammy Rosenbaum well. He had been "a frail boy, with a pale, thin face and big, dark eyes, who looked much older than his age—as so many children do who learned too early about life and never laughed much." Sammy was nine-years-old in 1939, when the Germans came to Rabka in the early days of the Polish campaign, and life became a nightmare for the Jews there. Until then life had been fairly normal—if it ever could be called normal for a poor Jew in Poland. Sammy's father was a tailor who worked long hours and made little money. People like the Rosenbaums were fair game for the authorities, and in Poland the hunting season lasted twelve months a year.

The family lived in two musty rooms and a tiny kitchen in an old, dark house. But they were happy, and very religious. Sammy learned to say his prayers. Every Friday night he would go with his father to the synagogue, after lighting the candles at home. Mother and Sammy's sister Paula, three years his senior, stayed at home and prepared dinner.

That sort of life became only a memory after the Germans occupied Poland. In 1940, the SS set up what it called a "police school" in former Polish Army barracks in the woods that surrounded Rabka. It was not an ordinary school; it was a training center for future cadres of SS killers. This was the early phase of exterminations. Executions were carried out by platoons of SS men who shot their victims. Sometimes they had to shoot fifty, a hundred, perhaps a hundred fifty people a day. SS men at Rabka were being hardened so they would become insensitive to the sight of blood, to the agonized shouts of women and children. The job must be done with a minimum of fuss and maximum of efficiency. That was a *Fuhrerbefehl*—the Fuhrer's order.

SS *Untersturmfuhrer* Wilhelm Rosenbaum from Hamburg was made school commander. Rosenbaum was a true SS type: cynical, brutal, convinced of his mission. He would walk around town with a riding crop. "When we saw him in the street we got so frightened that we would hide in the nearest house entrance," the woman from Rabka remembered. Early in 1942, SS man Rosenbaum ordered all Jews in Rabka to appear at the local school to "register." The sick and the elderly would soon be sent away. Others would have to work for the SS, the *Wehrmacht*, wherever they were sent.

Toward the end of the registration, SS *Fuhrer* Rosenbaum appeared in the schoolroom, accompanied by his two deputies, Hermann Oder and Walter Proch. (Both were among my first postwar "clients." I found Proch in 1947 in Blomberg-Mondsee, a village near Salzburg. He was sentenced to six years in prison. Oder, also an Austrian, was arrested in Linz in the big villa he had "requisitioned" from the former Jewish owner. He was later released by the Americans and is now a prosperous businessman in Linz. SS *Fuhrer* Rosenbaum disappeared after the war but remained near the top of my private "Wanted" list.)

In the schoolroom in Rabka, SS *Fuhrer* Rosenbaum looked through the list of names. "Suddenly, he beat his riding crop hard on the table," the woman from Rabka told me. "Each of us winced as though we had been whipped. SS man Rosenbaum shouted: 'What's that? Rosenbaum? Jews! How dare these *verdammte Juden* have my good German name? Well, I'm going to take care of it!'" Perhaps SS *Fuhrer* Rosenbaum would be surprised to discover that his good German name is generally considered a Jewish one, though there are, of course, people called Rosenbaum who are not Jewish.

He threw the list back on the table and strode out. From that day on everyone in Rabka knew the Rosenbaums would be killed; it was only a question of time. People in other places were known to have been arrested and executed because their name was Rosenberg, or because they were Jews and their first name happened to be Adolf or Hermann.

By that time, frightening rumors were being whispered in Rabka about the police school. Practice executions were said to be taking place in a clearing in the woods. Examinations were held, with the SS shooting people while with clinical detachment, SS Fuhrer Rosenbaum and his deputies observed the students' reactions. If a student flinched, he would be taken out of the execution squad and sent to a front-line outfit.

Mrs. Rawicz knew what she was talking about. After the registration she'd been sent to the police school as a charwoman. "When the SS men came back from the clearing in the woods I had to clean their boots, which were always covered with blood."

It was a Friday morning in June 1942. The eyewitnesses, two of whom now live in Israel, cannot remember the exact date, but they know it was a Friday. One of the eyewitnesses had been working in the house across from the playground behind the school. He saw what happened. Two SS men escorted "the Jew Rosenbaum," his wife, and their fifteen-year-old daughter Paula. Behind them came SS Fuhrer Rosenbaum.

"The woman and the girl were marched around the corner of the schoolhouse and then I heard some shots," the witness has said under oath. "I saw how SS man Rosenbaum began to beat our Rosenbaum with his riding crop. He shouted: 'You dirty Jew, I'll teach you a lesson for having my German name!' Then the SS man took his revolver and shot Rosenbaum the tailor. He shot him two or three times. I couldn't count the shots; I was too horrified."

Earlier, the SS men had come for the Rosenbaums in a small truck. Rosenbaum, his wife, and their daughter were around the table in the front room having breakfast. Sammy was already at a large stone quarry in nearby Zakryty, where he'd been sent as a forced laborer after his twelfth birthday. All Jewish men had to work, and Sammy was now classified as a man. But he was weak and undernourished and couldn't do much except sort out the stones and put the smaller ones on a truck.

The SS sent an unarmed Jewish policeman to the quarry for Sammy. They often sent Jewish policemen to arrest other Jews when they were too busy with their curriculum at the police school. The Jewish policeman later told the Jewish charwoman at the school exactly what had happened. He'd gone out to Zakryty in a small horse-drawn cart. He'd stopped the horse and waved at Sammy Rosenbaum. Everybody in the quarry stopped working and stared—the Jewish laborers and the two SS men who guarded them. Sammy put the big stone he held in his hands on the truck, and walked toward the cart. Sammy knew what was going to happen.

Sammy looked up at the Jewish policeman. "Where are they?" he asked—"Father, Mother, and Paula. Where?"

The policeman just shook his head.

Sammy understood. "They're dead." His voice was low. "I've known for a long time that it was going to happen. Because our name is Rosenbaum."

The policeman swallowed, but Sammy didn't seem to notice.

"And now you've come for me." He spoke matter-of-factly. There was no emotion in his voice. He stepped up and sat down on the seat next to the Jewish policeman.

The policeman was unable to say a word. He had expected the boy to cry, perhaps run away. All the while he was riding out to Zakryty the policeman had wondered how he could warn the boy, make him disappear in the woods, where the Polish underground might later help him. The two SS guards were watching with guns in their hands.

The policeman told Sammy what had happened that morning. Sammy asked if they could stop for a moment at his house. When they got there, he stepped down and walked into the front room, leaving the door open. He looked over the table with the half-filled teacups left from breakfast. He looked at the clock. It was half past three. Father, Mother and Paula were already buried, and no one had lit a candle for them. Slowly methodically, Sammy cleaned off the table and put the candlesticks on it.

"I could see Sammy from the outside," the Jewish policeman told Mrs. Rawicz. "He put on his skullcap, and started to light the candles. Two for his father, two for his mother, two for his sister. And he prayed. I saw his lips moving. He said *Kaddish* for them."

Kaddish is the prayer for the dead. Father Rosenbaum had always said *Kaddish* for his dead parents, and Sammy had learned the prayer from his father. Now he was the only man left in his family. He stood quietly, looking at the six candles. The Jewish policeman outside saw Sammy slowly shaking his head, as though he'd suddenly remembered something. Then Sammy placed two more candles on the table, took a match and lit them, and prayed.

"The boy knew that he was already dead," the policeman said later. "He lit the candles and said *Kaddish* for himself."

Then Sammy came out, leaving the door open, and quietly sat down on the cart next to the policeman, who was crying. The boy didn't cry. The policeman wiped away the tears with the back of his hand and pulled the reins. But the tears kept coming. The boy didn't say a word. Gently he touched the older man's arm, as if he wanted to comfort him—to forgive him for taking him away. Then they rode out to the clearing in the woods. SS *Fuhrer* Rosenbaum and his "students" were waiting for the little boy.

"About time!" said the SS man.

I told Mrs. Rawicz from Rabka that I had known about the SS police school since 1946. Several years earlier I had given the authorities in Hamburg all the facts and the testimony in the case against SS man Wilhelm Rosenbaum. Now there would be testimony for an additional case.

"Where is SS man Rosenbaum now?" she asked.

"Wilhelm Rosenbaum was arrested in 1964 and is now in prison in Hamburg awaiting trial."

She gave a sigh. "What's the use? They are all dead. And the murderer is alive." She signed the affidavit. "It makes no sense."

No tombstone bears Sammy Rosenbaum's name. No one might have remembered him if the woman from Rabka had not come into my office. But every year, one day in June, I light two candles for him and say *Kaddish*.

From *The Murderers Among Us.*
Reprinted by permission of the publisher.

Trapped in the Attic

(Excerpt)

By **Miriam Dansky**

Stories were one commodity we were never short of during our childhood years. My father told stories, long, circuitous tales, of his childhood in Poland: the family timber yard, the cheder, the chassidic courts. My mother told of her childhood in Hungary: the grocery store in Sarospotok, the picturesque town surrounded by mountains and vineyards. We grew up absorbing these stories like sponges, so that they permeated our souls.

It was only much later that we realized that these represented more than fairy tales with which to tuck us into bed. This realization came with the growing knowledge that certain basics were mysteriously absent from our secure and loving childhood. If there was so much that seemed solid and rooted, like our heavy bookcases, there was also something strangely missing. What was missing turned out really to be quite simple—grandparents, cousins, relatives of all shapes and sizes, the very people, or their offspring, who peopled these stories with their rampantly colorful personalities—in point of fact, the past. There was a gap, a hiatus, a disturbing lack of continuity, for my parents' stories never progressed beyond their childhood years . . .

We carried this reality around with us every waking moment. What had happened to it all? Why were we in autumn-leaved London and not in father's Chrzanow, or mother's Sarospotok? We had the feeling that something vast and inexplicable had happened to dislodge and dislocate them, and our curiosity grew and grew. We agreed with one another that something awesome lay at the bottom of it all.

There were certain telltale signs, certain glances that passed between my parents when they thought we weren't looking. We noticed other things too, such as my mother's inky blue-black tattoo on her forearm, which she never took pains to hide. Or my father, catching his breath sometimes, sucking in air as if there could never be enough for him...

Who could say that our parents' strangeness was different than that of others? How were we to know that my parents belonged to that species, rare enough in England, called Holocaust survivors?

That knowledge came much later, and then only by degrees, in what I can but describe as a gradual dawning. It seemed to seep in around us in our early school years like something dense and cloudlike. Yet, once we knew it, we knew that we had always known it. The gaps and crevices in my parents' storytelling were suddenly part of this huge, immeasurable black hole of history...

One does not survive eight labor camps to fritter away one's life aimlessly. If one survives while everyone, literally everyone perishes, one carries around a sense of duty and purpose like a cup of precious liquid. In this connection, there is a story that springs to mind concerning a certain student. He once asked a rabbi how to avoid unseemly thoughts which came to him when he should have been hard at work studying.

"My boy," the rabbi said kindly. "Go and get a wine goblet and fill it to the brim with liquid."

The boy thought this a little strange, but he complied.

"Now I want you to take a walk around town without spilling a drop."

The boy did this, but understandably with great difficulty. He then returned to the rabbi.

"Well, tell me my boy," he said. "What did you see in town?"

"Nothing," the boy said. "I was so busy concentrating on not spilling the liquid that I kept my head down all the time."

"You have answered yourself," the rabbi said. "If you will concentrate on your studies with the same degree of diligence, you will have no time for other distracting thoughts."

This story presents us with an image of my parents. They walked around, or so it seemed to me as I grew older and understood more, head down, intent on not squandering a drop of that precious liquid we call daily living, and which we often, G-d forgive us, take for granted.

"Take a minute of it for granted?" their disappointed looks would seem almost accusatory. "For this I survived eight concentration camps? For this I survived Auschwitz, Kole, Blechhamer, the IG Farben Industrie, Grkditz, Faulbruck, Markstedt, Funfteichen, Gerlitz, and finally Zittau where I was liberated?"

Imagine saying to my parents something as commonplace as, "I flunked my homework," or, "I got a bad mark in an exam" . . .

Sorry mother, sorry father. Sorry, for rocking the boat, sorry for denting the carefully constructed facade of a livable life into which you have invested no less than your youth, your tears, your lifeblood . . .

But out on the street, where the air was free, I would shout at the wind, shout at the trees, at anyone who would listen: Why does it have to matter so much? Why? Why is so much invested in me? Why must I be their past, their present and the future all rolled into one? I want to be perhaps a little irresponsible! I want to fail exams, or bend the spines of my books! . . .

Returning to the stories, it was at about the same time that we realized the huge potential of the word Shoah. From the whispered murmurings of schoolmates, or smatterings gleaned from newspapers, we began to understand the symbolism of what we had called, up to now, dead end. "All their stories," I confided to my sister, "come to a dead end."

Suddenly, we had an inkling why, one day, their world had simply stopped. At this, I began to imagine what would happen if our whole world as we knew it, were one day to simply "cave in." No more house, no more neighbors, no more school, and, of course, no more parents. In my dreams, it was just me and my very much younger sister, marooned in a world grown suddenly unrecognizable. What should we do? Where should we run? How to survive? And if all this happened to us, would we still be who we thought we were? Who or what would we be?

Even a beggar possesses a past, and with it the freedom to return. We would own less than the beggar, who in all weathers sat in his tattered coat on the cold park bench in Clapton Common, throwing bread to the birds.

How exactly had my parents survived? They must be endowed with some "special power," be somewhat superhuman. The "why" and "how" of their survival now began to haunt me day and night. We wondered, we surmised, we theorized; yet still we dared not step over the invisible dividing line that was their war experience. We had not heard their stories, the stories that mattered. For this, we would have to wait, with a terrible unassuaged longing for the truth.

That is how it transpired that one autumn day I sat with a tape recorder between us, notepad and pencil at the ready, nervously tapping my fingers on the heavy mahogany table. It was a strange situation. In a way, I was eager to know. Yet, as I stood on the brink of knowing, I was gripped with a terrible fear. Perhaps it would be better to leave the ghosts of the past undisturbed, for with knowledge comes responsibility. The question was—was I ready to hear my parents' stories?

Reprinted with permission from innernet.org.il.

Lesson 3 קדוש השם

In Their Death They Were Not Parted
The Mitzvah of *Kidush Hashem*

Introduction

In 1927, the sixth Lubavitcher Rebbe, Rabbi Yosef Yitzchak Schneersohn was arrested in Stalinist Russia for his activities to bolster Jewish observance in the Soviet Union. The Rebbe narrowly escaped a death sentence, and was sentenced to exile in a remote part of Russia. As he was about to board the train that would take him into exile, the Rebbe gave encouragement to his followers by making the following statement:

> This, however, all the nations of the world must know: Only our bodies were sent into exile and subjugated to alien rule; our souls are not subject to captivity and foreign rule. We must proclaim openly and before all that no one can impose their belief upon us in any matter affecting the Jewish religion, the Torah, G-d's commandments, and our customs. These cannot be subject to the coercion of others.
>
> *(SEFER HASICHOT 5627, P. 170)*

Many Jews throughout history demonstrated that no nation could force them to do something that was against Jewish ideals. This lesson will explore the way that Jewish tradition has informed and influenced the manner in which Jews—past and present—have dealt with the harsh oppression imposed upon them, yet found the strength to remain true to themselves and to G-d.

With All Your Soul

Learning **Activity**

1. Are there any values so important or precious to you that you would be willing to give up everything in order to maintain them?

2. Can you imagine any circumstances that would cause you to compromise on these values?

Text 1a

שְׁמַע יִשְׂרָאֵל ה׳ אֱלֹקֵינוּ ה׳ אֶחָד
וְאָהַבְתָּ אֵת ה׳ אֱלֹקֶיךָ בְּכָל לְבָבְךָ וּבְכָל נַפְשְׁךָ וּבְכָל מְאֹדֶךָ
דברים ו,ד–ה

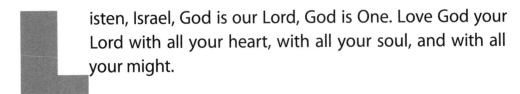

isten, Israel, God is our Lord, God is One. Love God your Lord with all your heart, with all your soul, and with all your might.

Devarim/Deuteronomy 6:4–5

TEXT 1B

רבי אליעזר אומר:

אם נאמר בכל נפשך למה נאמר בכל מאדך?

ואם נאמר בכל מאדך למה נאמר בכל נפשך?

אלא: אם יש לך אדם שגופו חביב עליו מממונו, לכך נאמר בכל נפשך

ואם יש לך אדם שממונו חביב עליו מגופו, לכך נאמר בכל מאדך

רבי עקיבא אומר: בכל נפשך אפילו נוטל את נפשך

תלמוד בבלי ברכות סא,ב

Rabbi Eliezer says, "Since it states 'with all your soul,' why state 'with all your might'? And since it stated 'with all your might,' why state 'with all your soul'? [The answer is] so that if there is a person whose body is more precious to him than his money, for this [person] it is stated 'with all your soul.' And if there is a person whose money is more precious to him than his body, for this [person] it was said, 'with all your might.'"

Rabbi Akiva says, "'With all your soul' [means] even if [G-d] takes your soul."

TALMUD, BERACHOT 61B

TEXT 1C

תנו רבנן: פעם אחת גזרה מלכות הרשעה שלא יעסקו ישראל בתורה

בא פפוס בן יהודה ומצאו לרבי עקיבא שהיה מקהיל קהלות ברבים ועוסק בתורה

אמר ליה: עקיבא, אי אתה מתירא מפני מלכות

אמר לו: אמשול לך משל

למה הדבר דומה

לשועל שהיה מהלך על גב הנהר

וראה דגים שהיו מתקבצים ממקום למקום

אמר להם: מפני מה אתם בורחים

אמרו לו: מפני רשתות שמביאין עלינו בני אדם

אמר להם: רצונכם שתעלו ליבשה

ונדור אני ואתם כשם שדרו אבותי עם אבותיכם

אמרו לו: אתה הוא שאומרים עליך פקח שבחיות

לא פקח אתה אלא טפש אתה

ומה במקום חיותנו אנו מתיראין

במקום מיתתנו על אחת כמה וכמה

אף אנחנו, עכשיו שאנו יושבים ועוסקים בתורה

שכתוב בה כי הוא חייך וארך ימיך (דברים ל,כ), כך

אם אנו הולכים ומבטלים ממנה, על אחת כמה וכמה

אמרו: לא היו ימים מועטים עד שתפסוהו לרבי עקיבא

וחבשוהו בבית האסורים

תלמוד בבלי ברכות ס'א,ב

ur Rabbis taught: Once the wicked Government [of Rome] issued a decree forbidding the Jews to study the Torah. Pappus ben Yehudah found Rabbi Akiva teaching the Torah to public gatherings.

Said Pappus, "Akiva, are you not afraid of the Government?"

He replied, "I will explain with a parable. A fox was once walking alongside a river and saw fish swimming in swarms from one side [of the river] to the other.

"Said the fox, 'From who are you fleeing?'

"They replied, 'From nets cast for us by the men.'

"The fox replied, 'Would you like to come up on to dry land so that you and I can live together in the way that my ancestors lived with your ancestors?'

"They replied, 'Are you the one that they call the cleverest of animals? You are not clever, but foolish. If we are afraid in the waters in which we can live, how much more [must we fear] dry land on which we would [certainly] die!'

"So it is with us," [concluded Rabbi Akiva]. "If such is our condition when we sit and study the Torah, of which it is written 'This is your sole means of survival and long life' (Deuteronomy 30:20); if we neglect the Torah how much worse off will we be!"

It is related that soon after this exchange, Rabbi Akiva was captured and imprisoned.

Talmud, Berachot 61b

Text 1d

רבי עקיבה הוה מותדין קומי טונוסטרופוס הרשע
אתת ענתה דקרית שמע שרי קרי וגחך
אמר ליה: סבא סבא, או חרש את או מבעט בייסורין את
אמר ליה: . . . לא חרש אנא ולא מבעט בייסורין אנא
אלא כל ימיי הייתי קורא את הפסוק הזה
ואהבת את ה' אלקיך בכל לבבך ובכל נפשך ובכל מאודך
רחמתיה בכל לבי, ורחמתיה בכל ממוני
ובכל נפשי לא הוות בדיקה לי
וכדון דמטת לי בכל נפשי
ואתת ענתה דקרית שמע ולא אפלגית עליה
בגין כן אנא קרי שמע וגחך

תלמוד ירושלמי סוטה ה,ה

Rabbi Akiva was being punished by the wicked Tornusrufus. The time for the recital of the *Shema* arrived. [Rabbi Akiva] began to recite it and laughed.

[Tornusrufus] said to him, "Old man, old man, you are either a sorcerer or you are making light of the suffering."

[Rabbi Akiva] replied, ". . . I am neither a sorcerer nor one who makes light of suffering. Rather, my whole life I have read the verse, 'And you should love the Lord your G-d with all your heart, with all your soul, and with all your might.' I have loved Him with all my heart, I have loved him with all my wealth, but I was not certain if I would be able to love Him with all my soul. Now a situation of 'with all my soul' faces me, and it is the time of the recital of *Shema,* and my mind is not divided on this issue. For this reason, I recite the *Shema* and laugh."

Jerusalem Talmud, Sotah 5:5

Charting the Contours of *Kidush Hashem*

Text 2

וְנִקְדַּשְׁתִּי בְּתוֹךְ בְּנֵי יִשְׂרָאֵל

ויקרא כב,לב

must be sanctified among the Israelites.

Vayikra/Leviticus 22:32

Text 3

כל בית ישראל מצווין על קדוש השם הגדול הזה
שנאמר ונקדשתי בתוך בני ישראל . . .
כיצד? כשיעמוד עובד כוכבים ויאנוס את ישראל
לעבור על אחת מכל מצות האמורות בתורה או יהרגנו
יעבור ואל יהרג
שנאמר במצות: אשר יעשה אותם האדם וחי בהם (ויקרא יח,ה)
וחי בהם ולא שימות בהם . . .

במה דברים אמורים בשאר מצות
חוץ מעבודת כוכבים וגלוי עריות ושפיכת דמים

אבל שלש עבירות אלו

אם יאמר לו עבור על אחת מהן או תהרג

יהרג ואל יעבור

במה דברים אמורים

בזמן שהעובד כוכבים מתכוין להנאת עצמו

כגון שאנסו לבנות לו ביתו בשבת או לבשל לו תבשילו . . .

אבל אם נתכוין להעבירו על המצות בלבד

אם היה בינו לבין עצמו ואין שם עשרה מישראל

יעבור ואל יהרג

ואם אנסו להעבירו בעשרה מישראל

יהרג ואל יעבור . . .

וכל הדברים האלו שלא בשעת הגזרה

אבל בשעת הגזרה, והוא שיעמוד מלך רשע כנבוכדנצר וחביריו

ויגזור גזרה על ישראל לבטל דתם או מצוה מן המצות

יהרג ואל יעבור אפילו על אחת משאר מצות

בין נאנס בתוך עשרה בין נאנס בינו לבין עובדי כוכבים

רמב"ם הלכות יסודי התורה ה,א–ג

The entire House of Israel is commanded to sanctify [G-d's] Great name, as it states, "I must be sanctified among the Israelites." . . . How is this [to be understood]? Should a gentile arise and force a Jew to violate one of the Torah's commandments at the pain of death, he should violate the commandment rather than be killed because it states regarding the *mitzvot*, "Which a man shall do and live by them" (Leviticus 18:5), [meaning] "live by them" and do not die by them. . . .

This is so regarding all *mitzvot* except idolatry, adultery, and murder. Regarding these three sins, if one is ordered, "Transgress one of these or you will be killed," [the Jew should let himself] be killed and not transgress. When does the above apply? [Transgressing a mitzvah in order to continue to live applies] when the gentile desires his own personal benefit. For example, he forces one to build a house or cook food for him on the Sabbath. . . . However, if his intention is solely to have the Jew violate the *mitzvot* [the following rules apply]: If he is alone and there are not ten other Jews present, he should transgress and not sacrifice his life. However, if he forces him to transgress [any mitzvah] in the presence of ten Jews, he should sacrifice his life and not transgress. . . .

All of the above distinctions apply under normal circumstances, but in times of an official decree of persecution, when, for instance, a wicked king like Nebuchadnezzar—or another like him—arises, and decrees against the Jews to nullify their religion or [even] a single one of the *mitzvot*, one should die rather than transgress any of the *mitzvot*, regardless of whether one is compelled [to transgress] in the presence of ten [other Jews] or only in the presence of non-Jews.

MAIMONIDES, MISHNEH TORAH,
LAWS OF THE FOUNDATIONS OF THE TORAH, 5:1–3

Rabbi Moshe ben Maimon (1135–1204). Better known as Maimonides or by the acronym Rambam. Born in Córdoba, Spain. After the conquest of Córdoba by the Almohads, he fled Spain and eventually settled in Cairo, Egypt. There, he became the leader of the Jewish community and served as court physician to the vizier of Egypt. His rulings on Jewish law are considered integral to the formation of halachic consensus. He is most noted for authoring the *Mishneh Torah*, an encyclopedic arrangement of Jewish law, and for his philosophical work, *Guide for the Perplexed.*

Table 3.1

What is the intent of the oppressor that is demanding that the Jew transgress a mitzvah?	What is the response required by the mitzvah of *kidush Hashem* with regard to most transgressions?	What is the response required by the mitzvah of *kidush Hashem* with regard to murder, adultery, or idolatry?
To gain pleasure	1	2
To force a violation of the Torah	3	4
To force a violation of the Torah at a time of religious persecution	5	6

TEXT 4

ne day, the supervisor of the train station came to the camp commander complaining that the Jews [interned in the labor camp] were stealing potatoes and conducting other actions of sabotage. For our "angel of death" this was enough. He gathered all the inmates to that field of misery and beat us with a murderous frenzy, incessantly cursing and insulting us all the while.

He soon tired of this exercise, but his predatory appetite had still not been satisfied, so he commanded Avraham Seif to choose thirty Jews to be hanged. Seif did not respond to the command. The incensed commander beat him with his whip. Seif turned to the commander and told him quietly but firmly, "You can shoot me; I will not kill my brothers."

The "angel of death"—who happened to be very short—was burning with rage and jumping like a flea. His face was red as a beet and he was puffing like a turkey. Still, Seif did not respond. He remained standing in his place without moving.

RABBI YEHOSHUA MOSHE ARONSON, ALEI MEROROT, P. 171

Rabbi Yehoshua Moshe Aronson (1907–1993). Rabbi and author. Appointed rabbi of Sanniki, Poland, in 1937. After the war, while still in the displaced persons camps in Austria, he wrote about his experiences in the Konin labor camp and about halachic dilemmas that arose during the war. His writing constitutes a rare documentation of a concentration camp from a rabbi's perspective. All of his writings have been collected and printed posthumously, titled *Alei Merorot*.

In the Holocaust All Are *Kedoshim*

TEXT 5

n the Janowska Road Camp, there was a brigadier (a foreman of a brigade) from Lvov by the name of Schneeweiss, one of those people one stays away from if he values his life. . . .

Even prior to the outbreak of World War II, he had publicly violated the Jewish holidays and transgressed against Jewish law. Here in Janowska, he was a cruel man who knew no mercy.

With a heavy heart, the rabbi (Spira), went before Schneeweiss. . . . "You are a Jew like myself . . . tonight is Kol Nidrei night. There is a small group of young Jews who do not want to transgress any of the thirty-nine main categories of work. It means everything to them. It is the essence of their existence. Can you do something about it? Can you help?"

The rabbi noticed that a hidden shiver went through Schneeweiss as he listened to the rabbi's strange request. . . . The stern face of Schneeweiss changed. For the first time since his arrival at Janowska, there was a human spark in it. . . .

"Tonight, I can't do a thing," said Schneeweiss . . . "I have no jurisdiction over the night brigade. But tomorrow, on Yom Kippur, I will do for you whatever I can." The rabbi shook Schneeweiss's hand in gratitude and left. . . .

In the morning, the rabbi and a small group of young Hasidim were summoned to Schneeweiss's cottage. "I heard that you prayed last night. I don't believe in prayers," Schneeweiss told them. "On principle, I even oppose them. But I admire your courage. For you all know well that the penalty for prayer in Janowska is death." With that, he motioned them to follow him.

He took them to the S.S. quarters in the camp, to a large wooden house. "You fellows will shine the floor without any polish or wax. And you, rabbi, will clean the windows with dry rags so that you will not transgress any of the thirty-nine major categories of work." He left the room abruptly without saying another word.

The rabbi was standing on a ladder with rags in his hand, cleaning the huge windows while chanting prayers, and his companions were on the floor polishing the wood and praying with him. . . . "The floor was wet with our tears. You can imagine the prayers of that Yom Kippur," said the Rabbi [after the war, when retelling this incident] to his Hasidim who were listening to his tale while he was wiping away a tear.

At about twelve o'clock noon, the door opened wide and into the room stormed two angels of death, S.S. men in their black uniforms, may their names be obliterated. They were followed by a food cart filled to capacity.

"Noontime, time to eat bread, soup, and meat," announced one of the two S.S. men. The room was filled with an aroma of freshly cooked food, such food as they had not seen since the German occupation: white bread, steaming hot vegetable soup, and huge portions of meat.

The tall S.S. man commanded in a high-pitched voice, "You must eat immediately. Otherwise you will be shot on the spot!" None of them moved. . . .

The German repeated the orders. The rabbi and the Hasidim remained glued to their places. The S.S. men called in Schneeweiss. "Schneeweiss, if the dirty dogs refuse to eat, I will kill you along with them."

Schneeweiss pulled himself to attention, looked the German directly in the eyes, and said in a very quiet tone, "We Jews do not eat today. Today is Yom Kippur, our most holy day, the Day of Atonement."

"You don't understand, Jewish dog," roared the taller of the two. "I command you in the name of the Fuhrer and the Third Reich, *fress!*"

Schneeweiss, composed, his head high, repeated the same answer. "We Jews obey the law of our tradition. Today is Yom Kippur, a day of fasting."

The German took out his revolver from its holster and pointed it at Schneeweiss's temple. Schneeweiss remained calm. He stood still, at attention, his head held high. A shot pierced the room. Schneeweiss fell. . . .

The Rabbi and the Hasidim stood as if frozen in their places. . . . Schneeweiss, the man who in the past had publicly transgressed against the Jewish tradition, had sanctified God's name publicly and died . . . for the sake of Jewish honor.

"Only then, on that Yom Kippur day in Janowska," said the Rabbi to his Hasidim, "did I understand the meaning of the statement in the Talmud, 'Even the transgressors in Israel are as full of good deeds as a pomegranate is filled with seeds.'"

YAFFA ELIACH, HASIDIC TALES OF THE HOLOCAUST, PP. 155–159

Yaffa Eliach. Professor of Judaic Studies at Brooklyn College, pioneer scholar in Holocaust Studies, and creator of the acclaimed "Tower of Life" at the United States Holocaust Memorial Museum in Washington. Born in Eishyshok in what is now Lithuania, she survived the Holocaust, and immigrated to Palestine with her aunt and uncle in 1946. Her more famous publications include *Hasidic Tales of the Holocaust* and *There Once Was a World*.

Questions for Discussion

1. Why do you think that Schneeweiss originally put himself at risk by agreeing to help the rabbi to observe Yom Kippur?

2. Why do you think that the Nazis cared if the Jews ate on Yom Kippur or not?

3. It is likely that Schneeweiss never studied the section of Jewish law concerning *kidush Hashem*, so why would Schneeweiss give up his life rather than eat and force other Jews to eat on Yom Kippur?

TEXT 6

ולכן אפילו . . . פושעי ישראל

מוסרים נפשם על קדושת ה' על הרוב

וסובלים עינוים קשים שלא לכפור בה' אחד

ואף אם . . . אין יודעים גדולת ה' . . .

ואין מוסרים נפשם מחמת דעת והתבוננות בה' כלל

אלא בלי שום דעת והתבוננות

רק כאלו הוא דבר שאי אפשר כלל לכפור בה' אחד

בלי שום טעם וטענה ומענה כלל

ליקוטי אמרים תניא, יח

Rabbi Shne'ur Zalman of Liadi (1745–1812). Known as "the Alter Rebbe" and "the Rav." Born in Liozna, Belarus and buried in Hadich, Ukraine. Chassidic Rebbe and founder of the Chabad movement, he was among the principle students of the Magid of Mezeritch. His numerous works include the *Tanya*, an early classic of Chassidism, *Torah Or* and *Likutei Torah*, and *Shulchan Aruch HaRav*, a rewritten *Code of Jewish Law*. He was succeeded by his son, Rabbi Dovber of Lubavitch.

Therefore, even the . . . transgressors among Israel, in the majority of cases, give up their lives for *kidush Hashem* and suffer harsh torture rather than deny G-d's oneness, although they . . . are ignorant of G-d's greatness. . . . By no means do they give up their lives by reason of any knowledge and contemplation of G-d. Rather, [they do so] without any knowledge or reflection, but as if it were absolutely impossible to renounce the one G-d, without any reason or rational argument whatsoever.

RABBI SHNE'UR ZALMAN OF LIADI, TANYA, CH. 18

Text 7

מצאתי בשל"ה

כשאומרים בתפלת נעילה שמע ישראל בקול רם ובכוונת הלב

יכוין כל אחד מישראל למסור נפשו על קדושת השם יתברך שמו

ונחשב לו הכוונה כאילו עשה בפועל

מחזור נוסח חב"ד, תפלת נעילה

have found [it written] in the *Shelah* (*Shenei Luchot Habrit*) that when in the *Ne'ilah* prayer, *Shema Yisrael* is recited aloud with heartfelt concentration, every Jew should have the intention of giving up his soul for the sanctification of G-d's name, may His name be blessed. This intention will be considered as if he had indeed [sanctified G-d's name] in actuality.

CHABAD YOM KIPPUR PRAYER BOOK, NE'ILAH PRAYER

TEXT 8

Although the Nazis were fighting with satanic hatred not only against "the Jews" but also against everything "Jewish," . . . they did not order us to transgress our religion. They did not give the Jews the choice of transgressing and surviving or holding onto the religion and being killed. They chose a policy of systematic liquidation of everyone who was called a Jew. The question is whether a Jew killed for being Jewish sanctifies G-d's name through his death. . . .

Where the gentile has a quarrel with the word "Jew" and the very concept of Judaism is what bothers him, the Jew's death is called *kidush Hashem*, even if the gentile does not force him to transgress his religion. Since all the nations of the world know with certainty that the Jews are G-d's people, their harassment and hatred of this nation is solely because of this. . . .

It is therefore clear to me that the deaths of the Jews who were killed in all sorts of savage ways merely for being Jewish were cases of *kidush Hashem*, because they were killed for being members of the chosen people, who have a relationship with G-d.

RABBI YEHOSHUA MOSHE ARONSON, ALEI MEROROT, PP. 305–306

Sacred Lives

TEXT 9

One morning, on Hoshana Rabbah as we were sawing wood, the wind carried in our direction piercing, tormented cries such as I had never heard before, even in the Janowska hell. The desperate clamor was coming closer and closer as if the weeping was filling up the entire universe and drowning it with painful tears.

"It is a children's Aktion, little angels from the entire vicinity . . . were brought here to meet their maker" said a katzetnik (camp inmate) who passed by, pushing a wheelbarrow, without even glancing in our direction. I thought the cries would shake the world's foundation. We continued sawing the wood as our eyes became heavier and heavier with tears.

Suddenly, just next to us, I heard the voice of a woman. "Jews, have mercy upon me and give me a knife." In front of us was standing a woman, pale as a sheet. Only her eyes were burning with a strange fire. I thought that she wanted to commit suicide. I looked around, and since I saw no German in sight, I said to her, "Why are you in such a rush to get to the World of Truth? We will get there sooner or later. What difference can one day make?"

"Dog, what did you say to the woman?" A tall young German who appeared from nowhere demanded an answer, while swinging his rubber truncheon above my head. "The woman asked for a knife. I explained to her that we Jews are not permitted to take our lives. For our lives are entrusted in the hands of God." I hastily added, "And I hope that you, too, will spare our lives." The German did not respond to my words. He turned to the woman and demanded and explanation from her. She answered curtly, "I asked for a knife."

As she was talking, she kept examining the German with her feverish eyes. Suddenly her eyes stopped wandering. Her gaze was fixed on the top pocket of the German's uniform. The shape of a knife was clearly visible through the pocket. "Give me that pocket knife!" she ordered the German in a commanding voice. The German, taken by surprise, handed the knife to the woman.

She bent down and picked up something. Only then did I notice a bundle of rags on the ground near the sawdust. She unwrapped the bundle. Amidst the rags on a snow-white pillow was a newborn babe, asleep. With a steady hand she opened the pocket knife and circumcised the baby. In a clear, intense voice she recited the blessing of the circumcision. "Blessed art Thou, O Lord our God, King of the Universe, who has sanctified us by thy commandments and hast commanded us to perform the circumcision."

She straightened her back, looked up to the heavens and said, "God of the Universe, you have given me a healthy child. I am returning to you a wholesome, kosher Jew." She walked over to the German, gave him back his blood-stained knife, and handed him her baby in his snow-white pillow.

YAFFA ELIACH, HASIDIC TALES OF THE HOLOCAUST, PP. 151–152

Key Points

1. *Kidush Hashem* is about life, not death. It is about maintaining a relationship with G-d, not about standing up to the oppressor.

2. During the Holocaust, many Jews viewed their lives against the backdrop of Jewish history and a culture of *kidush Hashem*.

3. *Kidush Hashem* became an important framework for some Jews in their battle with Nazism.

4. All who died during the Holocaust are deemed to be *kedoshim*.

5. The capacity for *kidush Hashem* is accessible to all because it resides in the essence of the Jewish soul.

6. *Kidush Hashem* is a statement that no one can force a Jew to deny the reality of G-dliness and to live a life that is not connected to the Divine reality.

7. We can express *kidush Hashem* in our lives today by actualizing our inner commitment to the type of life that connects us to G-d and to our Jewish souls.

Supplementary Texts

TEXT A

חדשים אחדים לפני שהגרמנים ימח שמם הוציאו לפועל את הרג הילדים היהודיים
הידוע בשם "קינדער אקציאן" בגיטו קובנה ביום ג' וד' ניסן תש"ד
כבר נפוצה השמועה הלא טובה בגיטו . . .

ההורים האומללים חיפשו עצות ותחבולות איך להבריח את ילדיהם עולליהם
מידי הרוצחים הטמאים כדי להצילם מטבח השמד הזה . . .

היו כאלה שמסרו את תינוקותיהם מדעת לכמרים למען יגדלו באמונתם כדי
להצילם, מתוך תקוה שאם ישארו בחיים הם יצליחו להוציא את ילדיהם מידי
הנכרים, והיו כאלה שמסרו את ילדיהם למכיריהם הנכרים שיחביאום עד לאחרי
המלחמה ואז יחזירום להוריהם היהודים אם יהיו בחיים.

ונשאלתי אם מותר לעשות כן מצד הדין מאחר שספק גדול הוא אם ההורים
ישארו בחיים והתינוקות הללו יטמעו בין הגויים
ולא ידעו את עמם ומולדתם . . .

תשובה . . . דודאי אסור בנידון דידן למסור את הקטנים העוללים ויונקים לכמרים
כדי להצילם מסכנת השמד והכליון הנשקף להם מידי הרוצחים הגרמנים ימח
שמם, אף על פי שעל הקטנים מצד עצמם אין החיוב של מצות קידוש השם
מכל מקום אסור לגדולים למסור אותם לעכו"ם . . .

ובנוגע לאלה שמסרו את ילדיהם למכיריהם הנכרים שיחביאום עד לאחרי המלחמה
ואז יחזירום להוריהם היהודים אם יהיו בחיים
אי יאות עבדי . . .

הרי אם לא ימסר התינוק לנכרים הלא בודאי יהרג, ואם ימסר לנכרים אלו הלא התינוק ישאר בחיים, ומאוד יתכן שגם ההורים ישארו בחיים . . .

ולא עוד אפילו אם ההורים לא ישארו בחיים מאוד יתכן שהנכרים הללו יחזירו את התינוק המופקד בידם למוסדות יהודים אחרי המלחמה ויש בזה הרבה צדדי ספק.

אם כן בודאי יש לנו להקל בזה ולהתיר להורים הנתונים בצרה ובשביה למסור את תינוקותיהם לנכרים מתוך התקוה שאחרי המלחמה הם יוחזרו לעמם ולמולדתם.

שאלות ותשובות ממעמקים, ה,ט

A few months before the Germans—may their name be blotted out—carried out the murder of the Jewish children, known as the *Kinderaktion,* in the Kovno Ghetto on March 27 and 28, 1944, the bad news circulated around the ghetto. . . . Anguished parents sought every conceivable way to get their children away from the murderers; to save them from the slaughter and destruction. . . .

Some were willing to hand their children over to priests—that they should grow up in the non-Jewish faith—in order to save them. They hoped that if they themselves would survive, they would manage to get their children back from the hands of the non-Jews. There were some who handed their children over to gentile friends to be hidden until after the war. Then—if the parents were still alive—they would be returned to them.

I was asked if it was permitted to do so since there was a great possibility that the parents would not survive, [which meant] that those children would be lost among the nations, and they would not identify with the Jewish people. . . .

[I ruled] that certainly parents could not give away their children to priests in order to save them from the impending death at the hands of the German murderers—may their name be blotted out. Although the children themselves had no obligation to fulfill the mitzvah of sanctifying G-d's name, it is nevertheless forbidden for adults to hand them over to the non-Jews. . . .

Regarding those that handed over their children to gentile *friends* to be hidden until after the war, when they will be returned to their Jewish parents, if they survived—was this proper to do? . . . If the children were not handed over to the gentiles they would surely be killed but if they were handed over to the gentiles, they would survive. It was conceivable that the parents would survive. . . . Even if the parents did not survive, it was very possible that the gentiles would return the children to Jewish institutions after the war.

Since there are a number of possibilities [that the child would return to Jewish hands after the war], therefore, certainly we can be lenient and allow the parents—subjected to pain and captivity—to hand their children over to gentile [*lay people*], in the hope that after the war they would indeed be returned to their people.

RABBI EFRAIM OSHRY, SHE'ELOT UTESHUVOT MIMA'AMAKIM, 5:9

Rabbi Ephraim Oshry (1914–2003). A young rabbinical scholar in Kaunas, the second-largest city in Lithuania when the Nazis invaded on June 23, 1941. He carefully recorded the halachic questions that Lithuanian Jews asked him during the war as well as his responses, writing them on bits of paper torn from cement sacks he carried on forced labor and burying them in tin cans. He dug up the cans after the war, using these notes as the basis for his collection of Holocaust responsa, printed in the five-volume *She'elot Uteshuvot Mima'amakim*.

TEXT B

During World War II, countless Jewish parents gave their precious children to Christian neighbors and orphanages in the hope that the latter would provide safe havens for them. The parents expected that they, or their relatives, would take these children back if they survived the war.

The few parents who did not perish in the Holocaust and were able to reclaim their children, often faced another horror. While the parents had summoned the strength to survive the slave labor and death camps, or had hidden out for years, those who took their children were busy teaching them to love Christianity and to hate Jews and Judaism.

To add insult to injury, many Jewish children who were taken in by orphanages, convents, and the like, had no parents or close relatives left after the Holocaust. When rabbis or distant relatives finally tracked down many of these children, the priests and nuns who had been their caretakers insisted that no children from Jewish homes were in their institutions. Thus, countless Jewish children were not only stripped of their entire families, they were also stripped of their souls.

In May, 1945, Rabbi Eliezer Silver from the United States and Dayan Grunfeld from England were sent as chaplains to liberate some of the death camps. While there, they were told that many Jewish children had been placed in a monastery in Alsace-Lorraine. The rabbis went there to reclaim them.

When they approached the priest in charge, they asked that the Jewish children be released into the rabbis' care.

"I'm sorry," the priest responded, "but there is no way of knowing which children here came from Jewish families. You must have documentation if you wish me to do what you ask."

Of course, the kind of documentation that the priest wanted was unobtainable at the end of the war. The rabbis asked to see the list of names of children who were in the monastery. As the rabbis read the list, they pointed to those that belonged to Jewish children.

"I'm sorry," the priest insisted, "but the names that you pointed to could be either Jewish or Gentile. Miller is a German name, and Markovich is a Russian name, and Swersky is a Polish name. You can't prove that these are Jewish children. If you can't prove which children are Jewish, and do it very quickly, you will have to leave."

One of the rabbis had a brilliant idea. "We'd like to come back again this evening when you are putting the children to sleep." The priest reluctantly agreed.

That evening the rabbis came to the dormitory, where row upon row of little beds were arranged. The children, many of whom had been in the monastery since the war started in 1939, were going to sleep. The rabbis walked through the aisles of beds, calling out, "*Shema, Yisrael, Hashem Elokeinu, Hashem Echad*!" (Hear, Jewish people, the Lord is our G-d, the Lord is One!")

One by one, children burst into tears and shrieked, "Mommy!" "Maman!" "Momma!" "Mamushka!" in each of their native tongues.

The priest had succeeded in teaching these precious Jewish souls about the Trinity, the New Testament, and the Christian savior. Each child knew how to say Mass. But the priest did not succeed in erasing these children's memories of their Jewish mothers—now murdered—putting them to bed every night with the Shema on their lips.

LISA AIKEN, THE HIDDEN BEAUTY OF THE SHEMA, PREFACE, PP. 17–19

Lisa Aiken. Born in Baltimore, Maryland and currently lives in Jerusalem. A clinical psychologist, she is also a noted inspirational speaker and author. Her books include *To Be A Jewish Woman* and *Why Me, God? A Jewish Guide to Coping With Suffering.*

Additional Readings

Angels Have No Shoes

By **Rabbi Emanuel Feldman**

Where have I seen them before, this array of shoes lying here before me?

The shoes belong to the Kohanim who removed them a moment ago when they mounted the *bimah* to pronounce the priestly blessing: new shoes and old, with laces and without, brown ones and black ones, dress shoes and casual.

This cluster of shoes lying beneath the *bimah*—why do I keep staring at them? Where have I seen them before?

In the Biblical sense, shoes are more than shoes. They play a weighty symbolic role in Jewish tradition, and they bear within themselves a subtext that far transcends protective covering for the feet.

Shoes play a central role in the Biblical *chalitzah* rite (Deut. 25:5-11); in the Book of Ruth, 3:8; in the laws of Yom Kippur, Tishah B'Av, and mourning. See also Gen. 37:28: After Joseph's brothers sold him for 20 pieces of silver, they used the coins (according to various Midrashim) to buy shoes for themselves—a fact alluded to by Amos 2:6: "They sold the righteous for silver, and the poor one for a pair of shoes."

One element concerning the mystery of shoes is worth examining. The shoe of the Torah, of course, is made from the skin of an animal (Talmud, Yevamot 102b, based on Ezekiel 16:10). When man wears the skin of an animal upon his feet, when he treads upon the earth by utilizing animal leather, he demonstrates that he is not just another animal. Instead, he is superior to and has the power to dominate the animal.

This is in fulfillment of God's will in Genesis 1:26, where man is told that he shall have dominion over the entire animal kingdom. And it is suggested by Psalms 8:7: "Thou makest man to have dominion over the works of Thy hands; Thou hast put all things under his feet . . . also the beasts of the field."

(Rabbi Shelomo Zalman Auerbach explains why only leather shoes are forbidden on Tishah B'Av and Yom Kippur and to mourners, while cloth shoes—which are usually much more comfortable—are permitted; the wearing of leather shoes symbolizes our dominion over the animals, but on such solemn occasions we are to be completely submissive to God, and it is inappropriate to express our dominion over anything.)

But there is more: Not only is man able to dominate the animal without; he is also endowed with the potential to dominate the animal within himself—his own natural impulses towards the beastly and physical. He need not be merely an upright beast.

He can, in short, become a spiritual, God-like creature. Man has been given the power to own the animal; he is not to be owned by the animal.

In addition to demonstrating man's dominion over the beast, the animal skin on man's feet separates him from the earth. Shoes thus represent man's spiritual potential. Man—though he emanates from the earth, walks the earth, and will return to the earth—possesses the ability to separate himself from that which is merely physical, and to reach for greater heights. An angel, bearer of spirituality, does not wear shoes. Nor does a beast, embodiment of animality. Only man—who can become either an angel or a beast—wears shoes in the hope that he will choose the former and not the latter.

Why, then, are the shoes removed when one finds himself on sacred ground, when one stands in the presence of God?

Sacred ground means that the earth, in this particular enclosure, has lost its physicality and has itself become holy. In such a circumstance, there is no need for man to separate himself from the earth, no need to express his dominance over the beastly. On the contrary, when the ground on which he stands becomes sacred and Godly, man is bidden to become as one with this ground and, as it were, to attach himself to the spirituality and the sanctity of this holy place. And so he removes from his feet the symbols of separation and dominance.

Thus it is that when Moses stands before the Holy One at the burning bush, he is told (Exodus 3:5): "Remove your shoes from upon your feet, because the place whereon you stand is holy ground."

Joshua, when he first enters Canaan, hears the identical command when he is confronted by the angel of God (Joshua 5:15). Remove your shoes, the angel says, as if to say that during this one moment of contact with the sacred, while you are being touched by the ultimate sanctity, you require no separators from the earth's physicality, no symbols of your dominance over the beast. For now, the very physicality and animality of the earth has been transmogrified into the spiritual.

Since one goes shoeless on holy ground, the ancient Kohanim went barefoot as they performed the sacrificial service in the Holy Temple. Their descendants, today's Kohanim, also remove their shoes before mounting the bimah to bless Israel. While today's removal of shoes is because of a special enactment by the Talmudic sage Rabbi Yochanan ben Zakai, one can recognize in this gesture a distant echo of what was done in the Holy Temple. In fact, Rabbi Yaakov Emden suggests (Mor Uketziah 54b) that today's Kohanim mount the bimah without their shoes because the place where the Kohanim now stand also represents holy ground.

Through my reverie I hear the chant of the Kohanim. "May the Lord bless thee and keep thee. May He cause His countenance to shine upon thee and be gracious unto thee. May He turn His face unto thee and give thee peace."

The Kohanim come down from the bimah and don their shoes again.

These shoes, where have I seen them before? I remember now where I have seen them. It was in that famous (infamous) black-and-white photograph of the crematoria. Shoes of men and women, shoes of little boys and of little girls piled ever so high, new shoes and old, with laces and without, dress shoes and casual, shoes that will never again be worn by their owners—a towering mound of forlorn and bereft and desolate shoes.

This is the place where Jewish boys and girls and their mothers and fathers, because they were all children of the One God, went up in smoke as fire offerings. But the thousands of shoes they left behind, wrenching as they are in their emptiness, can also, on a far different level, offer a small measure of solace and comfort.

Solace and comfort, for in that luminous moment when these Jews stood face-to-face with the ultimate holiness of *Kiddush Hashem* (sanctification of God's Name), they lost all connection to the universe of the earth and the animals. At that moment they transcended the need to demonstrate their moral and spiritual dominance over the beasts of the field and over the human beasts who murdered them.

And as they offered their souls to the Almighty One, as He reached down and brought them into His loving care for eternity, it was appropriate that their shoes be left behind—an ironic reminder that they now dwell in a more hallowed realm. Angels do not require shoes.

Reprinted with permission from innernet.org.

The Slaughter of Innocents

By **Liz Rosenberg**

In honor of the Chabad-Lubavitch Shluchim,
Rabbi Gabi and Rivky Holtzberg

The slaughter of innocents
appears to shatter this broken world.
The narrow bridge cracks.

Through the smallest slat, a thin flame
dances like a candle's ghost.

I see her small hands circle the flame three times.

I see her husband's shoulder near, and children gather
as if to warm themselves in this inextinguishable light.

Heart, believe it. Lean close
for a thousand thousand years.

One act of kindness lasts forever—
and these hands lit the way.

Reprinted with permission from chabad.org.

Lesson 4

Out of the Depths I Call to You
Finding Faith in Difficult Times

Introduction

Chana Eibeschutz-Eilenberg writes of her experience on the way to Auschwitz in 1944 (*Shema Yisrael*, p. 146):

> The train kept moving around the clock without pause. This was the nightmare journey to Auschwitz, more awful than human speech can describe. It was horribly crowded in the cattle car; we were suffocating. Mothers held their children in their arms with their last strength. Fathers fell to their knees, brought down by the weight of the small children clinging to their backs. The air was filled with weeping, cries and wails. The worst was the weeping of the little children. It drove some people insane.

> Suddenly, I heard my father's voice singing, "I believe with perfect faith in the coming of Mashiach." He went on to say some encouraging words to whoever was listening, offering them hope and reminding them not to sink into despair. When he was finished, he began to dance and ended up drawing everyone into the circle.

> An amazing thing happened then. The little children stopped crying, and the atmosphere in the car changed completely. This happened even though we all knew that we were on our final journey. . . .

> The men put on their talleisim and started the morning prayers. The singing and dancing had spread a feeling of calm over everyone and had shown me that nothing in the world can make Jews stop believing in the Creator.

In this lesson we will explore the issue of personal suffering and faith. What framework did Jewish tradition provide to Jews during the Holocaust to withstand the horror that they were experiencing? How did survivors of Auschwitz live a life of hope and meaning?

And what do their experiences tell us about finding meaning in a post-Holocaust world?

The Search for Meaning
Pain Is Emotional

TEXT 1

מִזְמוֹר לְדָוִד

אֵלִי אֵלִי לָמָה עֲזַבְתָּנִי

רָחוֹק מִישׁוּעָתִי דִּבְרֵי שַׁאֲגָתִי

אֱלֹהַי אֶקְרָא יוֹמָם וְלֹא תַעֲנֶה

וְלַיְלָה וְלֹא דֻמִיָּה לִי

תהלים כב,א–ג

A song of David.

My God, my God, why have You forsaken me?

[You are] far from my salvation [and] from the words of my moaning.

My God, I call out by day and You do not reply,

And at night I do not keep silent.

TEHILIM/PSALMS 22:1–3

Questions **for Discussion**

1. If G-d has truly abandoned King David, why is he still calling to G-d?

2. How would you comfort someone who feels abandoned by G-d?

למה עזבתני
רחוק מישועתי

Table 4.1

Event	Short Term Meaning of the Event	Long Term Meaning of the Event
1. The bookstore is out of Book 3 and the other students refuse to let you see or study from their book.	**Bad**	
2. You study the remaining three books and attend the exam. No questions on Book 3 are asked, so you win the prize. Your plane is leaving at 8:00 a.m. the next day!	**Good**	**Number 1 flips to good. Because you didn't have Book 3, you ended up being able to better answer the questions on the exam.**
3. You go home, throw a few things together for the trip, and go to sleep to recover from the exam. But bad weather and snow causes a power outage. Your alarm clock does not ring and you wake up at noon!	**Bad**	
4. Your plane is delayed to the following day because of the bad weather and snow on the roadways.	**Good**	**Number 3 flips to good because you got more rest and more time to prepare for the trip.**

Event	Short Term Meaning of the Event	Long Term Meaning of the Event
5. The following day, on your way to the airport, the taxi is involved in a car accident because of the snow on the roadways. Thank G-d, you are not hurt, but you miss your plane.	**Bad**	**All of the above scenarios now flip to bad because this whole thing has led to problems. The snow and ice is especially bad because it caused this accident.**
6. The plane that you were supposed to be on has engine trouble when flying to Europe and ends up stranding all of its passengers in Greenland for two weeks.	**Good**	**Not that the engine trouble is good, but the fact that you missed that flight is good.**
7. They put you on a plane to Paris the following day, but you are feeling sick from all that you have been through, and when you land in Paris you ask to be put on the next plane home.	**Bad**	**All of the above now flip to bad again.**
8. On the way home, you sit next to a wonderful individual. You talk the entire trip and end up getting engaged, married, and living happily ever after.	**Good**	**All of the above flip to good again.**

Pain and Purpose

TEXT 2

Any attempt to restore a man's inner strength in the camp had first to succeed in showing him some future goal. Nietzsche's words, "He who has a *why* to live for can bear with almost any *how*," could be the guiding motto . . . regarding prisoners. Whenever there was an opportunity for it, one had to give them a why—an aim—for their lives, in order to strengthen them to bear the terrible *how* of their existence. Woe to him who saw no more sense in his life, no aim, no purpose, and therefore no point in carrying on. He was soon lost. . . .

What was really needed was a fundamental change in our attitude toward life. We had to learn ourselves and, furthermore, we had to teach the despairing men, that *it did not really matter what we expected from life, but rather what life expected from us.* We needed to stop asking about the meaning of life, and instead to think of ourselves as those who were being questioned by life—daily and hourly. Our answer must consist, not in talk and meditation, but in right action and in right conduct. Life ultimately means taking the responsibility to find the right answer to its problems and to fulfill the tasks which it constantly sets for each individual. . . .

When a man finds that it is his destiny to suffer, he will have to accept his suffering as his task. . . .

No one can relieve him of his suffering or suffer in his place. His unique opportunity lies in the way in which he bears his burden.

VIKTOR FRANKL, MAN'S SEARCH FOR MEANING,
[POCKET BOOKS, 1985] PP. 97–99

Viktor Emil Frankl (1905–1997). M.D., PhD, was Professor of Neurology and Psychiatry at the University of Vienna Medical School. During World War II he spent three years in various concentration camps, including Theresienstadt, Auschwitz, and Dachau. Frankl was founder of the psychotherapeutic school called logotherapy. Frankl authored thirty-nine books, which have been published in thirty-eight languages. His most famous book, *Man's Search for Meaning*, has sold over nine-million copies in the U.S. alone.

TEXT 3

וַיֶּעְתַּר יִצְחָק לַה' לְנֹכַח אִשְׁתּוֹ כִּי עֲקָרָה הִוא

וַיֵּעָתֶר לוֹ ה' וַתַּהַר רִבְקָה אִשְׁתּוֹ

וַיִּתְרֹצֲצוּ הַבָּנִים בְּקִרְבָּהּ

וַתֹּאמֶר אִם כֵּן לָמָּה זֶּה אָנֹכִי

וַתֵּלֶךְ לִדְרֹשׁ אֶת ה'

וַיֹּאמֶר ה' לָהּ

שְׁנֵי גוֹיִם בְּבִטְנֵךְ וּשְׁנֵי לְאֻמִּים מִמֵּעַיִךְ יִפָּרֵדוּ

וּלְאֹם מִלְאֹם יֶאֱמָץ וְרַב יַעֲבֹד צָעִיר

בראשית כה,כא–כג

is wife was sterile, and Isaac pleaded with God for her sake. God granted his plea, and Rebecca became pregnant. But the children clashed inside her, and when this occurred, she asked, "Why is this happening to me?"

She went to seek a message from God. God's word to her was, "Two nations are in your womb. Two governments will separate from inside you. The upper hand will go from one government to the other. The greater one will serve the younger."

BEREISHIT/GENESIS 25:21–23

Living with Faith
Internalizing Faith

TEXT 4

גנבא אפום מחתרתא רחמנא קרי

תלמוד בבלי ברכות סג,א (גרסת עין יעקב)

A thief at the entrance to the tunnel [as he goes to steal] calls out [in prayer] to G-d.

TALMUD, BERACHOT 63A (VERSION OF EIN YA'AKOV)

TEXT 5

וְצַדִּיק בֶּאֱמוּנָתוֹ יִחְיֶה

חבקוק ב,ד

The righteous shall live by his faith.

HABAKKUK 2:4

Nurturing Faith

TEXT 6A

וזה נכלל גם כן בלשון אמונה
שהוא לשון רגילות
שמרגיל האדם את עצמו כמו אומן המאמן ידיו וכו׳

ליקוטי אמרים תניא, מב

Also implicit in the word *emunah* (faith), is [that it is] a term indicating "training" to which a person habituates himself, like a craftsman who trains his hands, and so forth.

RABBI SHNE'UR ZALMAN OF LIADI, TANYA, CH. 42

Rabbi Shne'ur Zalman of Liadi (1745–1812). Known as "the Alter Rebbe" and "the Rav." Born in Liozna, Belarus and buried in Hadich, Ukraine. Chassidic Rebbe and founder of the Chabad movement, he was among the principle students of the Magid of Mezeritch. His numerous works include the *Tanya,* an early classic of Chassidism, *Torah Or* and *Likutei Torah,* and *Shulchan Aruch HaRav,* a rewritten *Code of Jewish Law.* He was succeeded by his son, Rabbi Dovber of Lubavitch.

TEXT 6B

כמו אומן המאמן ידיו:
שיודע אותה בנפשו, יש לו כשרון לה
אלא שצריך לאמן ידיו שיבוא בפועל במעשה (בציור, עשיית כלים וכו׳)

הערה בשיעורים בספר התניא, מב

Like a craftsman who trains his hands: He is cognizant of the craft in his soul; he has a natural talent for it, but needs only to train his hands, so that it will find tangible expression in his actions (be it through art, or fashioning vessels, or the like).

RABBI MENACHEM MENDEL SCHNEERSON, NOTE IN LESSONS IN TANYA, CH. 42

Rabbi Menachem Mendel Schneerson (1902–1994). Known as "the Lubavitcher Rebbe," or simply as "the Rebbe." Born in southern Ukraine. Rabbi Schneerson escaped from the Nazis, and arrived in the U.S. in June 1941. The towering Jewish leader of the twentieth century, the Rebbe inspired and guided the revival of traditional Judaism after the European devastation, and often emphasized that the performance of just one additional good deed could usher in the era of Mashiach.

מִזְמוֹר לְדָוִד ה' רֹעִי לֹא אֶחְסָר

בִּנְאוֹת דֶּשֶׁא יַרְבִּיצֵנִי עַל מֵי מְנֻחוֹת יְנַהֲלֵנִי

נַפְשִׁי יְשׁוֹבֵב יַנְחֵנִי בְמַעְגְּלֵי צֶדֶק לְמַעַן שְׁמוֹ

גַּם כִּי אֵלֵךְ בְּגֵיא צַלְמָוֶת לֹא אִירָא רָע כִּי אַתָּה עִמָּדִי

שִׁבְטְךָ וּמִשְׁעַנְתֶּךָ הֵמָּה יְנַחֲמֻנִי

תַּעֲרֹךְ לְפָנַי שֻׁלְחָן נֶגֶד צֹרְרָי דִּשַּׁנְתָּ בַשֶּׁמֶן רֹאשִׁי כּוֹסִי רְוָיָה

אַךְ טוֹב וָחֶסֶד יִרְדְּפוּנִי כָּל יְמֵי חַיָּי

וְשַׁבְתִּי בְּבֵית ה' לְאֹרֶךְ יָמִים

תהלים כג

A song of David. The Lord is my shepherd; I shall not want. He causes me to lie down in green pastures; He leads me beside still waters. He restores my soul; He leads me in paths of righteousness for His name's sake. Even when I walk in the valley of the shadow of death, I will fear no evil for You are with me; Your rod and Your staff—they comfort me. You set a table before me in the presence of my adversaries; You anointed my head with oil; my cup overflows. May only goodness and kindness pursue me all the days of my life, and I will dwell in the house of the Lord for length of days.

Tehilim 23

Learning Activity

1. What feelings do you think King David is trying to express by calling G-d his shepherd?

2. If G-d is his shepherd, why is he walking through the valley of the shadow of death?

3. Contrast the earlier selection from Psalm 22 with Psalm 23—what has changed for King David in his relationship with G-d?

4. Do you find Psalm 23 comforting? Why or why not?

5. What does the "valley of the shadow of death" evoke in your own life?

Faith During the Holocaust

TEXT 8

And finally, think about the following:

A human being is not only the body we see, but also the invisible soul. That is the eternal thing within us, which remains—even when the body succumbs. Every suffering has an end. No pain endures forever. But your soul is immortal; [it] will overcome the suffering, in a world of peace and truth.

And thus there are three on which you can rely, wherever you go: God, the Jewish community, and your own soul. All three are eternal, immortal.

Choose life: that is the call of the most superb Jewish commandment. Keep up in every situation! Fulfill your obligation and task as a human being and as a Jew in faithfulness! With your entire will and strength!

Be strong! Chazak!

RABBI A. B. N. DAVIDS, SEPTEMBER 1942,
YAD VASHEM ARCHIVES, M 19/9-2

Rabbi Aharon Yisachar Davids (1895–1945). Named chief rabbi of Rotterdam, Netherlands in 1930. He led his community with dedication and strong leadership during the Holocaust. He was deported to Bergen-Belsen in 1943 and perished there in February 1945.

TEXT 9

The Germans came to Lublin to set up a "Jewish area" and ordered the chairman of the *Judenrat* to assemble the Jewish population in an open field outside the city for a "general parade." As the Jews presented themselves at the appointed time, the German commander ordered them to sing a gay and happy hasidic tune. The crowd was fearful and confused, but one hesitant voice started singing the moving song: *Lomir sich iberbeiten, Avinu shebaShamayim*, "Let us be friends again, our Father in heaven." The crowd remained unresponsive. The German soldiers threw themselves with murderous blows upon the Jews who would not obey their command. Suddenly, a voice broke from among the crowd singing the same tune with might and joy, but with the words now changed to: *Mir wellen sei iberleben, Avinu shebaShamayim*, "We shall outlive them, our Father in heaven." The song gripped the crowd. They sang it with enthusiasm and danced to it ecstatically. It became for them the hymn of Jewish eternity. The Germans, bewildered and at a loss, started shouting: "Stop it! Stop it!" Did they sense that it was the song of their doom?

ELIEZER BERKOVITS, WITH GOD IN HELL, PP. 92–93

Eliezer Berkovits (1908–1992). Rabbi, theologian, and educator. Born in Romania, he served in the rabbinate in Berlin before the war. In 1958 he became chairman of the Department of Jewish Philosophy at the Hebrew Theological College in Chicago. Author of *Faith After the Holocaust* and *With God in Hell*.

TEXT 10

Another entry in the diary of Leib Langfuss: "And the transports began arriving [in the Birkenau concentration camp] from Hungary, and two Jews turned to a member of our Kommando and asked him whether they should recite the *Viduy*, the last confession before dying. And my comrade said Yes. So they took a bottle of brandy and drank from it while shouting *l'chaim*, to life, to one another with true joy. And they insisted that my comrade drink too, but he felt too embarrassed, and ashamed. And he said no, but they refused to let him go. They pressed him to drink, to drink and to say *l'chaim*. And they said, 'You must live, for you must avenge us. You must. Therefore we say to you *l'chaim*, to life.' And they kept on repeating, *l'chaim, l'chaim,* we understand one another, don't we? *L'chaim.* And my comrade drank with them and he was so deeply moved that he began to weep. . . ."

I confess that ever since I have read these documents I find it difficult, even on Shabbat and on the Holy Days, to lift my glass and say *l'chaim.* But not to do so is tantamount to conceding defeat. So we continue to praise life. To do what others have done before us. Therein lies the strength of Jewish tradition: we repeat words and gestures that have come down to us through the centuries. We do it for ourselves, but not only for ourselves.

ELIE WEISEL, A JEW TODAY, PP. 181–182

TEXT 11

Voltaire said, "When all hope is gone, death becomes a duty." Not so for Jews. When all hope is gone, Jews invent new hopes. Even in the midst of despair, we attempt to justify hope. . . .

We owe it to our past not to lose hope. Say what you will, despair is not the solution. Not for us. Quite the contrary. We must show our children that in spite of everything, we keep our faith—in ourselves and even in mankind, though mankind may not be worthy of such faith. We must persuade our children and theirs that three thousand years of history must not be permitted to end with an act of despair on our part.

ELIE WIESEL, A JEW TODAY, PP. 165–167

Questions **for Discussion**

1. How do you allow the core of hope and faith that exists within us to become more evident in our day-to-day lives?

2. What is the meaning that motivates the way we live our lives? What can inspire our children to live more hopeful lives?

Key Points

1. Suffering does not need to be seen as a result of sin.

2. Since we only experience a thin sliver of the totality of human experience, it is impossible to know the long-term meaning of a given event.

3. Jewish tradition teaches that it is helpful to deal with painful situations by reframing the event in a way that gives it purpose.

4. It is a Jewish goal not only to believe in G-d, but also to express this faith in all aspects of life.

5. Faith and optimism need to be actively practiced in good times if they are to provide strength in difficult times.

6. Choosing life can be a powerful demonstration of *emunah* (faith).

Supplementary Texts

TEXT A

He was the baker at my children's summer camp, camp Massad in the Pocono Mountains. He did not speak much. . . . He began to tell me his story.

"You see, I had a little sister who was the most beautiful person on earth both in body and soul. There wasn't a thing in the world that was too difficult for me to do for my sister. When the Germans occupied our town, we hid her for we knew that they would take her away with the rest of the young women. . . . The knowledge that she was safe and with us gave us the strength to go on living in the most difficult times. . . .

"One day as we were returning home, a strange silence hung on the streets. . . . The closer we got to our building, the more we could sense that something was wrong. When we got there, we discovered that the door to our room had been broken in, everything was looted, and my sister was gone! While avoiding our eyes, neighbors told us that she had been taken by the Gestapo. Without thinking, I began to run to the Gestapo. My mother begged me to return; she did not want to lose two children in one day. But I just continued to run.

"I entered the Gestapo building as if it was the most natural thing for a Jew to do. I was greeted by a young soldier at the desk. 'What's your wish, Jew, to be shot now? If you are in great haste, I can accommodate you.'

"'You took my sister,' I said.

"'Who's your sister?'

"'The beautiful girl you just brought in.'

"'That's fascinating. Tell me, how do all ugly Jews have beautiful sisters?'

"The soldier at the desk called in another Gestapo man from the next room. He briefed him.

"'So she's your sister?' he said to me. . . .

"'Yes,' I said.

"'What do you want?'

"'Give me back my sister.'

"The German burst into wild laughter. 'What strange ideas Jews have these days,' he choked. Suddenly he stopped laughing. 'You know, Jew, I will let your beautiful sister go on one condition. If right now you will grow hair on the palm of your hand.'

"I opened the palm of my hand—it was covered with black hair. The Gestapo man's face twisted into a horrible grimace. He began to shout hysterically, 'You Jewish satan, devil, take your sister and run before I machine-gun the two of you!' . . . I grabbed my sister's hand and with all our strength we began to run, never looking back. We stopped for only a moment at our home to tell our parents that we were alive, and then we fled to the forest. . . ."

When he finished this story, he opened his clenched fist. His palm was covered with a thick growth of black hair. . . .

"You see," he went on, "when I was a very young man, a boy, I worked in a factory. My hand was caught in a machine. It was a terrible accident. How they managed to save my shattered hand I still marvel till this day. As you can see, there is not a task I can't perform with my hand, from the most difficult, strenuous movement to the most delicate. Apparently, the skin that was grafted onto my palm was from a hairy part of my body. In my late teens, hair began to grow on the palm of my hand. Doctors tell me today that this is impossible, but the palm of my hand did not go to medical school.

"But let me tell you something. Even if I had not had hair on the palm of my hand, if this had been the only way to save my sister's life, I would have grown hair on the palm of my hand right there before the German's eyes!"

YAFFA ELIACH, HASIDIC TALES OF THE HOLOCAUST, PP. 59–62

Yaffa Eliach. Professor of Judaic Studies at Brooklyn College, pioneer scholar in Holocaust Studies, and creator of the acclaimed "Tower of Life" at the United States Holocaust Memorial Museum in Washington. Born in Eishyshok in what is now Lithuania, she survived the Holocaust, and immigrated to Palestine with her aunt and uncle in 1946. Her more famous publications include Hasidic *Tales of the Holocaust* and *There Once Was a World*.

TEXT B

ne of the first American Jewish chaplains to arrive at the concentration camps was a well-known rabbi named Eliezer Silver. . . . With tears in his eyes, the rabbi went from survivor to survivor, speaking to them, comforting them, trying to infuse them with life . . . but there was one man who was very angry.

"I have no use for rabbis," he said bitterly. "After what I saw, I'm through with religion."

"Would you like to tell me about it?" the rabbi asked patiently.

"I'll tell you alright," he retorted. "There was a religious Jew in our camp who managed to salvage a prayer book. And do you know what he did with it? If anyone wanted to pray from his book, they had to give him their portion of bread. And you should have seen all the people whose bread he took! Well, after seeing that, I have no use for religious Jews."

"My son," Rabbi Silver answered gently, "instead of thinking about that one man who demanded bread for every prayer, why don't you think about the hundreds of Jews who were willing to give up their bread in order to pray from that prayer book."

REBBETZIN ESTHER JUNGREIS, THE COMMITTED LIFE, PP. 167–168

TEXT C

אמר רבא ואיתימא רב חסדא:

אם רואה אדם שיסורין באין עליו

יפשפש במעשיו

שנאמר: נחפשה דרכינו ונחקורה ונשובה עד ה' (איכה ג,מ)

תלמוד בבלי ברכות ה,א

Rava and some say Rav Chisda said, "If a person sees that afflictions are befalling him, he should investigate his deeds, as it is stated, 'Let us search and examine our ways and let us return to the Lord' (Lamentations 3:40)."

TALMUD, BERACHOT 5A

Additional Readings

The Survivor's Prayer

By **Zvi Yair**

My G-d, my savior
Who, in the valley of slaughter
When so many, my betters, fell
To my right and to my left,
Stamped the mark of life
Upon my brow
The brow of a lowly
And unworthy man
For who is to tell You
What to do?

And from then
Every throb of my heart
Is a psalm of thanks to You
My every breath of life
A song to Your name

Over this one thing
I implore You:
That my cup of gratitude
With a tear is laced
A tear of anguish and mourning
For the millions
For whom Your cloud muted
Their screams issuing
From the pits of death

I implore You
Over the echo of sorrow
In the trumpet of my praise
Over the trickle of pain
In my outpourings of thanks

Please
Forgive the tear

Reprinted with permission from chabad.org.

Yom Kippur Sermon

Delivered in the Feldafing DP Camp, 1945

By **Rabbi Yekutiel Yehuda Halberstam,**
the Rebbe of Klausenberg

"*Ashamnu*—Did we sin?

"*Bagadnu*—Were we unfaithful? . . . Were we, God forbid, unfaithful to God and did we fail to remain loyal to him?

"*Gazalnu*—did we steal? From whom did we steal in Auschwitz and Mühldorf? . . .

"*Maradnu*—We rebelled? Against whom? We rebelled against you, Master of the Universe? . . .

"This *Vidui* (confession) was not written for us," he concluded, closing his *machzor* [holiday prayer book] . . .

But, he thundered anew, "We are guilty of sins that are not written in the *machzor* . . . How many times did many of us pray, Master of the Universe, I have no more strength, take my soul so I will not have to recite *Modeh Ani* anymore? . . . We must ask the Almighty to restore our faith and trust in Him. 'Trust in God forever.' . . . Pour your hearts out to Him."

Rabbi Yekutiel Yehuda Halberstam (1905-1994), the rebbe of Sanz-Klausenberg, was born into a prestigious rabbinic family and studied in his youth with the greatest rabbis in Poland. In 1921 he married the daughter of R. Chaim Tzvi Teitelbaum, the chief rabbinic judge of Sighet. He was chosen five years later as the rabbi of Klausenberg (Cluj). During the Holocaust the Klausenberger Rebbe lost his wife and eleven children. Despite these losses, he continued to lead a religious life and was a source of inspiration for many Jews. After the Holocaust he became a leader of ultra-Orthodox survivors and struggled to revive Jewish life in the DP camps. He established yeshivas and seminaries, and married a second wife, the daughter of Rabbi Shmuel Dovid Ungar, the chief rabbinic judge of Nitra, one of the leading rabbis of the generation. After his arrival in Israel, the Klausenberger Rebbe established important centers of Klausenberg-Sanz Chassidism in Netanyah and Jerusalem.

Reprinted with permission from yadvashem.org.

Forgiveness

By **Jay Litwin**

These were the days before Yom Kippur. I was lonely and couldn't figure out why. The loneliness had been there for months.

Things were good with my wife and kids. I'd been on the phone with my sisters and in close contact with my friends.

So, what was the source of this loneliness?

I was missing G-d.

I was and had been feeling distant from Him. A strange feeling for me. Even in my late teens I had been able to connect with Him when I needed to. He always answers my calls. Sometimes I don't even need to call. I just feel his companionship as I journey through life.

But these last months had been lonely. I had been separate from Him, unable even to call out. And I didn't know why.

Just before Yom Kippur, I received an e-mail from a friend. He's not a religious Jew, though we discourse often about G-d and Torah. He's a writer and has a way with words. We also share the same disease, and talk much about our symptoms, history, fears, treatments and aches. There's a special something that happens with people who share the same disease. We never have to worry about boring each other. All our concerns and obsessions about the daily changes in our health or symptoms, our latest internet discoveries about new cures and clinical trials may bore others, but are continuously fascinating to us.

At the end of this email my friend wrote: "Jay, this Yom Kippur, I don't think you should go to shul and ask G-d for forgiveness. This Yom Kippur you should stay home and G-d should come crawling on His knees and beg you to forgive Him for what He's done to you."

When I read these lines I laughed. My friend is a sacrilegious provocateur. He believed what he said, but he mainly wrote those words to shock me. I filed his words, but paid them little attention.

As Yom Kippur drew close, I continued to wonder what was taking place between G-d and me. I worried that this day of prayer and fasting would be void of the usual connection that Yom Kippur brings.

And then in a flash I realized that I was angry at G-d. And had been for some time. I was angry about my disease and I was angry that I was not yet healed. I was angry about my pain. And I was angry at the disruption to my life, the fear, the worry and anxiety that my disease was causing my family and those who loved and cared about me. I was angry about the whole thing, and He, being the boss of everything that happens in the world, was responsible and to blame.

And so, I entered Yom Kippur angry at G-d.

I put on my *kittel* and my *tallit* and I went to shul. I had received permission from my doctors and rabbi to fast. I beat my chest and listed my sins. I asked forgiveness. And yet, no matter how long the list of sins was, no matter how much I sought forgiveness, I could not find any act so heinous as to deserve the punishment that I felt was being inflicted upon me.

I prayed for G-d's forgiveness, and in my prayer book I read the words that promised His forgiveness. He would forgive me, I read, because that was His nature. He is a forgiver. He loves me. He wants me to be close to Him. And so He forgives me not for any reason, not because I deserve it, but simply because that is who He is. He is merciful and forgives and wipes the slate clean so that we—He and I—can be close again for the coming year.

I read these words, nice words, yet my anger remained.

Then I again remembered the email. In his cynicism, my friend had hit the mark: I needed to forgive G-d. I needed to rid myself of my anger and blame for the sickness He had given me. I needed to wipe the slate clean so that He and I could be close once again.

But how? On what basis should I forgive Him? If He was human, I could forgive Him for His imperfections, His fallibility, His pettiness, His upbringing, His fragility and vulnerability. I could try to put myself in His shoes, to understand His position. But He is G-d, perfect and complete! Acting with wisdom and intention. How could I forgive Him?!

As I continued my prayers throughout the day, with my anger and inability to forgive foremost in my mind, the words in my prayer book began to transform from pleas for forgiveness to instructions on how to forgive. Could it be that on this Yom Kippur, G-d was teaching me how to forgive Him? Were these words lessons on forgiveness from the Master of Forgiveness?

The instructions seemed clear: Forgive for the sake of forgiveness. Forgive not because there is a reason that you understand (for you may never understand My ways) nor because I deserve it (for the ways that I manifest are often terrible and frightening). Forgive solely out of love, so we can be close once again. Forgive because you, created in My image, are also a forgiver. I created you with that capacity so that always, no matter what happens in your life, you and I can be close, so that you and whomever you love, despite what transpires between you, can always reunite and begin again, clean and pure, ready for a new start.

The message and instructions were there and I began to hear through the prayers G-d speaking to me, reaching out for reconciliation, waiting for my forgiveness, providing instruction on how to forgive Him.

Again I remembered my friend's provocative e-mail. No, G-d was not crawling. But was He begging? Was He beseeching me for forgiveness and reconciliation? Was our unity more important to Him than any sin I had committed against Him or any pain He had inflicted upon me?

Still, I could not do it. Even seeing the extent to which

He was reaching out to me, I was incapable of forgiveness. Though I wanted to forgive, on this day of truth, I saw that I could not. What He had done to me remained too terrible, too intentional to forgive.

As the closing *Ne'ilah* prayer approached, I was in despair. It all seemed hopeless. When I presented my case before my invisible set of internal of judges I carry with me, I was judged right, He guilty. He deserved my distance and rejection and I would stubbornly and righteously continue it.

As the sun began to set I felt completely alone. The loneliness was intolerable.

The feeling reminded me of times when I argue with my wife. We fight about some injustice or hurt that has occurred. I present my case before my internal judges and I am proven right. I withdraw in righteousness, punish her with rejection and distance. Sometimes it will last a few hours, sometimes a couple of days. But finally, the loneliness sets in. The distance becomes unbearable. The withdrawal demands an end. My desire for reconciliation and reunification overpowers any need to be right or to punish. And so, without needing to even speak about what it was we were fighting about, eventually we forgive each other so that we can be together again, loving again, carrying on our lives and relationship and family in good will and with a fresh start. We don't forgive because of any reason, nor out of our acceptance of each other's human pettiness or frailty or imperfection. We forgive simply from the desire to love and reunite. Simply so we can be together again. So that things will be the way they should.

And in the last minutes of Yom Kippur, out of my unbearable loneliness and separation from G-d, I found my ability to forgive. I forgave simply so that we—G-d and I—could be close again. So that we would return to the unity that is meant to be between us. Out my love for Him, my need of Him, my inability to carry on without Him I found the capacity somewhere in me. I reached out to Him in forgiveness and in that moment the pain and blame began to recede.

For me, Yom Kippur has not ended. This forgiveness business is not so easy as to be learned and actualized in a day. My anger and resentment, frustration and intolerance still flare, still cause damage. On my bad days it is hard for me to accept all that is happening, changing, challenging my life. But some new dynamic has entered the process. A softening. An acceptance. A letting go. A . . . forgiveness.

For, you see, the last thing I want during the fragility of this time in my life is to be separate from G-d or from those whom I love or from the rising sun or a star-filled night.

I don't want anger and blame to ruin any moment of my life nor rend me from the unity with which G-d has created the world and that only I have the power to destroy.

Thankfully, G-d has provided me with the capacity to forgive and, now, in these days since Yom Kippur, he has provided me with the opportunity to reveal that forgiveness. He knows that both He and I, and all those that He and I love, will eventually, continuously do unforgivable things to each other. And despite the pain we will cause each other, we will need to forgive each other.

To not forgive would be an unbearable breach of the unity of creation.

Reprinted with permission from chabad.org.

Lesson **5**

A Tree of Life to Those Who Hold Fast to It
Halachic Questions of the Holocaust Era

Introduction

Throughout Jewish history, Torah and Halachah (Jewish law) have served as a moral compass for Jewish life. During the Holocaust era, many Jews continued to look to Jewish tradition for direction. They would consult with a learned expert in Jewish law who would answer their questions. Sometimes these answers were recorded in the form of responsa (written decisions of halachic authorities on questions of Jewish law and practice) that were unearthed after the Holocaust.

The responsa literature opens a fascinating historical window into the real-life issues that concerned Jews in the midst of the Holocaust. In this lesson, we will explore the concerns, the questions, and the courage of Jews who were able to bring a ray of sanity and morality into a world suffused with darkness.

עץ חיים היא

Living Law

Learning Activity

Imagine that you are going to a distant country far from Western civilization. You will be living there for a number of years, amidst a foreign culture. Because of space constraints, you can only take one thing with you that will help remind you of your culture and your identity.

What will you choose to take?

TEXT 1

לוּלֵי תוֹרָתְךָ שַׁעֲשֻׁעָי אָז אָבַדְתִּי בְעָנְיִי
לְעוֹלָם לֹא אֶשְׁכַּח פִּקּוּדֶיךָ כִּי בָם חִיִּיתָנִי
לְךָ אֲנִי הוֹשִׁיעֵנִי כִּי פִקּוּדֶיךָ דָרָשְׁתִּי
לִי קִוּוּ רְשָׁעִים לְאַבְּדֵנִי עֵדֹתֶיךָ אֶתְבּוֹנָן
לְכָל תִּכְלָה רָאִיתִי קֵץ רְחָבָה מִצְוָתְךָ מְאֹד
מָה אָהַבְתִּי תוֹרָתֶךָ כָּל הַיּוֹם הִיא שִׂיחָתִי
מֵאֹיְבַי תְּחַכְּמֵנִי מִצְוֹתֶךָ כִּי לְעוֹלָם הִיא לִי

תהלים קיט, צב–צח

ere not Your Torah my occupation, then I would have perished in my affliction.

I shall never forget Your precepts for through them You have sustained me.

I am Yours; save me for I sought Your precepts.

Concerning me: the wicked hoped to destroy me; I shall ponder Your testimonies.

Of every finite thing I have seen the end; Your commandments are very broad.

How I love Your Torah! All day it is my conversation.

Each of Your commandments makes me wiser than my enemies, for it is always mine.

TEHILIM/PSALMS 119:92–98

Question for Discussion

Based on these verses, what did King David "take along with him" as he endured much suffering?

TEXT 2

Torah, as its Hebrew root implies, is a form of [the Hebrew word] *hora'ah*—teaching. It teaches man the path he should follow, and is indeed a guide to fulfilling the commandments. Yet it is also far more than that. It is a comprehensive guide, the expression of Judaism's conception of everything in the world. . . . Hence, whether the subject is concrete and practical or abstract and spiritual, whether it expresses an immediate and living need or is entirely theoretical and without practical application, since it is related to Judaism's world view, it is related to Torah, and Torah does indeed deal with it. . . .

The ultimate purpose of Torah is not, then, only to scrutinize the commandments and reach practical conclusions regarding them; it is, rather, to provide a comprehensive world view, bringing out both the essential relationship of Torah to every subject and also the subjects' connections with each other.

RABBI ADIN STEINSALTZ (EVEN-YISRAEL),
THE TALMUD: A REFERENCE GUIDE, P. 2

Rabbi Adin (Even-Yisrael) **Steinsaltz** (1937–). Born in Jerusalem, Steinsaltz is considered one of the foremost Jewish thinkers of the twentieth century. Praised by *Time Magazine* as a "once-in-a-millennium scholar," he has been awarded the Israel Prize for his contributions to Jewish study. He is the founder of the Israel Institute for Talmudic Publications, a society dedicated to the translation and elucidation of the Talmud.

Text 3a

כִּי יִפָּלֵא מִמְּךָ דָבָר לַמִּשְׁפָּט

בֵּין דָּם לְדָם בֵּין דִּין לְדִין וּבֵין נֶגַע לָנֶגַע

דִּבְרֵי רִיבֹת בִּשְׁעָרֶיךָ

וְקַמְתָּ וְעָלִיתָ אֶל הַמָּקוֹם אֲשֶׁר יִבְחַר יְהֹוָה אֱלֹהֶיךָ בּוֹ

וּבָאתָ אֶל הַכֹּהֲנִים הַלְוִיִּם

וְאֶל הַשֹּׁפֵט אֲשֶׁר יִהְיֶה בַּיָּמִים הָהֵם

וְדָרַשְׁתָּ וְהִגִּידוּ לְךָ אֵת דְּבַר הַמִּשְׁפָּט

דברים יז,ח–ט

If you are unable to reach a decision in a case involving capital punishment, litigation, leprous marks, [or any other case] where there is a dispute in your territorial courts, then you must set out and go up to the place that God your Lord shall choose.

You must approach the Levitical priests [and other members of] the supreme court that exists at the time. When you make inquiry, they will declare to you a legal decision.

DEVARIM/DEUTERONOMY 17:8–9

Text 3b

ואפילו אינו כשאר שופטים שהיו לפניו אתה צריך לשמוע לו אין לך אלא שופט שבימיך

רש"י שם

Although this judge may not be [of the same stature] as other judges who preceded him, you must listen to him. You have only the judge of your time.

RASHI, AD LOC.

Rabbi Shlomo Yitschaki (1040–1105). Better known by the acronym Rashi. Rabbi and famed author of comprehensive commentaries on the Talmud and Bible. Born in Troyes, Champagne, France, Rashi studied in the famed *yeshivot* of Mainz and Worms. His commentaries, which focus on the simple understanding of the text, are considered fundamental to Torah study. Since their initial printings, the commentaries have appeared in virtually every edition of the Talmud and Bible. Many of the famed Tosafists of France are among Rashi's descendants.

TEXT 4

הנני החתום משיב לשואלוני על דבר הקדושין מהעלמה שנתקדשה ושניהם היו
אנוסים לעבור על תורת משה על ידי גוים וגם העדים כיוצא בהם.
רואה אני שהיא צריכה גט שאף ישראל משומד לרצונו שקדש, קדושיו קדושין
שנאמר חטא ישראל (יהושע ז,יא)
אף על פי שחטא ישראל הוא (סנהדרין מד,א) וכל שכן האנוסים לבם לשמים
והרי אלו הוכיח סופן על תחלתן
שחזרו ויצאו משם כשמצאו הצלה . . .
ושלום שלמה ב"ר יצחק

תשובת רש"י, הובא בארחות חיים, הלכות קידושין יג

erewith do I, the undersigned, answer him who has questioned me concerning the marriage of a certain girl who was married, and both [the bride and the groom], as well as the witnesses [to the ceremony], had been forced by Gentiles to [disavow and] violate the [precepts of the] Torah.

I am of the opinion that this woman requires a Jewish bill of divorcement [before she can marry another man]. Even the marriage of someone who voluntarily become an apostate and then married is legal and binding [according to Jewish law]. For it is said, "Israel has transgressed" (Joshua 7:11), meaning that "even though he has transgressed, he is still an Israelite" (Sanhedrin 44a).

How much the more is this true in the case of the forced converts who at heart are still loyal to G-d. In this particular case their final conduct reflects their original attitude, for when they were able to find some form of escape they left and returned to Judaism....

Peace! Shlomo the son of Rabbi Isaac

RESPONSUM OF RASHI, CITED IN ORCHOT CHAIM, HILCHOT KIDUSHIN, 13

Primary Sources

TEXT 5

I was a young rabbi in the Kovno ghetto of Lithuania, whose great Jewish minds were known throughout the Jewish world. People, the plain people, approached me with their questions. Because life was not normal and there was a war on, they were not always sure what the Torah required of them. Source books were not available, and I could not rule on these questions the way I would have in normal times. My memory had to serve me. But I did write down the questions and my brief rulings on paper torn from cement sacks which I hid in cans that I buried in the ghetto soil to preserve them. If I survived, I thought, I'd expand the notes into full-length responses.

When we realized that we were the targets of the Germans just because we were Jews—that our Jewishness was being attacked—then our Jewish pride came to the fore . . . I am not speaking of wonderworking rabbis who secretly and humbly had mastered the Talmud and Kabalah, but simple Jews whose faith in the Almighty was the core of their being. Such a Jew simply follows the dictates of the Torah as he or she knows best. And when they don't know, they approach a rabbi, whose authority and wider knowledge and accessibility to sources is recognized and relied upon. And so, Jews approached me.

Through the Divine watchfulness of God, I survived and was able to return and forage for the cans of questions and answers I had hidden away. . . .

Rabbi Ephraim Oshry (1914–2003). A young rabbinical scholar in Kaunas, the second-largest city in Lithuania when the Nazis invaded on June 23, 1941. He carefully recorded the halachic questions that Lithuanian Jews asked him during the war as well as his responses, writing them on bits of paper torn from cement sacks he carried on forced labor and burying them in tin cans. He dug up the cans after the war, using these notes as the basis for his collection of Holocaust responsa, printed in the five-volume *She'elot Uteshuvot Mima'amakim*.

I was asked detailed, astonishingly moving questions . . . The world at large may not understand this. But the greatness of Jews can be seen in these very concerns . . . Can the modern Jew fathom it? Can the world fathom it? . . . Does one laugh perplexed? Does one gasp amazed? Because it is amazing . . .

Rabbi Ephraim Oshry,
Responsa from the Holocaust, Introduction, pp. XIII–XIV

Text 6

שאלה: ביום מר . . . הלא הוא יום י"ג לחודש מרחשון של שנת תש"ב, בעת העברת הפעולה הגדולה "אקציע" בלע"ז, של הובלת למעלה מעשרת אלפים איש כצאן טבחה לשחיטה . . .

נשאלתי אז בזמן ההוא מהשרידים האומללים שנשארו בחיים . . . האם מוטלת עליהם החובה לברך ברכת הגומל

על החסדים הטובים שגמל אתם הא-ל להצילם מפעולת השמדה זו, או מכיון שעדיין לא חלפה מעליהם הסכנה . . . ויושבים הם כאסירי עני וברזל סגורים ומסוגרים בתוך חומות הגיטו המוקף מלבד זאת בגדר של תיל מחושמל, ואין יוצא ואין בא, כי מלבד כל זאת השכין האויב בכל שערי ומבואי הגיטו שומרים מזוינים במכונות יריה לשמור את דרך הגיטו . . .

ואם כן לפי זה דינם של השרידים האומללים הללו הוא

כדין יושבי בית האסורים שעדיין לא נושעו ממצוקתם

שאלות ותשובות ממעמקים א,ז

n the tragic day . . . the 8th of Marcheshvan 5702 [October 29, 1941], at the time of the large scale operation that was called *Aktion,* when more than 10,000 people were taken away [from the Kovno Ghetto] to be butchered like sheep . . .

I was asked by some of the miserable survivors . . . whether they were obligated to recite the *Hagomel* blessing to thank G-d for His kindness in allowing them to be saved from this destruction. Or [perhaps were they not obligated to recite the blessing] because they were still in danger . . . They remained locked and imprisoned within the ghetto walls surrounded by an electrified barbed wire fence; no one was allowed to come or go. Besides for this, there were armed guards stationed at the ghetto gates guarding the exits . . . Hence, they were essentially like prisoners who had still not been freed from their distress.

Rabbi Ephraim Oshry, She'elot Uteshuvot Mima'amakim, 1:7

Text 7

ובעת תפילת הבוקר כשהשליח ציבור ר' אברהם יוסף הי"ד התחיל לומר את ברכות השחר . . . משהגיע לברכת "שלא עשני עבד" קרא בקול מר לאדון האדונים, איך אוכל לומר ברכה זו בשעה שנמצאים אנחנו בעוצר ושבי . . . איך יוכל עבד לברך ברכת בן חורין בשעה שמוט עבדות נתון על צוארו ומוסרי שביה נתונים על גופן, איך יכול עבד נתון למרמס חרפת אנוש המחסר לחמו ומימיו ומשביעו ראש ולענה, איך יכול עבד כזה לברך ליוצרו ולומר "שלא עשני עבד" . . . ככה דיבר האיש מדי יום ביומו בעת ברכת השחר, ורבים מתפללים מרוב שיחם וכעסם סייעו על ידו, ונשאלתי אז לחוות את דעתי, דעת תורה האם יש להמנע מלומר ברכה זו, דמתחזי כשיקרא, ואדרבא איסורא איכא, או דילמא אין לנו לשנות ממטבעו שטבעו הכמים בסדר התפלה והברכות

שאלות ותשובות ממעמקים ג,ו

During the morning prayer, when the cantor Reb Avraham Yosef (may G-d avenge his blood), was reciting the blessings that are said in the morning . . . and he reached the blessing [Blessed are you Lord, Sovereign of the Universe] "Who has not made me a slave," he shouted bitterly to the Master of all masters, "How can I recite this blessing when we are incarcerated and captured? . . . How can a slave make the blessing of a free man when the burden of slavery is upon him? How can a slave, repeatedly abused and demeaned, lacking his bread and water, praise his Creator by uttering, 'Who has not made me a slave'?"

He would do this every day during the morning blessings. And many of those who joined him in prayer, because of their anger, would support him. I was then asked for the Torah ruling on this question: should the blessing be omitted because it seemed to be a lie—in which case it would be forbidden to recite it—or was it forbidden to alter [or skip] any part of the prayer text established by our sages?

RABBI EPHRAIM OSHRY, SHE'ELOT UTESHUVOT MIMA'AMAKIM, 3:6

TEXT 8A

Rabbi Zvi Hirsh Meisels . . . was the scion of a distinguished Hasidic and rabbinic family and was the *rav* [rabbi] of Veitzen in Hungary. Before being transported to Auschwitz he had already achieved a considerable reputation as a halachic scholar and was the author of a volume of responsa. . . .

He tells of the events which took place in Auschwitz on the eve of Rosh Hashana in 1944. The Nazi commander of Auschwitz had determined to keep alive only those boys between the ages of fourteen and eighteen who were big enough and strong enough to work. The others would be sent to the crematorium. . . . Fourteen hundred boys . . . were imprisoned in a special cellblock under the guard of the Jewish *kapos*. . . .

The next morning, the first day of Rosh Hashanah, fathers or other relatives who had heard of the fate that awaited the children tried to persuade the *kapos* to release them. The *kapos* replied that an exact count had been taken of the boys, and they would have to pay with their own lives if even one were to be found missing. Some of the relatives still had valuables concealed in their clothing or on their bodies, and they offered them to the *kapos* in return for the lives of their children. . . . Succumbing to greed, the *kapos* agreed to release some of the prisoners. But, they warned, for each prisoner released they would have to seize some other Jewish boy who had escaped the *selektion* . . . so that the count would be full when the block's inmates were taken to the crematoria.

Although they knew that their sons' lives would be spared only at the cost of others, fathers made whatever deals they could to save their own children.

RABBI IRVING J. ROSENBAUM, HOLOCAUST AND HALAKHAH, PP. 3–4

Rabbi Irving J. Rosenbaum (1922–2005). Longtime Chicago Loop Synagogue leader, educator, and founder of the Davka Corporation, which develops Judaic software. In 1961 he was named the first executive director of the Chicago Board of Rabbis. He authored *The Holocaust and Halakhah*. Was named Hebrew Theological College's president in 1977.

Text 8b

הנה ניגש אלי איש יהודי . . . שאמר לי כדברים האלה. רבי, הבן יחיד שלי, היקר
לי מבבת עיני, נמצא שמה בתוך הנערים הנידונים לשריפה, ויש בידי היכולת
לפדותו, והיות שידוע לנו, בלי שום ספק, שהקאפו״ס יתפסו אחר במקומו, על
כן אני שואל מהרבי שאלה להלכה ולמעשה לפסוק לי הדין על פי התורה אם
אני רשאי לפדותו, וכאשר יפסוק כן אעשה.

שאלות ותשובות מקדשי השם, ג–ו

Rabbi Tzvi Hirsh Meisels (1904–1974). Served as rabbi in Vac, Hungary before the Holocaust. Best known as the author of *Mekadshei Hashem*, a collection of halachic responsa from various rabbis killed during the Holocaust. During the war, he and his entire community were sent to Auschwitz. There he served as spiritual mentor to thousands.

was approached by a man who said the following: "Rabbi, my only son, more precious than the pupil of my eye, is there among those condemned to the crematorium. I have the ability to ransom him. But since we indubitably know that [if he is released] the *kapos* will take another in his place [who will be killed], I therefore ask of the Rabbi a question which demands a response to an actual situation. Render a judgment in accordance with the Torah. May I ransom him? Whatever your ruling, I will obey it."

RABBI TZVI HIRSH MEISELS,
SHE'ELOT UTESHUVOT MIKADSHEI HASHEM, PP. 3–6

Questions for Discussion

1. What does the man's question say about his worldview?

2. What do you think the answer should be?

More Precious than Gold

Jews did not sit and weep [in Theresienstadt]. They revealed super-human steadfastness by secretly assembling in the darkness of night in order to study Torah, to participate in courses on Jewish subjects, and to listen to lectures on eternal questions, the mysteries of existence beyond the reach of human understanding. . . .

"I shall never forget these meetings," wrote Dr. [Leo] Baeck. "We would assemble in pitch darkness. To light a candle or even a match would have brought immediate disaster upon all of us. Nevertheless, in the midst of the all that darkness I sensed light. The faces of these Jews were illuminated by an unearthly radiance, as one was talking to them about matters of the spirit and the eternal questions, about God, about Jews and the world, about the eternity of Israel. I sensed a light in that darkness, the light of the Torah. . . . I often contemplated my people . . . their faces I could not distinguish, but I saw great light."

ELIEZER BERKOVITS, WITH GOD IN HELL, PP. 11–12

Eliezer Berkovits (1908–1992). Rabbi, theologian, and educator. Born in Romania, he served in the rabbinate in Berlin before the war. In 1958 he became chairman of the Department of Jewish Philosophy at Hebrew Theological College in Chicago. Author of *Faith After the Holocaust* and *With God in Hell*.

Text 10

נשאלתי שאביע את דעתי, דעת תורה כדת מה לעשות בנוגע לדלהלן: היות שבבית החולים הזה נמצא בחור חולה . . . והגרמנים לאחר שקטעו את רגלו הימנית הכניסוהו לבית חולים זה על מנת שישוב לאיתנו לאחר הניתוח, וברצונו של בחור זה לשפוך את שיחו לפני קונו בכל יום תמיד, לכן נפשו בשאלתו שישלחו לו לבית החולים זוג של תפילין למען יוכל להתפלל בהם כמצווה עלינו בתורתנו, אכן מכיון שיצא הקול, קלא דלא פסיק, שהגרמנים נוהגים שבאם אחד מהחולים מבריא ויוצא מבית החולים הם לוקחים ממנו את חפציו האישיים ושורפים אותם באש, ונשאלתי אם מותר לשלוח לבחור הזה תפילין, שהרי באם יתרפא הגרמנים ישרפו אותם יחד עם שאר חפציו, ואם כן בזה שאנו שולחים לו את התפילין הוי כאילו אנו גורמים לשריפתם . . .

תשובה: . . . ומותר לנו לשלוח לבחור דן את התפילין למען יוכל לקיים מצות "וקשרתם לאות על ידך והיו לטוטפות בין עיניך" (דברים ו,ח) . . . כי אין זה כלל בטוח שאכן אמת הוא הדבר שהגרמנים נוהגים לשרוף את חפצי כל יוצאי בית החולים, וקול זה יתכן שאינו אלא קול של פחדים ומורא . . . מכיון שלא ברור כלל שהקול הוא קול אמת בודאי מותר לשלוח לו את התפילין . . .

ולכן מכל הנזכר לעיל הוריתי שיש לשלוח לבחור דן זוג תפילין כשירות כדי שיוכל לקיים מצוה גדולה זו ולהרנין בזה את לבו ורוחו . . . והד"ר דאווידאוויץ שהיה רופא בבית החולים הזה העיד שהוא היה באותו מעמד כשהביאו לו את התפילין, וכשהניחם בפעם הראשונה היתה שמחתו גדולה עד איז קץ כאילו הוא יוצא מאפילה לאור גדול ומשעבוד לגאולה.

שאלות ותשובות ממעמקים, ג,א

was asked to render a halachic decision on the following: In the hospital [of the Kovno Ghetto] there was a boy that was ill . . . The Germans had placed him in the hospital to recover after amputating his leg. This boy wished to pour out his heart in prayer each day. Therefore, he asked that a pair of *tefilin* be sent to him in the hospital so that he should be able to pray as mandated by Jewish law. However, there was a persistent rumor in the ghetto that the Germans burned every patient's personal possessions upon his recovery and dismissal from the hospital. I was asked whether it was permitted to send this boy *tefilin* for should he recover, the Germans would burn them along with his other belongings. This would mean that by sending him the *tefilin,* the senders would caused the [*tefilin*] to be burned. . . .

Reply: . . . It is permitted to send *tefilin* to this boy so that he may fulfill the commandment "Bind [these words] as a sign on your hand, and let them be an emblem in the center of your head" (Deuteronomy 6:8). . . .It is not definite that the Germans will burn the personal belongings of those discharged from the hospital. It is possible that this rumor is merely a product of fright and fear. . . . Because the rumor is unverified . . . it is therefore certainly permitted to send him the *tefilin*. . . .

Based on the above, I ruled that they should send to this boy a valid pair of *tefilin* so that he would be able to fulfill this mitzvah, and in this way, his heart and spirit would be calmed. . . Dr. Davidovitch, who was a doctor in this hospital, testified that he was present when the boy was presented with the *tefilin*. When the boy donned them for the first time his joy knew no bounds; it was as if he had emerged from darkness to light and from captivity to freedom.

Rabbi Ephraim Oshry, She'elot Uteshuvot Mima'amakim, 3:1

Key Points

1. Halachah (Jewish law) provides a means for Jews to apply the teachings of Torah to every area of life, from the most mundane concerns to the most monumental decisions.

2. Reading halachic responsa can provide sociological and psychological insight into historical events and the lives of Jews in past generations.

3. Holocaust responsa reflect both a profound awareness of the depths of suffering, as well as a powerful affirmation of the freedom of the spirit that transcended those horrific circumstances.

4. Love of the Torah and observance of *mitzvot* was a precious heritage that brought solace and meaning to many Jews during the Holocaust.

Supplementary **Texts**

TEXT A

בימי הרעה והמצור בהיותנו כלואים בגיטו קובנה ושום קשר לא היה לנו עם החוץ

אפסו אזלו לנו בגלל כך כל תשמישי קדושה שאי אפשר היה להשיגם בשום אופן,

והנה באו לפני מספר אנשים ודמעתם על לחיים ושאלוני כדת מה לעשות, מאחר

שמזוזותיהן נפסלו ואי אפשר להשיג מזוזות אחרות כדי לקובען על פתחיהם.

ותוכן שאלתם היא אם דירותיהם בגיטו חייבות הן במזוזה,

או דילמא מאחר שהגיטו הוא סגור ומסוגר אין יוצא ואין בא, וכולו מוקף הוא,

בגדר של חוטי ברזל מחושמל וצריחים ומגדלים שעליהם הופקדו שומרים לשמור

לבל יגשו ויתקרבו יושבי הגיטו אל הגדר וכל הקרב אל הגדר היה נהרג מיד במכונות

היריה שהיו בידי השומרים, ואם כן דינם של יושבי הגיטו כדין יושבי בית האסורים,

ויש לדעת אם בית אסורים חייב הוא במזוזה דגם בית האסורים לדירה יחשב או

דלמא בית אסורים פטור הוא ממזוזה.

שאלות ותשובות ממעמקים, א,יג

During the days of evil siege when we were imprisoned in the Kovno ghetto without any link to the outside world, we ran out of all of our mitzvah supplies [such as *tefilin* and *mezuzot*]. A number of people came to me with tears on their cheeks, asking me what to do since their *mezuzot* had become invalid. It was impossible to obtain [new] valid *mezuzot* to place on their doors.

Their underlying question was whether the ghetto apartments really required *mezuzot*. The ghetto was locked and there was no way in or out. It was surrounded by an electrified barbed-wire fence and by watch towers occupied by machine gun-armed guards who made sure that no one could even approach the fence without being shot.

Perhaps, then, the dwellers of the ghetto were really no more than prisoners. Thus, the question is whether a prison needs a *mezuzah*, because even a prison can be considered a place of dwelling, or is it exempt from requiring a *mezuzah*?

Rabbi Ephraim Oshry, She'elot Uteshuvot Mima'amakim, 1:13

Questions **for Discussion**

1. Why would people living under such harsh conditions be concerned about whether or not their doors had kosher *mezuzot*?

2. What do you think a *mezuzah* represented in their lives?

Text B

ויהי היום ותעבור השמועה לא טובה במחנה הכלואים לאמור, שהנה הגרמנים החליטו לקחת מספר רב של אנשים על מנת להעבירם למחנה אחר, זאת אומרת למחנה השמדה. ובעקבות השמועה הזאת עשתה שמועה אחרת לה כנפים, שהנה מספר רב של כלואי הגיטו בורחים בחשכת הלילה ליערות כדי להצטרף לחבורות הפרטיזנים העושים נקם בגרמנים ומרבים בהם חללים, כי זוהי הדרך היחידה שנשארה ליהודים הנחשבים אצל הגרמנים כצאן לטבח יובל, והיא לעמוד על נפשם על ידי צירוף לחבורות הפרטיזנים הלוחמים בהם בחרוף נפש.

אולם דא עקא, כי הדרך ליערות היא הרת סכנות, כי מלבד שהגיטו עצמו מוקף הוא בגדר תיל מחושמל שכל הנוגע בו קובע את נפשו, ובמרחק ידוע מזה בנויים מגדלי תצפית עליהם עומדים חיילים גרמנים כשבידיהם מכונות ירייה דרוכות, הם עומדים וצופים יום ולילה . . .

מלבד זאת היו ביערות פלוגופת פרטיזנים כאלה שלא רצו בכלל לקבל לתוכם יהודים, כי גם הם היו שונאי ישראל גדולים למרות שנלחמו עם הגרמנים, ויהודי שנפל לידי פלגות הפרטיזנים כזאת שילם לא אחת בחייו.

ולזאת נשאלתי אז . . . אם מותר מצד הדין לאחד מכלואי הגיטו לסכן את עצמו

ולברוח ליערות, כי אולי ה' יהיה בעזרו ויצליח על ידי בריחתו להשאר בחיים,
כי כאן בתוך הגיטו הסכנה הנשקפת לחייו היא ודאית ואילו על ידי בריחתו הוא
יכניס את עצמו רק לספק סכנה . . .

או דילמא יש מקום לשקול להיפך ולומר, שהחיים בגיטו כפי שהם עכשיו אין
בהם סכנה, כי ישנה גם שמועה האומרת שאלה שנשארו בגיטו עד עכשיו לא
יאונה להם כל רע אם רק יעבדו וימלאו את כל מה שהגרמנים דורשים מאתם,
ולעומת זאת גדולה היא מאוד הסכנה לבורחים לא רק מצדם של הגרמנים אלא
גם מצדם של גויי הארץ הליטאים המתנכלים לתפוס יהודים כאלה להמיתם או
למוסרם לידי הגרמנים.

שאלות ותשובות ממעמקים, ד, י

ne day, a rumor spread through the ghetto that the
Germans had decided to transfer a large number of
people to a death camp.

On the heels of this rumor came another one that a
large number of ghetto prisoners were planning to escape that
night to join the partisan units in the forests who were battling
against the Germans. They felt that this was the only way for Jews
to defend their lives against the Nazi onslaught.

The problem, however, was that the road to the forest was extremely
dangerous. Besides for the fact that the ghetto was surrounded by
an electrified barbed-wire fence—touching it was suicidal—and
beyond that there were watchtowers with machine gun-armed
German sentries on duty day and night . . . there were partisan
groups in the forests that refused to accept Jews. Many were anti-
Semites themselves despite the fact that they were fighting the
Germans. [It was known that] more than once that a Jew who fell
into their hands paid with his life.

Thus I was asked . . . whether Halachah permitted a ghetto prisoner to put himself at risk by escaping into the forest. Perhaps G-d
would help his escape and he would survive. Here in the ghetto, the

apparent danger to life was absolute [because people felt that it was just a question of time until they would be killed], whereas by escaping, there was only the possibility of forfeiting one's life [since one might survive]. . . .

On the other hand, one might argue the opposite: life in the ghetto posed no immediate danger, for there were rumors that those who remained in the ghetto would come to no harm so long as they worked and fulfilled all the German demands. Conversely, the danger to those escaping to the forest was very great, not only from Germans but also from the Lithuanians who either handed such Jews back to the Germans or killed them themselves.

RABBI EPHRAIM OSHRY, SHE'ELOT UTESHUVOT MIMA'AMAKIM, 4:10

TEXT C

The Torah contains not merely a set of laws, but also canons of interpretation as well as principles according to which possible internal conflicts may be resolved. Maimonides records the doctrine that the Torah will not be altered, either in its entirety or in part, as one of the Thirteen Principles of Faith. . . .

Once revealed, the Torah does not remain in the heavenly domain. Man is charged with interpretation of the text, resolution of doubts, and application of the provisions of its laws to novel situations. . . .

The foregoing should not in any sense generate the impression that subjective considerations or volitional inclinations may ever be allowed consciously to influence scholarly opinion. Torah study requires, first and foremost, intellectual honesty. . . . It is a travesty of the halakhic process to begin with a preconceived conclusion and then attempt to justify it by means of halakhic dialectic. Neither Hillel nor Shammai nor any of their spiritual heirs engaged in sophistry in order to justify previously held viewpoints. The dialectic of halakhic reasoning has always been conducted in the spirit of "*yikov ha-din et ha-har*—let the law bore through the mountain." The law must be determined on its own merit and let the chips fall where they may.

RABBI J. DAVID BLEICH,
CONTEMPORARY HALAKHIC PROBLEMS, VOL. II, INTRO, PP. XIII–XV

Rabbi Dr. J. David Bleich (1936–). Authority on Jewish law and ethics and bioethics. Professor of Talmud at the Rabbi Isaac Elchanan Theological Seminary, an affiliate of Yeshiva University, as well as head of its post-graduate institute for the study of Talmudic jurisprudence and family law. A noted author, he is most famous for his four-volume *Contemporary Halakhic Problems* and *Time of Death in Jewish Law*.

TEXT D

Jacob Frankel, an accountant, describes what transpired in Buchenwald:

"Do not think that the most expensive commodity in Buchenwald was bread. My experience taught me that there was a much more valuable kind of merchandise there—a pair of *tefillin*. I myself took part in a transaction involving the extraordinary price for a pair of *tefillin* of four complete rations of bread. To tell the truth, this was a partnership venture in which all of us, the *hasidim* of Gur, were involved. . . . A Ukrainian *kapo* had stolen a pair of *tefillin* from the SS storehouse and was prepared to sell them—for not less than four rations of bread. . . . I went to the *kapo* and informed him I was prepared to give him two rations as a down payment. He refused and wanted the full payment in advance. So another *hasid* . . . became my partner. It took several days until the two of us were able to save up four rations of bread. But the *kapo* kept his word and brought us a small pair of *tefillin* wrapped in paper. We quickly inspected them and then prayed in them with an ecstasy which it is impossible ever to experience again in our lives . . ."

Rabbi Joshua Aronsohn describes how *tefillin* were put on in Auschwitz:

"When we arose in the darkness of the night, and we had just managed to wash, the block leaders and their helpers were hurrying us along to the forced-labor details. There were long queues of prisoners waiting in line, not for bread or coffee, but to fulfill the *mitzvah* of *tefillin*. We appointed a special "guard" whose job it was to make sure that no one kept the *tefillin* on for longer than it took him to say the one verse *shema yisrael,* so that more would be able to fulfill the *mitzvah*."

Moshe Brachtfeld writes:

"After some time we were taken to another camp. . . . They did not have even one pair of *tefillin*. How great was their joy when they discovered that we had brought a pair with us. About five hundred Jews recited the benediction that first day, and so it was every day thereafter. The pressure was so great that we were compelled to divide the set of *tefillin*. One group used only the *shel rosh*, the head *tefillah*, and the other the *shel yad*, the hand *tefillah*.

"Understandably, each group recited only the one benediction appropriate in each case. There was no other way; we felt it was better that each one should fulfill at least part of the *mitzvah* than that only some should be able to fulfill it completely. This was really an elixir of life for us.

"I recall a Jew from Munkacs, Reb Aharon Veider, who arose at two o'clock in the night so that he could pray in the *tefillin*. He was able to pray as much as he desired without interruption. Then at about

3:00 a.m. toward morning, the round of those who put on *tefillin* had already begun. It lasted usually until 5:30, the time of the block inspection. I and my brother were the last to get there. Nonetheless, we saw to it that the *tefillin* were brought to the place where we worked. There tens of Jews were able to use the short noon-hour break to put on the *tefillin* in a concealed place."

RABBI IRVING J. ROSENBAUM, THE HOLOCAUST AND HALAKHAH, PP. 79–81

TEXT E

've got candles! Candles for the Sabbath. Would you like to light Sabbath candles?" she whispered into my ear. I looked at my friend with astonishment.

"Don't you believe me?" she asked. Then trying to convince me she continued, "I've got real Sabbath candles! At work I found grease which I dissolved in the boxes and here I've got real candles."

I forgot the hunger, the SS guards, the high voltage wire fence, the whip and the machine guns facing us. I was in a daze. This information set my heart on fire. Can you imagine a spark of Sabbath candles in the abyss of darkness? . . .

That evening, she gave me two candles. They were plain and inexpertly done, for me, however, they were a priceless treasure. I saw in them my child that had been so brutally torn away from me. I saw in them my own childhood and I felt as if I had regained part of my lost soul. I had been thinking, where does the power of these lie? How could these crude little candles kindle in my heart such a flaming fire? It was a sensation I could not explain. But somehow I felt that souls of Jewish women of the past and present generations have an inseparable bond with candles. Or is it because I saw my mother's covered face? . . .

That Friday evening, after work, fourteen girls gathered in my room, prepared to welcome the Sabbath Queen. . . .

I lit the candles, passed my palms over them. But before I had a chance to cover my eyes, heavy steps were heard from the outside corridor.

The steps were of the SS commander. For a split second our hearts stopped beating. I covered my eyes and hastily made the blessing. Then I added in a barely audible voice, "G-d Almighty! It is clear to you that what I did was not for my pleasure or for my honor. But for Your reverence . . . the reverence of the holy Sabbath . . . for all to know and to remember . . . that G-d created the heaven and earth in six days and on the seventh day He rested."

I had hardly finished when a command was heard: "Out to the waiting trucks!"

While the girls ran out a thought pierced my mind: "Would all the girls be punished because I lit the candles?"

I ran after them. Coming closer I saw them removing loaves of bread from the truck. A shipment of bread had come and we were ordered to bring it to the kitchen. I raised my eyes to Heaven and thanked G-d for the miracle that had happened in front of my very own eyes.

Anna Eilenberg-Eibeshitz,
Remember: A Collection of Testimonies, pp. 135–137
Testimony of Miriam Weinstock

TEXT F

n her testimony at the Eichmann trial, Rivkah Kuper describes the light of Shabbath candles at Auschwitz:

"When we arrived on the eighteenth of January, 1943 we were put into the block at Birkenau. They had previously been horse stables. . . . Among the first things we sought were two ends of candles. Friday night we gathered together on the top tier of our block. There were then about ten or twelve girls. . . . We lit the candles and began quietly to sing Sabbath songs . . . we heard choked sobbing from the tiers of bunks all around us. At first we were frightened, then we understood. Jewish women who had been imprisoned months, some of them years, gathered around us, listened to the songs. Some asked us if they might also recite the blessing over the candles. . . . From then on, every *Shabbat* we lit the candles. We had no bread, there was nothing to eat, but somehow we managed to get the candles."

RABBI IRVING J. ROSENBAUM, THE HOLOCAUST AND HALAKHAH, P. 97

Additional Readings

The "Holocaust" of the Books

By **Esther Farbstein**

Before the Holocaust, the bookcase formed the heart of a Jewish house. Torah study and the reading of books were part of daily life, and the books were treated with special care and respect. According to Jewish law, nothing should be put on top of religious books and, of course, one must not sit on them. Not only a scholar, but anyone carrying books has the right of way. Furthermore, rescuing books from fire and water takes precedence over rescuing other belongings. The same is true when redeeming pledges.[1] Buying books, and especially lending them to others so that the latter can study, is considered a special virtue. Even in the poorest communities, libraries were established in the local *batei midrash* and were available for study day and night. In addition, there were renowned libraries in some private homes, such as that of Rabbi Yitzhak Elchanan Spector, the nineteenth-century rabbi of Kovno, whose love of and expertise in books and manuscripts were legendary. His library included extremely rare volumes. The Rebbe of Ger, Rabbi Avraham Mordechai Alter—a prominent bibliographer and owner of rare books and many manuscripts—had thousands of books.[2]

Libraries also served as agencies of the Enlightenment and of the surrounding culture, as well as centers of sociocultural activity. Some of these had a general Jewish hue; others—such as the Bund libraries—reflected the worldview of a specific segment of society. Two of the largest concentrations of Jewish books and manuscripts were in Vilna; the Strashun Library (founded in 1893), with some 25,000 books, half of them rabbinical literature;[3] and the library of the YIVO

Scientific Institute (founded in 1925), which housed various collections in Yiddish and specialized in Yiddish culture. YIVO's chief librarian was Zelig Kalmanowicz (who subsequently kept a diary in the Vilna ghetto that was published posthumously).[4]

It was no coincidence that the 1935 burning of Jewish books in Germany marked a turning point in anti-Jewish activity and was repeated in various places. In 1941 or 1942 Rabbi Shimon Huberband wrote:

"Hundreds of thousand of Jewish holy books have been destroyed during the current war, including many rarities, expensive manuscripts, and old, valuable communal records. . . .

"When the evil ones entered cities, they ripped to shreds, burned, and annihilated tens of thousands of books. . . .

"In various provincial cities, there are still a few holy books somehow remaining. But the same cannot be said for the cities and towns from which Jews have been expelled. The holy books in those cities have been totally lost."[5]

The Nazis bragged about this. When they burned the big library of the Chachmei Lublin Yeshiva, they wrote:

"We took special pride in destroying the biggest Talmudic seminary of all the Polish yeshivas, which sent out rabbis to the Jews in all corners of the world. . . . We brought the big library to the Lublin marketplace and set fire to it. For twenty hours the books burned.

---

[1] Assaf, "*Am ha-Sefer veha-Sefer.*"

[2] See Abramovich, "*ha-Admor mi-Gur.*"

[3] The Strashun Library was founded by Rabbi Mathias Strashun, a scholar and book collector, based on the library

that he had received from his father, Rabbi Shmuel Strashun, author of *Hagahot ha-Rashash al ha-Shas.* Among other things, it contained five incunabula and hundreds of old books. The library was housed first in the great synagogue of Vilna and then in a special building erected in the synagogue courtyard. Rabbi Yitzhak Rubinstein, the city rabbi, was in charge of the library; the catalog was compiled under the supervision of Prof. Joseph Klausner.

[4] See Cohen, "*Sifriyot Yehudiyot ve-Kor'eihen.*"

[5] Huberband, Kiddush Hashem, 215.

The Jews of Lublin gathered round the blazing books and wailed bitterly; we were almost deafened by their screams. We brought the army orchestra to play our national songs extremely loudly, until the Jews' wailing was swallowed up in the pounding of the drums and the cheers of the soldiers."[6]

The book-burnings and abuse of religious texts marked the start of a protracted, planned, and comprehensive assault on Jewish books, culminating in the ghetto period.

Despite the difficulty of the move to the ghetto and the worries about survival, Jews managed to take books with them and even to have libraries in most ghettos. In Kovno, a city of Torah scholars of all hues, the city rabbi, Avraham Dov-Ber Shapiro, initiated a special project to move books to the ghetto—especially those from Rabbi Yitzhak Elchanan Spetor's library—in the carts that were to transport the Jews' meager belongings (in August 1941).

"Shulamit and Izzy Rabinowicz, loyal friends of ours in the ghetto who left many books in their home, did something great. Years later, Shulamit told me how, when they moved into the ghetto, they were still wavering between their many pieces of furniture and their large library, some of which had come from their grandfather, the noted Rabbi Yitzhak Elchanan. Even then, she decided that the books took precedence. They set up a special hiding place behind an inside staircase. During the next two years I was one of the regular beneficiaries of this cache."[7]

Leib Garfunkel writes:

"What self sacrifice it took to move the books from the city to the ghetto. . . . This can all be understood and appreciated only by someone who was an eyewitness to all these tribulations and evils."[8]

Similar things occurred in Cracow and elsewhere:

"In the move to the Plaszow ghetto . . . trucks and wagons loaded with furniture and boxes, carriages . . . and hand-carts . . . made their way over the Podgorski bridge. . . . Father [Rabbi Yehoshua Ehrenberg] started gathering abandoned books that were lying around and moved a few cartloads of them to the ghetto. . . . 'Where will we put all these books?' Mother said in astonishment. But father managed to convince her, saying, 'Torah is the best merchandise. It's a mitzvah to rescue them! A wise man will take mitzvot.'"[9]

To a large extent, the nature of the books in the ghetto reflected the ghetto population. The list of titles, the language, the popularity of the books, the reading habits, and the librarians are all integral parts of the history of the Holocaust and the story of spiritual heroism.[10]

"No matter how tight the space, a little corner was always found for books. The Jews of Kovno guarded them scrupulously and with veneration. Books were the sole pleasure that the Jews, immersed in grueling forced labor, still had; as it says, 'This is my solace in my affliction.'[11] Reading and studying the books made them forget their troubles and tribulations, at least for a moment. . . . It was not uncommon to see a group of Jews paving the airfield or chopping wood and discussing literature, music . . . while in snow or mud up to their knees."[12]

One library in Warsaw operated under the auspices of the soup kitchens. The librarian would personally supply books to sick or housebound children.

"One of the 'thirty-six [saints]' of the Jewish book was Leib Shor . . . and Bashia Berman, a librarian by profession. . . . While some public activists were losing sleep worrying about how to find bread and shelter for the burgeoning camps of poverty-stricken, hungry, and homeless Jews, these two were worrying about where to get spiritual sustenance for the Jews. They were

---

[6] *Die Deutsche Jugend Zeitung*, quoted in *Hatzofeh*, Jan. 6, 1941.

[7] Eilati, *Lahatsot et ha-Nahar*, 88.

[8] Garfunkel, *Kovna ha-Yehudit*, 127-129.

[9] Frenkel, Ehrlich, and Abramovich, *Devar ha-Yeshua*, 51.

[10] For a comprehensive study of books during the Holocaust, see Shavit, *Hunger for the Printed Word*; see also Eibeshitz, "Ha-Sefer bi-Tekufat ha-Shoah."

[11] Psalm 119:50.

[12] Schulgasser, "Hashmadat ha-Sefarim."

the first to realize the extreme importance of books as a weapon in the war against despair. Ostensibly, they could have said, 'Who needs books when there's nothing to eat, when we don't know what the day will bring?' But experience proved the opposite. Never did people give such expression to their hunger for books as during the occupation. . . . This hunger came partly from a longing to forget the constant danger . . . and partly from a longing to exercise their mental powers. . . . And if this was true of the adults, how much more so was it true of the children. Especially Jewish children in the ghetto. These children had been robbed of the world—the river, the green tree, freedom of movement—and they could find all these again in the magical world of the printed word."[13]

Libraries were also established by youth movements and political parties in the Warsaw ghetto. Alter Shnur (Itzinger), a teacher and writer in the Lodz ghetto, called the ghetto "the city of the books." The main library was the Sonnenberg Library, which even before the war had been situated in Baluty, the old Jewish quarter where the ghetto was built. It contained some 7,500 books, including books in German for refugees who had been deported form Germany and textbooks for children.[14]

In Theresienstadt, the library was created gradually in cultural/linguistic stages, as Jews from various places were brought there; at first most of the books were in Czech, afterwards some in German were added, and finally books in Danish where brought in. There were also books there that had been confiscated from libraries in Germany, including that of the Orthodox rabbinical seminary in Berlin, books taken from the residents of Theresienstadt, and so on. The library was headed by Prof. Emil Utitz, an apostate Jew deported from Prague to the camp in 1942. At its peak in 1944, seventeen people worked there, of whom only two survived. An estimated two-hundred-thousand books went through this library; some of them were not returned and some were even taken on the final journey when Jews were deported form Theresienstadt. Next to the library was a reading room, which was "paradise" to the prisoners, especially the elderly. When the Nazis carried out their "beautification" of the ghetto for propaganda purposes—the climax of deception in this ghetto—they took advantage of this library, temporarily enlarging it, photographing it, and afterwards shrinking it and liquidating it along with the rest of the ghetto.[15]

Booksellers' stands were a common feature in the larger ghettos. Most of the books were sold to readers thirsting for books. Reuven Ben-Shem wrote in his diary on June 10, 1941: "On several occasions I saw Jews who had not a cent for bread bargaining over the price of a book."[16] Mary Berg, a young girl in Warsaw, wrote in her diary in late 1942: "All of us threw ourselves on the books with the same impatience with which we throw ourselves on food."[17] And at an event marking the hundred-thousandth book borrowed in Vilna, Isaac Rudashevski wrote in his diary, "The reading of books in the ghetto is the greatest pleasure for me. The book unites us with the future, the book unites us with the world."[18]

As conditions worsened, books were also sold for reuse as paper. This was one manifestation of the harsh struggle for survival:

---

[13] Auerbach, Be-Hutsot Varsha, 167. Bathia (Bashia) Berman, born in 1907, worked in the Polish national library and in municipal libraries in Warsaw before the war. She took a special interest in Jewish libraries and conducted a study of the subject in 1934. She was particularly interested in children's literature. When she was deported to the ghetto, she stayed in touch with librarians in Aryan Warsaw. In the ghetto she collected books from stands where they were being offered for sale, from house committees, and from libraries, and hid them in what were purportedly game areas. She was especially concerned about street children, children hiding in the forests, and children in CENTOS homes. The image of her marching with suitcases of books for children was etched in the memories of survivors from Warsaw. At some point she recruited volunteer girls to assist her; they took care of the books and helped her deliver them to homes and families. These books were enjoyed by thousands of children. See Temkin-Berman, "Sifriyot Yehudiyot be-Varsha," 521-524.

[14] Shavit, Hunger for the Printed Word, 81-83, based on the Chronicle of the Lodz Ghetto and other sources.

[15] Ibid., esp. 120-130.

[16] Reuven Feldshuh (Ben-Shem), handwritten diary, Yad Vashem Archives, 033/959.

[17] Berg, Warsaw Ghetto, 204.

[18] Rudashevski, Diary of the Vilna Ghetto, 106. According to testimony, even during the Aktionen in the Vilna ghetto the library was full of readers (Kruk, Last Days, 504 [Apr. 6, 1943]).

"Jewish holy books are now very inexpensive. This is due to the poverty of the Jewish population. After selling their household items, Jews finally also sell their holy books. On all the street corners, one finds carriages full of holy books, being sold for dirt-cheap prices, literally for pennies."[19]

The mistreatment of religious books raised halachic questions, which were discussed at a meeting of the Lodz rabbinical board on March 18, 1942. One rabbi there described the trade in books for personal reuse and the condition of religious books in need of repair or halachically permitted disposal that had been left in the homes of the deportees.[20] Elsewhere, Rabbi Ya'akov Avigdor of Drohobycz in eastern Galicia wrote:

"On more than one occasion, I buried hundreds of slain martyrs with my own hands and placed in their graves packages of Torah-scroll parchments that had been ripped to shreds and were rolling around outside. I said, 'He who avenges the honor of the Torah scrolls will also avenge the honor of the martyrs.' But here is not the place to talk about this; neither the ink nor the paper would suffice."[21]

From the summer of 1941, around the time of the start of the Final Solution, the Germans imposed special orders regarding books, which were no less upsetting than the book-burnings. The Jews called these the "edicts of the books" and the *Aktionen* of the books." These orders were applied all over Europe as part of Operation Rosenberg (Einsatzstab Reichsleiter Rosenberg, or ERR for short).[22] The idea was twofold: to wipe out Jewish culture and to preserve books in an international library of Judaism, thereby establishing a "scientific conceptual basis" for the belief in a worldwide Jewish problem and for Nazi anti-Semitism. The library would be a memento of the annihilation of the nation that embodied the spirit of these books. To this end, the Nazis employed specially-trained people who knew Hebrew and who carried out the order with the help of Jewish forced laborers. Books that the Nazis considered valuable were sent to Frankfurt, the center of ERR activity. The others were sent to be shredded for the German paper industry or other uses. Hundreds of thousands of books (some say millions) were accumulated in German hands. Not for naught did the Germans boast that this would be the largest Jewish library in the world. When the bombing of Germany began, some of the books were moved to the occupied lands or stored underground. Thousands seem to have been destroyed in the bombing. A small portion was found after the war in Germany; they were used by the survivors and later sent to the National Library in Jerusalem and Jewish libraries around the world.[23]

The "*Aktionen* of the books" left a deep imprint on the ghetto inhabitants and remained in the survivors' memories as an unhealed wound. On February 18, 1942, the residents of the Kovno ghetto were ordered to hand over their books to the Germans. As Rabbi Shmuel Rose, a survivor who had previously been at the Slobodka Yeshiva wrote:

"That bitter day is still firmly etched in our memories. Our enemies acted shrewdly with us, not merely destroying us but also grieving us terribly so long as the breath of life was in us because taking the book from the 'People of the Book' is a deep, incurable wound to the Jewish soul. . . . The . . . enemy's ambition was to wipe out the name of Israel, Heaven forbid, not only from life, but from the book as well."[24]

---

[19] Huberband, *Kiddush Hashem*, 215.

[20] Minutes of a meeting of the Lodz rabbinical board, Mar. 18, 1942, Yad Vashem Archives, JM M-49/95.

[21] Avigdor, *Tehiyat Ya'akov*, in *Helek Ya'akov*, 67.

[22] The ERR operated under the auspices of the Institut zur Erforschung der Judenfrage (Institute for the Study of the Jewish Question) from March 1941. It was founded and headed by Alfred Rosenberg, one of the most radical Nazi ideologues. The ERR actually functioned from October 1940—even before it was officially established—confiscating art treasures in France. Afterwards it looted holy objects, books, and libraries in Eastern Europe. This institute was responsible for the cultural plunder of European Jewry.

[23] See Shunami, "Parshiyot." Among the people sent from Eretz Israel after the war to sort and assess the books found was Prof. Gershom Scholem. See also Cohen, "Ha-Sifriyot Sheli."

[24] Rose, *Shirat Shmuel*, 102. The document was written shortly before the printing of the Munich Talmud was completed on the day after Sukkot 1948. It was signed by Rabbi Samuel A. Snieg, chairman of the rabbinical association committee in Munich, and Rabbi Shmuel Rose, a

At first the Germans ordered the Jews to make up a precise list of the books and held the Jewish police responsible for the enforcement. However, some of the ghetto inhabitants resisted handing over their books:

"And those Jews, persecuted almost beyond endurance, who had already broken-heartedly sacrificed their jewelry and furs, decided wordlessly, each separately and all together: This will not be."[25]

As Rabbi Oshry described it:

"We decided to protect our holy books with no less and perhaps with greater determination than we protected our lives. . . .

". . . Jews of all classes and strata displayed great self-sacrifice on behalf of Jewish books, even risking martyrdom to hide Torah scrolls. Workmen—shoemakers, tailors, carpenters—were elevated by this battle to the highest level of sanctity.

"Jewish children stood no lower. They sensed in this battle a deeper aspect—that it was a battle over Jewish eternity. The ghetto-Jew was inspired and purified and elevated to the loftiest heights. . . .

"Young men and old men dug pits and hid volumes of the Talmud, of Maimonides' codes, of responsa works, and many other seforim. These people as well as others hid on their premises single volumes of Talmud or the Torah for personal study. I recall how much self-sacrifice Bertshik Bricker, whom we called Bertshik the glazier, used in hiding volumes of Talmud and other works.

"I recall how, after the decree was issued, I asked my youngsters in the Tiferes Bachurim, 'Where will we get volumes of the Torah and Talmud to study?'

The youngsters stood up and declared, 'Don't worry, Rebbi, each of us will hide a *chumash* (volume of Torah) or *gemora* to study from!'"[26]

Others made a different tough decision:

"We will never commit such an abomination, come what may. We will not deliver the holy books into the Nazis' impure hands—no mater what it takes to prevent them from being desecrated by the Germans. It was hot in the ghetto that night, very hot. Jews leaned over their small iron stoves; instead of taking out the books to the accursed Germans, they preferred to do it with their own hands and pay them their final respects. . . . The pages curl and shrink with a dull sound, as if emitting what was written on them, as if to say, 'Your toil and efforts are in vain. You will not succeed in annihilating us. Many have already tried that to no avail.' Brokenhearted, we take solace in the fact that we did not betray our books and hand them over to the impure ones. We completed the sacred work and paid our last respects to the holy texts. It was a night of watchfulness in the ghetto, and it was hot, very hot."[27]

Such actions were carried out in various places. Rabbi David Kahane describes the resistance to the plunder of books in Lvov.

"The Religious affairs Department . . . had at its disposal a 'collecting group'; its members went to the remaining study houses, gathering the Torah books, holy vessels, and other articles such as chandeliers, lamps, and books not yet despoiled by the Aryans. They were all stored in the spacious and warm cellars at 12 Bernstein Street. With successive additions this grew to be a one-of-a-kind museum that boasted rare holy books, as well as marvelous examples of applied crafts used in synagogues. Many exhibits exemplifying all that the Jews of Lvov had assembled with diligence and veneration over the past six hundred years of their history could be found there."[28]

After a few months the hiding place was discovered, and the Germans moved everything to a processing facility for raw materials.

In Warsaw the ghetto archives organized the collection and hiding of books, with the participation of leading

member of the committee. It was printed in the foreword to the first Talmud published there.

[25] Schulgasser, "Hashmadat ha-Sefarim."

[26] Oshry, *Annihilation of Lithuanian Jewry*, 74-75.

[27] Schulgasser, "Hashmadat ha-Sefarim."

[28] Kahane, *Lvov Ghetto Diary*, 40.

rabbis, such as Rabbi Yehuda Leib Orlean and Rabbi Eliezer Friedenson.

"Apparently, he [Rav Avraham Weinberg] was taken in the middle of his *shiur*, since a number of *Gemaras Bechoros* are laid out on his table, still open at the page at which they were disturbed. . . . I order my team to leave the *Gemaras* as they are, untouched, as if they were holy relics."[29]

In Drohobycz the local rabbi himself hid his books:

"Through real self-sacrifice, I was able to bury all my books—about eight thousand volumes—in a large pit. Today I can disclose that they are in a pit beneath the house standing at 2 Czackiego Street in Drohobycz. There I also buried the books that I had written and printed. Unfortunately, even today there is not a shred of hope of getting them out of there because the city of Drohobycz is in an area governed by Soviet Russia."[30]

The Germans knew of the book collections in Vilna, and they sent experts from the ERR to find them. The liquidation of the Strashun Library began in August 1941, with the help of Dr. Johannes Pohl, an expert in Hebrew books who had worked at the National Library of the Hebrew University in Jerusalem from 1933 to 1936. Two prominent librarians were murdered after refusing to hand over the list of books. The chief librarian, Chaikel Lunski, was jailed and ordered to disclose the location of the incunabula. Yitzhak Strashun, a member of the library's founding family, hanged himself. Pohl ordered the Vilna Judenrat to choose twenty scholars, at least five of them experts in Judaica; those chosen included Zelig Kalmanowicz, Abraham Sutzkever, Szmerke Kaczerginski, Rachel Poupko-Krinski, and Herman Kruk. These librarians, assisted by ghetto inhabitants and librarians outside the ghetto, managed to save some very valuable books in a bold, large-scale operation that they called the "bridge of paper." Some of them were smuggled into the ghetto, others were hidden, and many were marked as valuable so that the Germans would not destroy them. Many of these books were sent to Frankfurt and later found in storerooms there.

"We each hid a book, pending the Germans' departure, this might be the last book we would read. The books were endangered. . . . We wanted to save them without risk to life. . . . It was rare for us to leave YIVO without a book. We were the bridge of paper."[31]

The YIVO library building became a center for sorting and collection and for the rescue of books. "We walled [them] up; we buried [them] in basements and caves. . . . We would hide under our clothes and bring into the ghetto . . . fifteenth- and sixteenth-century manuscripts and dozens of other documents," wrote Abraham Sutzkever.[32] The sight of the books made Kalmanowicz think of "the war of Gog and Magog at its height." Kruk wrote: "Who in fact purges whom, we or the Germans? The game depends on who takes whom first. If we do in the Germans, we are the winners; if they us, we are the losers here."[33]

In Kovno, too, Jewish forced laborers were called upon to help the Nazis understand and assess the content of the books. One of them, Rabbi Avraham Gerstein, asked Rabbi Oshry in February 1942: In a case of duress, is it permissible to study Torah with the murderers who are looting the Jews' spiritual treasures? Rabbi Oshry replied that it was permitted due to the risk to life. In fact, he did it himself:

"Since I was in charge of the book warehouse, the evildoers asked me to explain to them the glosses of Rabbi Yitzhak Elchanan [Spector], which were written in the margins of his Talmud. . . . They also asked me to read and explain to them one of his responsa, which was bound together with the tractate Berachot in his Talmud. . . . Due to the danger, I was compelled to comply with these enemies' request . . . because for all the reasons I have mentioned, there is no prohibition . . . in the situation that we were in."[34]

[29] Seidman, *Warsaw Ghetto Diaries*, 184-186, 237.

[30] Avigdor, *Helek Ya'akov*, 15.

[31] Rachel Krinski, quoted in Shavit, *Hunger for the Printed Word*, 95.

[32] Sutzkever, *Geto Vilna*, 100. See also Klausner, "Batei Eked Sefarim;" Kalmanowicz, *Yoman be-Geto Vilna*, esp. Aug. 26, 1943; Fishman, *Embers Plucked from the Fire*.

[33] Kruk, *Last Days*, 358.

[34] Oshry, *Mi-Ma'amakim*, vol. 1, question 14. For an English summary, see Oshry, *Responsa from the Holocaust*, 60-61. See also Eibeshitz, "Sefarim bi-Yemei ha-Shoah."

The plunder of books took place in all the occupied lands. Special units were sent to Hungary in 1944, and members of the Jewish labor companies, recruited as auxiliary forces for the Hungarian army, were brought in to carry out the edict in the communities of greater Hungary.[35]

In a comprehensive, planned, and brutal operation, the Nazis managed to destroy the treasures of Jewish literature. In Kovno, more than a hundred thousand volumes in Hebrew, Yiddish, and other languages were plundered.[36] The big libraries in Vilna, Gora Kalwaria (Ger), Amsterdam, and Paris—the Jews' pride and joy—were emptied out. The same occurred in the yeshivas, rabbinical seminaries, and private collections. Of the Gerrer Rebbe's huge library, not a trace remains.

The campaign against books, unparalleled since the Middle Ages, raises the question of the Germans' intent. What did this campaign have to do with racist hatred? What was the connection between it and the war against the Jews?

We can discern a few stages in the Nazis' policies regarding the books and thus identify a process of ideological radicalization in this context. At first, the book-burnings were spontaneous outbreaks of hatred for Jewish culture and Jewish symbols. The Nazis forced the Jews to watch these events and often to take an active part in them, so as to weaken their emotional resistance even before their physical strength was depleted. This aim was also clear in their decision to dispossess the Jews of their books in the ghetto, in order to take away their spiritual foothold and deprive them of the refuge and strength that the books gave them. This calculated plan and its comprehensive implementation prove that the Nazis wanted to liquidate not just the Jews but Judaism as well, along with its values and the morality that it had given the world, and they therefore viewed books as appropriate targets of violence. The roots of this struggle were in the foundations of their racial theory, which stressed the cultural character ingrained in each race. For many Jews, the war against Jewish books reflected the immeasurable difference between Judaism and Nazism and the struggle on the spiritual level as well—in the form of Germanism versus Judaism, impure against pure—with the book perceived as representing the Jewish spirit.[37]

Whether consciously or unconsciously, Jews sense that this was the Germans' intent, and many of them regarded protecting books as an act of resistance against the Nazis and their aims. "They accepted having everything else taken from them, but not the Book. When it came to fighting for a Torah scroll, to hiding a Torah scroll, the weakest Jew demonstrated that he was a vigorous hero," wrote Rabbi Oshry of Kovno.[38] Tuvia Borzykowski, a librarian from Radomsko who became one of the commanders of the Warsaw Ghetto Uprising, wrote:

"Perhaps rescuing a library from the Nazis will seem like an odd, strange act: a world is collapsing, and the future of the Jews—perhaps the future of all humanity—hangs in the balance. What value, then, does a Jewish library in some remote town have? . . . without putting too much thought into whether or not anyone needs the rescued books. This library was cultivated over the years. . . . I was one of the people who took part in building it and its last librarian. . . . It was hard for me to abandon it. Perhaps there was a bit of rebellion in this: the Germans were fighting not only against living Jews but against their culture as well. . . . It took weeks to hide the library. . . . Of course, we ran the risk of being caught by the Gestapo. . . . We managed to move a few hundred books. . . . I brought the last of the books up to the attic . . . and prayed, 'Just as I was able to arrange them, may I be able to see them.'"[39]

The books met the same fate as the people: the vast majority of these treasures, collected over the generations in European Jewish communities, were lost.

The connection between the Jews and the written word was not severed even in the concentration camps; the yearning for books appears in various testimonies. Behind the fences, there were extraordinary

[35] Cohen, "Ha-Sifriyot Sheli;" Scheiber, "Goral Sifriyot u-Sefarim."

[36] Garfunkel, *Kovna ha-Yehudit*, 128-129.

[37] See Prager, "ha-Merida ha-Natsit be-Historya;" Prager, "Ha-Yahadut ve-Chol Hash-pa'atah."

[38] Oshry, *Annihilation of Lithuanian Jewry*, 72.

[39] Borzykowski, *Bein Kirot Noflim*, 227-229.

encounters between Jews and the written word. Although these cases were few in number, they were so dramatic and symbolic that it is worth quoting some accounts verbatim.

In a labor camp in Estonia, where Meir Dworzecki of Vilna had been sent, Hebrew letters suddenly appeared:

"Hebrew letters in the ruined fields of Estonia: Who planted and disseminated you? Who lost you on this final journey? From which brother in fate are you? Have you brought lost greetings from an anonymous brother? . . . And at night the pages—these holy texts—were brought to a camp barrack; they were spread out, smoothed over, and recognized: the tractate Rosh Hashanah, chapter 2, page 25. . . . People read them as a newly arrived visitor would read. The pages became a book and a newspaper for the denizens of the camp barracks. And the pages contained a story: about the debate among the Sages regarding when the holidays occur. . . . And when fate made me and the rest of the people from the camp roam, they took the pages, the holy texts, with them. It's a newspaper, it's a book, it's the fraternal ring sent to the Jews by fate, in order to attach them to the chain of generations. Thus they brought the holy texts with them over the Baltic Sea, to the Stutthof camp near Danzig, a camp of eighty thousand people. When Rosh Hashanah came, and a north wind lashed half-naked bodies with bitter cold, freezing them in their thin prison garb, hundreds of bodies pressed and crowded in, body against body, one against another, between the barracks. . . . And when the living heat of people flowed like a current from one body to another, suddenly a voice was heard: 'Let's study in the meantime!' Rabbi Yehoshua was suffering but he said, 'If we come to challenge the conclusion of the court of Rabban Gamliel, we must challenge the conclusions of every single court.'"[40]

---

[40] Dworzecki, *Bein ha-Betarim*, 55, 57-58. Some people have questioned the reliability of this account, (originally written in Yiddish), seeing it as an exaggeration and a description of something impossible. However, new testimonies on these subjects, such as Weiss Halivni's (below), indicate that such incidents did occur, including the discovery of pages with such symbolic and relevant content. Even if we regard the description as semi-literary, it is significant in that it conveys the feeling of the encounter between the

Far from Estonia, there was another encounter with pages of holy texts. In Auschwitz, a young boy—David Weiss—spotted a page with Hebrew letters used to wrap a sandwich, which a German was munching heartily. Despite his hunger, it was not the bread that caught his attention but the wrapping:

"His sandwich was wrapped in a page of *Orach Chaim*, a volume of the *Shulchan Aruch*, Pesil Balaban's edition. . . . As a child of a poor but scholarly home, I had always wanted to have this edition. . . . Here, of all places, in the shadow of the tunnel, under the threatening gaze of the German, a page of the *Shulchan Aruch*, with fatty spots all over it, met my eyes. The page was from the laws of Passover. . . . Upon seeing this wrapper, I instinctively fell at the feet of the guard, without even realizing why; the mere letters propelled me. With tears in my eyes, I implored him to give me this bletl, this page. For a while he didn't know what was happening; he thought I was suffering from epilepsy. . . . This was, I explained to him, a page from a book I had studied at home. Please, I sobbed, give it to me as a souvenir. He gave me the bletl and I took it back to the camp. On the Sundays we had off, we now had not only Oral Torah but written Torah as well. . . . The bletl became a rallying point. We looked forward to studying it whenever we had free time, more so even than to the phylacteries. . . . Mr. Finkelstein volunteered to keep the bletl and, of course, produced every second Sunday, when we were off. He must have carried it on his person; I'm sure he slept with it. The bletl was always with him and secure. Knowing that the bletl was with Mr. Finkelstein, we felt secure as well."[41]

In the Janowski camp, Jews found pages from the tractate Ketubot, as Rabbi David Kahane of Lvov attests:

"I had a dear friend, David Shapiro, a native of a remote village in the Carpathian mountains. He was a self-taught scholar, a well-read man, an ardent Czurtkow Hasid, and, above all, a noble and dear soul. One day he returned from work carrying a rare and dangerous find. He had found the buried remains of the Talmudic tractate Ketuboth. Only the last two chapters were intact.

Jew and the printed page in the depths of hell, an encounter documented in several testimonies.

[41] Weiss Halivni, *The Book and the Sword*, 68-70.

That night we conducted a Talmud study session and became absorbed in a very interesting tale. "Rabanan taught: a person should always live in the land of Israel, even in a city predominantly pagan, and must not live outside the land of Israel even in a city inhabited mostly by Jews. For he who lives in the land of Israel, it is as if he has God, whereas he who lives outside the land of Israel, it is as if he does not have God" (Ketuboth 60:b)."[42]

In the Sarzysko "yellow death" camp, Rabbi Yitzhak Finkler, the Rebbe of Radoszyce, had pages from the Talmudic tractate Bechorot hidden in his mattress; a few young men would gather around him to study these pages.[43]

Such events demonstrate that the special relationship between the People of the Book and the book remained intact. Thus the prophecy "neither hunger for bread nor thirst for water but [hunger] to hear the words of the Lord" was fulfilled.

From *Hidden in Thunder*, vol. 2.
Reprinted by permission of the publisher.

---

[42] Kahane, *Lvov Ghetto Diary*, 113.
[43] Granatstein, *One Jew's Power*, 116-117.

לילה כיום יאיר

Lesson 6

When Night Will Shine like Day
Ensuring a Brighter Tomorrow

Introduction

In this lesson, we bring our study full circle, from a focus on G-d and the Holocaust to a discussion of humanity and the Holocaust. In his memoirs, *All Rivers Run to the Sea* (p. 403), Elie Wiesel relates the following conversation that he had with the Lubavitcher Rebbe, Rabbi Menachem Mendel Schneersohn:

> "Rebbe," I asked, "how can you believe in God after Auschwitz?" He looked at me in silence for a long moment, his hands resting on the table. Then he replied, in a soft, barely audible voice, "How can you not believe in God after Auschwitz?" Whom else could one believe in? Hadn't man abdicated his privileges and duties? Didn't Auschwitz represent the defeat of humanity? Apart from God, what was there in a world darkened by Auschwitz? The Rebbe stared at me, awaiting my response. I hesitated before answering, "Rebbe, if what you say is meant as an answer to my question, I reject it. But if it is a question—one more question—I accept it."

Does Auschwitz mean the defeat of humanity? What does the Holocaust teach us about people? What does it teach us about the things in which people put their trust? What does the Holocaust tell us about the human capacity for evil and goodness?

In this lesson, we will explore the meaning of living life in a post-Holocaust world.

The Pity of It All

TEXT 1

הִגְדַּלְתִּי מַעֲשָׂי בָּנִיתִי לִי בָּתִּים נָטַעְתִּי לִי כְּרָמִים

עָשִׂיתִי לִי גַּנּוֹת וּפַרְדֵּסִים וְנָטַעְתִּי בָהֶם עֵץ כָּל פֶּרִי . . .

כָּנַסְתִּי לִי גַּם כֶּסֶף וְזָהָב וּסְגֻלַּת מְלָכִים וְהַמְּדִינוֹת

עָשִׂיתִי לִי שָׁרִים וְשָׁרוֹת וְתַעֲנֻגוֹת בְּנֵי הָאָדָם שִׁדָּה וְשִׁדּוֹת

וְגָדַלְתִּי וְהוֹסַפְתִּי מִכֹּל שֶׁהָיָה לְפָנַי בִּירוּשָׁלָ͏ִם אַף חָכְמָתִי עָמְדָה לִי

וְכֹל אֲשֶׁר שָׁאֲלוּ עֵינַי לֹא אָצַלְתִּי מֵהֶם

לֹא מָנַעְתִּי אֶת לִבִּי מִכָּל שִׂמְחָה כִּי לִבִּי שָׂמֵחַ מִכָּל עֲמָלִי וְזֶה הָיָה חֶלְקִי מִכָּל עֲמָלִי

וּפָנִיתִי אֲנִי בְּכָל מַעֲשַׂי שֶׁעָשׂוּ יָדַי וּבֶעָמָל שֶׁעָמַלְתִּי לַעֲשׂוֹת

וְהִנֵּה הַכֹּל הֶבֶל וּרְעוּת רוּחַ וְאֵין יִתְרוֹן תַּחַת הַשָּׁמֶשׁ

קהלת ב,ד–יא

 made myself great works; I built myself houses, and I planted myself vineyards.

I made myself gardens and orchards, and I planted in them all sorts of fruit trees. . . .

I accumulated for myself also silver and gold, and the treasures of the kings and the provinces; I acquired for myself various types of musical instruments, the delight of the sons of men, wagons and coaches.

So I became great, and I increased more than all who were before me in Jerusalem; also my wisdom remained with me.

And [of] all that my eyes desired I did not deprive them; I did not deprive my heart of any joy, but my heart rejoiced with all my toil, and this was my portion from all my toil.

Then I turned [to look] at all my deeds that my hands had wrought and upon the toil that I had toiled to do, and behold everything is vanity and frustration, and there is no profit under the sun.

KOHELET/ECCLESIASTES 2:4–11

Question for Discussion

In this reading, King Solomon describes the futility of his life pursuits. Why would King Solomon have such a negative assessment of his many accomplishments?

Our customers were the first front to be mobilized against us in this war of destruction. Our employees became the second front. The loyalty of our employees was systematically undermined—this showed itself when they were branded as "friends of the Jews" by the Sturmer. To facilitate their terrorization, the employees' full addresses were printed in the paper. The intimidation, the fear of being publicly marked as a "slave of the Jews" (Judenknecht), discouraged all those in our firm who had so far remained loyal to the enterprise. At the same time, it encouraged those who were inclined to sabotage, to betray, and to spy. They went as far as to listen to our phone conversations, to "check" our mail and to search our garbage bins. Eventually—apart from the few Jewish workers who were isolated in any case—only a few of the hundreds of employees remained loyal to us and were not intimidated by the risks involved.

The third front in this destructive fight was the press. Increasing numbers of newspapers and magazines refused to publish our advertisements. Once we were prevented from publishing ads in any German newspaper or magazine, we were deprived of our most efficient means of advertisement . . .

The fourth front stabbing us in the back was our former suppliers and contractors. They increasingly refused to deliver to us.

At the same time, all authorities and party offices—such as the "Trustees of Labor," the Labor Front, the Gestapo, and the customs agencies—created a fifth front against us with summons, house searches, and inspections, all with the purpose of shattering our position. In addition to them were the state and local tax agencies. . . .

In 1938, like vultures surrounding someone condemned to death, a great number of mediators and negotiators suddenly appeared on the scene. Based on experience they had gained in conducting successful Aryanizations, they came up with advice and disguised threats. . . .

Walther Kohl, owner of the Max Kohl retail business, soon proved to be the most serious bidder. . . . Mr. Kohl, naturally, like all Aryan buyers of Jewish enterprises, got a much lower purchase price than he would have gotten under normal circumstances. He was nevertheless convinced that he had saved us by buying our firm. . . .

Finally, state secretary Brinkmann, responsible for such matters in the Reich's Economic Ministry, demanded a sum of 200,000 RM for the official "approval of the Aryanization." The sum was raised by us and Kohl.

A commercial publication to our customers in October 1938 already carried the sentence "Grunfeld, now under German ownership."

Annegret Ehmann et al., Juden In Berlin, pp. 289–291

TEXT 3

Shortly before the onset of the Inquisition, a Spanish Jew boasted that the kings and lords of Castile had the advantage over their many adversaries in that their Jewish subjects "were amongst the most learned, the most distinguished in lineage, in wealth, in virtues, and in science." During the Weimar Republic—the high point of their integration and assimilation into German life—German Jews might have claimed the same.

There has rarely been a confluence of two cultural, ethnic, or religious traditions that proved so richly creative at its peak. Frederic Grunfeld writes that had the end not been so awful we would now hail the decades before the Nazi rise to power as "a golden age second only to the Italian Renaissance." In literature alone, German Jews accounted for such luminaries as Heine, Borne, Kafka, Werfel, Zweig, Wolfskehl, Broch, and Kraus; in the sciences, Willstater, Haber, Ehrlich, Einstein, and Freud; in music, Mahler, Weill, Schoenberg, and Mendelssohn's grandson Felix Mendelssohn-Bartholdy . . . .

The Jews of Germany never ceased in their effort to merge German and Jewish identity. The heartstrings of their affection were tied early; their overriding desire was to be complete Germans. Many succeeded.

AMOS ELON, THE PITY OF IT ALL, PP. 6–8

Amos Elon (1926–2004). Israeli essayist and author. Served for many years as a correspondent for the Israeli daily newspaper, *Ha'aretz*. His 2002 book, *The Pity of It All,* is a portrait of German Jewry from the mid-eighteenth century until the rise of Hitler.

The Tree of Knowledge
of Good and Evil

TEXT 4A

e was born here in 1923, and has been here ever since.

He lived at this very spot?

Right here.

Then he had a front-row seat for what happened?

Naturally. You could go up close or watch from a distance. They had land on the far side of the station. To work it, he had to cross the track, so he could see everything.

Does he remember the first convoy of Jews from Warsaw on July 22, 1942?

He recalls the first convoy very well, and when all those Jews were brought here, people wondered, "What's to be done with them?" Clearly, they'd be killed, but no one yet knew how. When people began to understand what was happening, they were appalled, and they commented privately that since the world began, no one had ever murdered so many people that way.

While all this was happening before their eyes, normal life went on? They worked their fields?

Certainly they worked, but not as willingly as usual. They had to work, but when they saw all this, they thought: "Our house may be surrounded. We may be arrested too!"

Claude Lanzmann (1925–). Paris-based filmmaker, writer, and journalist. Best known for his creation of the documentary film *SHOAH,* a complex oral history about the systematic murder of six million European Jews by the Nazis.

Were they afraid for the Jews too?

Well, he says, it's this way: if I cut my finger, it doesn't hurt him. They knew about the Jews: the convoys came in here, and then went to the camp, and the people vanished.

Interview with Czeslaw Borowi, Treblinka, Poland
Claude Lanzmann, Shoah: The Complete Text of the Acclaimed Holocaust Film, pp. 17–18

Text 4B

id he hear screams behind his locomotive?

Obviously, since the locomotive was next to the car. They screamed, asked for water. The screams from the cars closest to the locomotive could be heard very well.

Can one get used to that?

No. It was extremely distressing to him. He knew the people behind him were human, like him. The Germans gave him and the other workers vodka to drink. Without drinking, they couldn't have done it. There was a bonus—that they were paid not in money, but in liquor. Those who worked on other trains didn't get this bonus. He drank every drop he got because without liquor he couldn't stand the stench when he got here. They even bought more liquor on their own, to get drunk on.

Interview with Henrik Gawkowski, Malkinia, Poland
Claude Lanzmann, Shoah: The complete Text of the Acclaimed Holocaust Film, p. 25

Questions for Discussion

1. Did Czeslaw Borowi and Henrik Gawkowski have a sense of morality (could they distinguish between right and wrong)?

2. What elements of their testimony led you to this conclusion? (The transcript can be used as a reference.)

3. Henrik drove the train to the concentration camp. Czeslaw farmed his field next to the concentration camp. Based on their testimony would you use words such as "good" or "evil" to characterize Henrik and Czeslaw? Why or why not?

TEXT 5

Understandably with the history of Nazi Germany, it has been tempting to paint pictures in stark black and white, clearly delineating good and evil—for was not the Third Reich the most thoroughly evil political system ever created? However, life is not like that. Human beings are bundles of paradoxes, and the choices they are forced to make rarely are clear-cut. In order to understand the nature of politics and the social history of the Third Reich, it is necessary to appreciate that even under Hitler everyday life was characterized by contradictions and paradox. . . .

As we are well aware, the Nazi regime was probably the most criminal, barbarous, and immoral that the world had ever seen. Yet . . . . the Nazi regime appeared to many of its subjects to offer a remarkably effective "law and order" government. . . .

An understanding of the history of the Third Reich, and of the wider implications that it has for understanding other societies, lies precisely in trying to make sense of a society in which people who may have despised corrupt and arrogant Nazi Party bosses, feared Gestapo agents or informers in their workplaces . . . might at the same time have felt pleased that Germany was able to rearm . . . be grateful that they were back at work after years of unemployment, or be extremely impressed by the holiday programs offered by the "Strength through Joy" organization. . . .

The history of Nazi Germany is also about ambiguities—about the deeply disturbing compromises which made up the lives of people of varying degrees of decency struggling to survive in the most indecent of times. . . . [This] is not to suggest that a regime which unleashed a world war and murdered millions of people in cold blood was no different from any other political regime. It is, however, to suggest that the history of Nazi Germany might have more to tell us about society and politics elsewhere than many people may care to admit.

RICHARD BESSEL, LIFE IN THE THIRD REICH, INTRODUCTION, PP. XVII-XXI

Richard Bessel. Professor of Twentieth Century History at the University of York, England. His books include *Life in the Third Reich* and *Germany After the First World War*.

TEXT 6A

It is comforting to believe that health care professionals who have pledged an oath to "do no harm" and who are minimally concerned with the morality of their own conduct could not kill babies or conduct brutal, often lethal, experiments on starving inmates in concentration camps. It is comforting to think that it is not possible to defend involuntary euthanasia, forced sterilization, and genocide in moral terms. It is comforting to think that anyone who espouses racist, eugenic ideas cannot be a competent, introspective physician or scientist. Such beliefs are especially comforting to ethicists. Nazi medical crimes show that each of these beliefs is false.

It is commonly believed that only madmen, charlatans, and incompetents among doctors, scientists, public health officials, and nurses could possibly have associated with those who ran the Nazi party. . . .

Once identified, the myths of incompetence and madness make absolutely no sense. How could flakes, crackpots, and incompetents have been the only ones supporting Nazism? Could the Nazis have had any chance of carrying out genocide on a staggering, monumental scale against victims scattered over half the globe without the zealous help of competent biomedical and scientific authorities? The technical and logistical problems of collecting, transporting, exploiting, murdering, scavenging, and disposing of the bodies of millions from dozens of nations required competence and skill, not ineptitude and madness.

ARTHUR CAPLAN, WHEN MEDICINE WENT MAD, PP. 55–56

Arthur Caplan. Emanuel and Robert Hart Professor of Bioethics and Philosophy at the University of Pennsylvania. His research interests include transplantation research ethics, genetics, and reproductive technologies. A frequent commentator on national radio and television, Caplan is also the author or editor of more than twenty books, including *When Medicine Went Mad.*

TEXT 6B

The Holocaust occurred with the intellectual support and involvement of the medical and scientific establishment of the most scientifically and technologically advanced society of its time. The Holocaust, unlike many other instances of mass killing, was scientifically inspired, supervised, and mediated genocide.

ARTHUR CAPLAN, WHEN MEDICINE WENT MAD, P. 63

TEXT 7

I recall very clearly how I felt about 10 years ago, when I read *Doctors of Infamy* . . . for the first time. Several chapters in that book describe the horrible infectious disease experiments carried out by the Nazis in Buchenwald. . . . When I started reading, I remember feeling horror, anger, and dismay. But as I continued reading, I became engulfed by curiosity. That was the frightening thing! After so many years, my curiosity as a scientist overwhelmed all other emotions (about Jews and relatives) and I kept looking for answers that would have helped my ancient research. . . . It is hard to explain to the layman, even to the philosopher, how the motives and methodology of applied research generate a kind of scientific morality in which the greatest good is a "breakthrough."

VELVEL W. GREENE, WHEN MEDICINE WENT MAD, P. 158

Velvl Greene. Earned a PhD in bacteriology and biochemistry at the University of Minnesota, where he was Professor of Public Health and Microbiology for many years. In 1986, he and his family settled in Israel, where he directed the Sir Immanuel Jakobovits Center for Jewish Medical Ethics.

TEXT 8

Rabbi Dr. Jonathan Sacks (1948–). Born in London, chief rabbi of the United Hebrew Congregations of the Commonwealth. Attended Cambridge University and received his doctorate from King's College, London. A prolific and influential author, his books include *Will We Have Jewish Grandchildren?* and *The Dignity of Difference*. Recipient of the Jerusalem Prize in 1995 for his contributions to enhancing Jewish life in the diaspora. Knighted in 2005.

In terms of ethics, Judaism was the first religion to insist upon the dignity of the person and the sanctity of human life. For the first time, the individual could no longer be sacrificed for the group. Murder became not just a crime against man, but a sin against God. "Whoever sheds the blood of man, by man shall his blood be shed, for in the image of God has God made man" (Genesis 9:6). Already prefigured here is the phrase in the American Declaration of Independence that speaks of all human beings as "endowed by their Creator with certain unalienable rights." We cannot give up what is not ours. The sanctity of life is written into the structure of the universe by the terms of creation. It is a non-negotiable standard by which all human conduct is to be judged.

Rabbi Jonathan Sacks, Radical Then, Radical Now, pp. 72–73

Text 9

ear Teacher: I am a survivor of a concentration camp. My eyes saw what no man should witness:

Gas chambers built by learned engineers.

Children poisoned by educated physicians.

Infants killed by trained nurses.

Women and babies shot and burned by high school and college graduates.

So I am suspicious of education.

My request is:

Help your students become human. Your efforts must never produce learned monsters, skilled psychopaths, educated Eichmanns.

Reading, writing, and arithmetic are important only if they serve to make our children more humane.

Haim Ginott, Teacher and Child, p. 317

Haim G. Ginott (1922–1973). Began his career as an elementary school teacher in Israel in 1947 before immigrating to the U.S. There he attended Columbia University in New York City, earning a doctoral degree in clinical psychology in 1952. Ginott's books, *Between Parent and Child, Between Parent and Teenager,* and *Teacher and Child,* have been popular for many years and were translated into thirty languages.

TEXT 10

Rabbi Menachem Mendel Schneerson (1902–1994). Known as "the Lubavitcher Rebbe," or simply as "the Rebbe." Born in southern Ukraine. Rabbi Schneerson escaped from the Nazis, and arrived in the U.S. in June 1941. The towering Jewish leader of the twentieth century, the Rebbe inspired and guided the revival of traditional Judaism after the European devastation, and often emphasized that the performance of just one additional good deed could usher in the era of Mashiach.

Those who fulfill the Seven Noachide Principles are called the "Pious Among the Nations of the World," a title which reflects the qualities of kindness and love. . . .

In order for educational endeavors [aimed at promoting these principles] to meet with success, it requires . . . [each individual to] serve as a living example to others by modeling these principles [in day-to-day life] in an all-consuming manner.

RABBI MENACHEM MENDEL SCHNEERSON, TORAT MENACHEM 5746, VOL. 3 PP. 64–65

The Path of the Righteous Gentile

TEXT 11A

Samuel P. Oliner (1932–). Emeritus Professor of Sociology at Humboldt State University. Was a 12-year-old Jewish boy in Poland when the Nazis forced him and his family into the ghetto at Bobowa. He managed to escape and a Polish peasant took him in, disguised his identity, and found him a job. In collaboration with his wife, Dr. Pearl Oliner, he conducted a landmark study exploring the experiences and motivations of those uncommon individuals who aided Jews during the Holocaust.

For most rescuers, then, helping Jews was an expression of ethical principles that extended to all of humanity and, while often reflecting concern with equity and justice, was predominantly rooted in care. . . . Most rescuers explain their actions as responses to a challenge to their fundamental ethical principles. This sense that ethical principles were at stake distinguished rescuers from their compatriots who participated in resistance activities only. For these resisters, hatred of Nazis and patriotism were most often considered sufficient reasons for their behavior; for rescuers, however, such reasons were rarely sufficient.

SAMUEL AND PEARL OLINER, THE ALTRUISTIC PERSONALITY, P. 170

TEXT 11B

They were and are "ordinary" people. They were farmers and teachers, entrepreneurs and factory workers, rich and poor, parents and single people, Protestants and Catholics. Most had done nothing extraordinary before the war nor have they done much that is extraordinary since. Most were marked neither by exceptional leadership qualities nor by unconventional behavior. They were not heroes cast in larger-than-life molds. What most distinguished them were their connections with others in relationships of commitment and care. . . .

SAMUEL AND PEARL OLINER, THE ALTRUISTIC PERSONALITY, P. 259

TEXT 12A

Rescuers' commitment to actively protect or enhance the well-being of others did not emerge suddenly under the threat of Nazi brutality. . . . More rescuers integrated such values into their lives well before the war began—and remained committed to them long after it ended.

SAMUEL AND PEARL OLINER, THE ALTRUISTIC PERSONALITY, P. 170

TEXT 12B

To a large extent, then, helping Jews was less a decision made at a critical juncture than a choice prefigured by an established character and way of life. As Iris Murdoch observes, the moral life is not something that is switched on at a particular crisis but is rather something that goes on continually in the small piecemeal habits of living. Hence, "at crucial moments of choice most of the business of choosing is already over."

Many rescuers themselves reflected this view, saying that they "had no choice" and that their behavior deserved no special attention, for it was simply an "ordinary" thing to do.

SAMUEL AND PEARL OLINER, THE ALTRUISTIC PERSONALITY, P. 222

Beyond Never Again Revisited

TEXT 13

I went to Israel. . . . Along with a group of businessmen I was with, I had the opportunity to have an audience with Rabbi Finkel, the head of the yeshiva there. I had never heard of him and didn't know anything about him. We went into his study and waited 10 to 15 minutes for him. Finally, the doors opened. . . .

Then he asked, "Who can tell me what the lesson of the Holocaust is?" He called on one guy, who didn't know what to do—it was like being called on in the fifth grade without the answer. And the guy says something benign like, "We will never, ever forget. . . ." And the rabbi completely dismisses him.

I felt terrible for the guy until I realized the rabbi was getting ready to call on someone else. All of us were sort of under the table, looking away—you know, please, not me. He did not call me. I was sweating. He called on another guy, who had such a fantastic answer: "We will never, ever again be a victim or bystander."

The rabbi said, "You guys just don't get it. Okay, gentlemen, let me tell you the essence of the human spirit.

As you know, during the Holocaust, the people were transported in the worst possible, inhumane way by railcar. They thought they were going to a work camp. We all know they were going to a death camp.

After hours and hours in this inhumane corral with no light, no bathroom, cold, hours and hours, they arrived at the camps. The doors were swung wide open, and they were blinded by the light. Men were separated from women, mothers from daughters, fathers from sons. They went off to the bunkers to sleep.

As they went into the area to sleep, only one person was given a blanket for every six. The person who received the blanket, when he went to bed, had to decide, "Am I going to push the blanket to the five other people who did not get one, or am I going to pull it toward myself to stay warm?"

And Rabbi Finkel says, "It was during this defining moment that we learned the power of the human spirit, because we pushed the blanket to five others."

Howard Schultz (1952–). Chairman and CEO of Starbucks, the largest coffeehouse chain in the word, and former owner of the Seattle Supersonics.

And with that, he stood up and said, "Take your blanket. Take it back to America and push it to five other people."

HOWARD SHULTZ, A BLANKET TRUST, HERMES MAGAZINE, SPRING 2001

Key Points

1. The smooth integration of Jews into pre-war German society in the political, cultural, economic, and social realms was short-lived after the Nazi rise to power.

2. It is easy to rationalize evil actions by noting the benefits of taking an evil course of action.

3. Since human beings have both good and evil impulses, even "good" people will often take part in evil pursuits if this is promoted by their society.

4. The resolve to take a stand against evil must be fostered before challenging times arrive.

5. Most righteous gentiles who risked their lives in order to save Jews did so because it challenged fundamental ethical principles that had been ingrained in them since childhood.

6. We can encourage societies to rise up against evil in their midst by teaching universal moral principles and making character education a priority.

7. Ultimately, a response to the Holocaust is expressed not only in the creation of a society that condemns genocide, but also in the individual actions performed on behalf of our families, our communities, and our world that make this universe a more G-dly place.

Supplementary Texts

TEXT A

One principle must be absolute for the SS man: we must be honest, decent, loyal, and friendly to members of our blood and to no one else. What happens to the Russians, what happens to the Czechs, is a matter of utter indifference to me. Such good blood of our own kind as there may be among the nations we shall acquire for ourselves, if necessary, by taking away the children and bringing them up among us.

Whether the other races live in comfort or perish of hunger interests me only insofar as we need them as slaves for our culture; apart from that it does not interest me. Whether or not 10,000 Russian women collapse from exhaustion while digging a tank ditch interests me only insofar as the tank ditch is completed for Germany.

We shall never be rough or heartless where it is not necessary; that is clear. We Germans, who are the only people in the world who have a decent attitude to animals, will also adopt a decent attitude to these human animals, but it is a crime against our own blood to worry about them and to bring them ideals.

I shall speak to you here with all frankness of a very serious subject. We shall now discuss it absolutely openly among ourselves, nevertheless we shall never speak of it in public. I mean the evacuation of the Jews, the extermination of the Jewish race.

It is one of those things which is easy to say. "The Jewish race is to be exterminated," says every party member. "That's clear, it's part of our program, elimination of the Jews, extermination, right, we'll do it."

And then they all come along, the eighty million good Germans, and each one has his decent Jew. Of course the others are swine, but this one is a first-class Jew. Of all those who talk like this, not one has watched, not one has stood up to it.

Most of you know what it means to see a hundred corpses lying together, five hundred, or a thousand. To have gone through this and yet—apart from a few exceptions, examples of human weakness—to have remained decent fellows, this is what has made us hard. This is a glorious page in our history that has never been written and shall never be written.

HEINRICH HIMMLER, SPEAKING TO SS OFFICERS, POSEN, OCTOBER 4, 1943

TEXT B

ואהבת לרעך כמוך (ויקרא יט,יח)

רבי עקיבה אומר: זהו כלל גדול בתורה

בן עזאי אומר: זה ספר תולדות אדם (בראשית ה,א) זה כלל גדול מזה

תלמוד ירושלמי נדרים ט,ד

You must love your neighbor as [you love] yourself" (Leviticus 19:18). Rabbi Akiva says, "This is a great principle of the Torah."

Ben Azai says, "'This is the book of the chronicles of Adam [on the day that God created man, He made him in the likeness of God'] (Genesis 5:1). This is a greater principle of the Torah."

JERUSALEM TALMUD, NEDARIM 9:4

y friend, an author of a book about the Holocaust, survivor of Auschwitz . . . Yehiel Feiner . . . never appeared in public after the Holocaust, except at the trial of Eichmann in Jerusalem. [His testimony] was the shortest, because he fainted after a moment or two.

But [he] was one of the most impressive witnesses. He described the picture—in Auschwitz, when people came out of the trains. A place where there were no flowers; children were not being born at that place. And he called it a different planet—Auschwitz.

I had more than two or three conversations with him later. I opposed him. I opposed this thinking and this expression—that Auschwitz was on a different planet.

It was here. On our planet. In our homeland Poland, on this continent—Europe, and it happened here. It was done by people who loved music, violins, pianos. Flowers they loved. They brought up their own children—after brutally killing babies and children of the Jewish people en masse.

RABBI YISRAEL MEIR LAU, SPEECH TO THE EUROPEAN PARLIAMENT, BRUSSELS, NOVEMBER 10, 2008

Rabbi Yisrael Meir Lau (1937–). Chief rabbi of Tel Aviv-Jaffa, and former chief rabbi of the State of Israel. Born in Piotrków Trybunalski, Poland to Rabbi Moshe Chaim Lau, who was rabbi of the town. At the age of eight he was liberated in Buchenwald by American forces. His writings include *Do Not Raise Your Hand Against the Boy*, his best-selling autobiographical account of his Holocaust experiences. In 2005 Rabbi Lau received the Israel Prize for Lifetime Achievement.

Text D

כִּי תִרְאֶה חֲמוֹר שֹׂנַאֲךָ רֹבֵץ תַּחַת מַשָּׂאוֹ וְחָדַלְתָּ מֵעֲזֹב לוֹ עָזֹב תַּעֲזֹב עִמּוֹ

שמות לג,ה

 f you see the donkey of someone you hate lying under its load, you might want to refrain from helping him, but [instead] you must make every effort to help him [unload it].

SHEMOT/EXODUS 23:5

Text E

אוהב לפרוק ושונא לטעון

מצוה בשונא כדי לכוף את יצרו

תלמוד בבלי בבא מציעא לב,ב

 f a friend's animal needs to be unloaded, and an enemy's animal needs to be loaded, it is a mitzvah to [first help] the enemy, in order to subdue one's evil inclination.

TALMUD, BAVA METSIA 32B

TEXT F

The only justice would be if I could bring back, if not six million, at least one person to life. But I cannot. The only other justice I would accept would be—and I mean it very profoundly—very sincerely, the coming of the Messiah. . . .

I don't feel any theology of the Holocaust is possible except this one: if the Messiah were to come.

HJC (interviewer): . . . The victims have spoken, the perpetrators have spoken, the indifferent have spoken. God has not spoken. Is the only way, then, for God to speak with the coming?

EW: The only way. The only way: the coming of the Messiah. This is the only response possible because otherwise, nothing is a response.

INTERVIEW WITH ELI WIESEL,
TELLING THE TALE: A TRIBUTE TO ELIE WIESEL, P. 43

Elie Wiesel (1928–). Professor of the Humanities at Boston University. Born in Sighet, Transylvania, he was deported by the Nazis to Auschwitz at the age of fifteen. Wiesel is the author of more than forty books of fiction and non-fiction, including the acclaimed memoir *Night*, which has appeared in more than thirty languages. In 1986, Wiesel won the Nobel Prize for Peace. Soon after, Wiesel and his wife established The Elie Wiesel Foundation for Humanity. For his literary and human rights activities he has received numerous awards including the Presidential Medal of Freedom and the U.S. Congressional Gold Medal.

Additional Readings

Lessons of the Holocaust

By **Dennis Prager**

Between 1939 and 1945, the Nazi German regime, with help from millions of other Europeans, murdered almost every Jew in Europe. But for all its notoriety, for all the words devoted to narrating its inexpressibly horrible details, for all the references to it in modern moral and theological discourse, it seems that nothing has actually been learned from the Holocaust.

There are at least two reasons for this. One is that just about everyone who writes or speaks about the Holocaust describes it as "incomprehensible" (an "eruption of the irrational" by "a nation gone mad")— and it is not possible to derive any lessons from the incomprehensible.

The other reason is that the lessons of the Holocaust are too frightening, too disturbing to confront.

These reasons are related: an easy way to avoid confronting evil is to label it incomprehensible.

The Holocaust Is Comprehensible

Historians, theologians, and others who call the Holocaust incomprehensible do so for a variety of reasons. One is that most of those who write about the Holocaust are essentially secular and humanist in their approach to understanding human nature. Such individuals tend to have a relatively optimistic view of human nature (humanists believe in humans). They see good as normal and rational, and evil as mad or irrational. If this is their view regarding daily evil, it is infinitely more so regarding the systematic torture and murder of millions of innocent men, women and children.

Another reason is that these writers regard the motivation for the Holocaust—anti-Semitism—as irrational. Therefore, for most observers, something irrational (anti-Semitism) caused something incomprehensible (the Holocaust).

But what if these two suppositions are wrong?

What if evil is neither irrational nor incomprehensible? And what if anti-Semitism is neither irrational nor incomprehensible? In such cases, the Holocaust may be quite comprehensible. And so it is.

Since evil is part of human nature—evil may be as "normal" as good—eruptions of evil are hardly incomprehensible. The questions historians and thinkers need to ask is not why men do evil, but under what circumstances is evil likely to express itself, how can we work to prevent it, and why do the evil so often focus first on Jews?

As for anti-Semitism, throughout their history, Jews have regarded it as a quite comprehensible reaction against a people that brought God and universal moral law into the world. The Talmud explained Jew-hatred nearly 2,000 years ago by noting how similar the Hebrew words for hatred (*seenah*) and Sinai (*see-nai*) sound. The great hatred of the Jews emanates from Sinai, where the Jews received God-based ethical laws to which all mankind is held accountable.

The Catholic historian of anti-Semitism, Father Edward Flannery, also understood this. "It was Judaism," he wrote, "that brought the concept of a God-given universal moral law into the world. . . . The Jew carries the burden of God in history, [and] for this has never been forgiven."

In *The Jewish Mystique*, Ernest van den Haag similarly summarized the root of anti-Semitism: "[The Jews'] invisible God not only insisted on being the one and only and all-powerful God . . . he also developed into a moral God. . . . The Jews have suffered from their own invention ever since."

Even anti-Semites have acknowledged this. The father of German racial theory, Houston Stewart Chamberlain, wrote, "The Jew came into our gay world and spoiled everything with his ominous concept of sin, his law, and his cross."

He was echoing Richard Wagner's words: "Emancipation from the yoke of Judaism appears to us the foremost necessity."

And Hitler defined his mission as the destruction of the "tyrannical God of the Jews [and His] life-denying Ten Commandments."

The Nazi attempt to murder all the Jews was precisely what the Nazis called it: "The Final Solution to the Jewish Problem." Hitler concluded that all previous solutions—assimilation, conversion, persecution, and expulsion—had failed to rid the world of the Jewish problem. Only the actual killing of every Jew would work.

Thus, evil, which permanently lurks within human nature, has a long record of detesting the people and religion that first declared war—divine war—against it. Understanding this, neither evil nor anti-Semitism is incomprehensible.

On Human Nature

The most obvious, and perhaps the most important, lesson to be derived from the Holocaust is that the human being is not basically good. To me, this is so obvious that I feel foolish noting it. Yet, few people—Jews included—have incorporated this basic principle into their views on life.

It is this lingering belief in human goodness that has led to the contemporary predilection for blaming anything except human nature—society, socioeconomic forces, class warfare, weapons, parents, television—for the evil that people do. Jews who are estranged from Judaism and its view of the human being locked in a permanent battle between his good and evil inclinations are among the most delinquent in this area. That is why the question I most frequently hear from Jews about the Holocaust is, "How can I believe in God after the Holocaust?"

That question is surely worthy of a response (see "God and the Holocaust," *ULTIMATE ISSUES*, Vol. 3, No.4), but it is a question that lets the real culprits—people—off the hook. God did not throw children onto pyres of fire; God did not build the gas chambers, or man the death camps, or conduct freezing experiments on fully conscious men and women. People did.

Whenever I meet someone who claims to find faith in God impossible, but who persists in believing in the essential goodness of humanity, I know that I have met a person for whom evidence is irrelevant. Yet, those who continue to believe in humanity—after the Holocaust, Communist genocides in the Ukraine, Cambodia and elsewhere, black slavery and so much more evil—are considered rational, while those of us who believe in God are dismissed as elevating faith over reason.

One wonders what human beings would have to do in order to shake people's faith in humanity. How many innocent people have to be murdered and tortured? How many women need to be raped? We have developed elaborate alibis for people who inflict the most horrible cruelties on other people. The most common is that such people are "sick." But Hitler and his followers were not necessarily sick. They were all evil.

On What Is Important

Given the Holocaust and all the genocide-like mass murders of this century—in Armenia, the Ukraine and many other parts of the Soviet Union, Uganda, Cambodia—only faith in man's innate goodness can explain why people are not obsessed with one issue—how to make good people. This is not simply some abstract moral question—it is an issue of pure self interest: if we do not make good people, we or our children will be hurt. On purely selfish grounds, this ought to be our greatest concern.

All our other social preoccupations—better education, conquering poverty, fighting drugs—are less important than raising the next generation to be good people. Yet, instilling goodness in young people is for most individuals and societies, including our own, a lower priority than instilling brightness, talent, patriotism, happiness, religious faith, or some other value independent of goodness. As absurd as most people's reluctance to learn this lesson is, the Jews' inability to learn it is beyond belief. If any group should be preoccupied—no, obsessed—with instilling good in people it ought to be the Jews, the targets of the Holocaust, and the most consistent targets of evil in history. Yet in America today, Jews, more than any other group, support *value-free* education; Jews, more than any other group (polls consistently indicate that Jews are the most secular group in America), believe that people need not feel morally accountable to God and religion; Jews, in short, more than any other group, believe in humanity.

On Education and Art

Another unsettling conclusion from the Holocaust is that two of the most esteemed Western values—education and art—are morally irrelevant. The only education that can make people more moral is moral education (preferably on a religious foundation). There is no correlation between any other education and human decency. Two major studies of Nazis during the Holocaust confirm this observation.

Professor Peter Merkl of the University of California at Santa Barbara studied 581 Nazis and found that Germans with a high school education "or even university study" were more likely to be anti-Semitic than those with less education (*Political Violence Under the Swastika*, Princeton University Press, p. 503).

A study of the makeup of 24 leaders of Einsatzgruppen, the mobile killing units that killed nearly 2 million Jews prior to the use of the gas chambers, showed that the great majority were well educated: "One of the most striking things about the Einsatzgruppen leadership makeup is the prevalence of educated people, professionals, especially lawyers, Ph.D.s . . ." (Irving Greenberg in *Auschwitz: Beginning of a New Era*? Ktav, p. 17).

These findings should not surprise us. Almost the only support for the other great butcher—Joseph Stalin—also came from the well educated. For the many in our society who link Ph.D.s and university education with human decency, these lessons are important indeed. And, again, if there is one group that needs to learn this lesson, it is the Jews. No group venerates education, degrees, titles and elite universities more than Jews—despite the fact, moreover, that some of the greatest hostility to Jews, today in the guise of anti-Zionism, is found at these universities.

The same holds true for art. It is very sobering that the most artistically cultivated society in Europe unleashed the Holocaust. The commandant of Auschwitz was an accomplished pianist who played Schubert's *Lieder* on the piano each day after supervising the day's gassing of thousands of Jewish families and the indescribable medical experiments on Jews and Russian prisoners of war. One of the greatest conductors of this century was the Berlin Philharmonic's Herbert Von Karajan. His interpretations are noted for their beauty. Yet, Von Karajan had joined the Nazi Party in 1932, even before the Nazi Party came into power, and rose to *kappelmeister* under Hitler.

To cite one of many other possible examples, Norway, which suffered terribly at the hands of the Nazis, had almost no Nazi supporters. One of the very few who did support Nazism, even while the Nazis ruled over Norway, was that country's most gifted writer, Knut Hamsun, winner of the Nobel Prize for Literature.

For those in our society who associate artistic greatness with human greatness, or who crave board membership on an art museum but would never sit on the board of a Jewish or other religious day school, the Holocaust teaches an extremely important lesson.

On Religious Evil and Secular Evil

The most common argument against religion is that it has been used to commit much evil, e.g., the Crusades, the Inquisition, Khomeini, and religious conflicts in Northern Ireland and Lebanon. This is true, and religious people cannot explain it away by claiming that all these people were not really religious. People can be both religious and evil. Moreover, many religious people who are not evil do not regard fighting evil and promoting goodness as important as promoting right faith. And while all major religions seek the good, not all are equally concerned with good and evil. Salvation, faith, surrender to God, ego denial, and attaining truth are some other, more important, concerns.

On the other hand, another lesson of the Holocaust is that the amount of evil committed by secular ideologies dwarfs religion-inspired evil. In this century alone, more innocent people have been murdered, tortured, and enslaved by secular ideologies—Nazism and Communism—than by all religions in history.

Yes, Christianity laid the foundations of Western Jew-hatred—foundations that were used well by Hitler and the Nazis. But it was Nazism, a secular and anti-Christian ideology, not Christianity, that built the gas chambers. That many Christians were either evil enough to actively support Nazism or merely foolish enough not to appreciate how anti-Christian—not to mention evil—Nazism was tells us much about those Christians, but it does not negate the secular and anti-Christian nature of Nazism. (Even today, after all the revelations about Communist evils, including repeated attempts to destroy Christianity and other religions, there are Christians who refuse to see the evil and anti-Christian nature of Communism.)

Thus, centuries of Christian anti-Semitism on the one hand and the Nazi hostility to Jewish and Christian values on the other proved lethal to Jews. God without ethics and ethics without God are both dangerous to Jews—and to the world.

On Pacifism

I have never understood how a person could know the horrors of Auschwitz and yet embrace pacifism, the belief that all killing is wrong. The Allied soldiers who killed Nazis saved millions of innocent people from being murdered and from fates even worse than murder. Those soldiers engaged in the holiest, most moral behavior that men could have engaged in between 1939 and 1945. So long as there is evil that can only be stopped by killing, the Holocaust must forever banish pacifism from the vocabulary of moral people.

Of course, it is tragic that nations spend precious funds on armaments, but armaments are not the moral problem. Nations that do evil are the moral problem. The tanks, grenades, and bombers that liberated Auschwitz were instruments of mercy as surely as bandages and medicines.

From *Ultimate Issues*, July-September 1989.
Reprinted by permission of publisher.

Finding One's Way

By **Dr. Tamar Frankiel**

Some years ago, as I was waiting to give a lecture before a group at my synagogue, the rabbi came up to me and said confidentially, I hope you aren't going to talk too much about other religions. He was referring to my work in comparative religion. I had spent fifteen years studying and had a master's and a Ph.D. in the subject. But at his remark, I was startled. What do you mean? I asked. Well, you know, Jews don't bother with that stuff. Actually, I wasn't planning to talk about anything except Jewish material. But I rapidly began reviewing and censoring my speech in my mind. I had two reactions, one resentful: Is he trying to tell me how to think? And one fearful—maybe I'm not really kosher—not Orthodox enough.

My two opposite feelings were hints of what was almost my double personality. First, I was a creation of the secular world: I had spent years learning the ropes of academia; I knew the challenge of intellectual life, the stimulation from University colleagues. At the same time, I had accepted the way of Torah. I wanted most of all to grow in my relation to G-d, to develop a deep spiritual practice. Up to this point, I had believed that my previous studies had enriched my understanding of Judaism. I found in Jewish practice many echoes of what I had learned. The setting aside of sacred times, the holiness of certain places, rich symbolisms of the natural world and ancient cultures, complex systems of sacrifice—the religions of the world were full of these phenomena, and I was finding them alive in Judaism.

But now I began to wonder. Were there conflicts between my studies in comparative religion and my life as a practicing Jew? If I had been a computer technician or a doctor, perhaps it would not have been so great a problem. But I was studying things that seemed very alien to a Jewish philosophy and way of life. I loved teaching about everything from Buddhism to Judaism, from bizarre rituals to esoteric philosophy. I saw the world through the lenses of my studies of the history of religions, sociology and psychology. But perhaps these were not things I should be thinking about. I even considered giving it up entirely.

I had the good sense, at one point, to ask a rabbi if I could continue to seek professional work in my field. I received his approval, so my concerns about making a living were relieved. But many personal and intellectual issues remained. Some of these issues turned out to be superficial, and my problems quickly disappeared; others were deeper and required considerable inner work and intellectual searching to resolve them.

Many people, for example, assumed that it would have been difficult for me to believe in G-d or to practice one religion exclusively. They thought studying comparative religion discourages a person from believing in one G-d and promotes a relativistic morality wherein all beliefs and practices are equal. Comparative religion supposedly teaches that all religions are really one—they have basically the same myths, the same ethics, and the same ultimate purpose. But this is not really true of serious scholarship in comparative religion. True, for purposes of classroom teaching, questions of belief are temporarily set aside. The instructor does not put forward a particular religious viewpoint, because s/he must encourage students to ask significant questions fearlessly, and to develop the intellectual discipline to think through to some answers and to criticize all answers.

The result of this teaching method—it is a method, not a conclusion—is that many university students come away with the idea that there are no respectable religious answers to questions of goodness, truth, or divine reality; that every argument has its counter-argument; and that truth is relative. Simplified even further, some students hold (and vehemently affirm to their teachers) that anyone's opinion is as good as anyone else's in religious matters, so how can the teacher dare give low grades for their opinions! This argument ad absurdum shows its own fallacy: it is not that there are no answers, but that one must be very careful about putting forward one's own culturally limited viewpoint as the answer.

But then, are there answers to ultimate questions in the study of comparative religion? No one so far has been willing to stake a scholarly reputation on a definitive answer, for there is always an element of faith involved. Yet, in my opinion, there has been progress. The inquiry has proceeded to the point where a simple atheism is no longer possible. Over and over again, the attempts to explain away religion as a function of social, psychological, or political forces have been demonstrated as inadequate. Positivists still struggle to come up with a more adequate explanation, but more and more scholars have left that narrow-minded enterprise behind. In that respect, the field is more open to serious discussions of faith than it was twenty years ago. For me, the further I inquired into the matter, the easier it was to accept a belief in G-d. In 1970, I was an agnostic if not an atheist; in 1980, I had no difficulty believing, though I was still searching for how to conceive of a relationship to the G-d I believed in.

G-d was one thing; accepting a Torah way of thought was another. Sometimes I wondered if I was consenting to my own brainwashing. Everything is in Torah, I was told. You don't need to go anywhere else. For someone who has sampled the richness of other traditions and the works of great authors, this seemed impossible. I considered it a statement coming from very intelligent but very narrow-minded individuals, designed not to encourage discussion and exploration but to cut it off. For after all, I didn't know much Torah—I only knew that strange other stuff, the ways of thinking taught in universities—so what could I say? Go and learn, they told me.

I went and learned. And I found that the deeper I went into Torah, the fewer conflicts I found within myself. For example, I was interested in depth psychology and its relation to religion. I found in Chassidic teachings and in certain commentators on the *Chumash* (Bible) ideas that preceded Freud and Jung by scores, if not hundreds, of years. I was interested in associations of symbols and the use of language. I found the poetry of the *Siddur* (prayer book) and *Tehillim* (Psalms) not merely beautiful but inspiring and challenging. And to see a mind at work on the intricacies of language, one need go no further than the *Likkutei Moharan* of Rabbi Nachman of Breslov. I liked sociology and anthropology: it surprised me to find that our sages were enormously sophisticated in such areas: they knew about crowd psychology, social pressure to conform, radical differences in cultural viewpoints, and the difficulties of being fair and objective.

Was everything really in Torah, then? Certainly the phrase didn't mean that Chinese history or modern art was in Torah. But everything I needed to know to improve the quality of my life was in Torah, from spiritual inspiration and intellectual challenge, to depth of ethical thinking and practical advice.

Still I had problems arising from my scholarly background—for example, the matter of similarities among religions. I had learned to look at the larger patterns which many religions seem to have—for example, similar symbolism, common ways of marking off sacred space or sacred time.[1] Traditional Jewish thought simply didn't recognize such parallels as having significance. It took me some time to understand why.

The history of Judaism is replete with examples of having to fight the incursions of other religions. We need only remember the golden calf: This is your G-d, O Israel, who took you out of Egypt! Together with all the great commentators, we wonder how the Jews who had just received the Ten Commandments at Sinai could have fallen for that one. Later on, we have the famous contests organized by Elijah between the Baal of Canaan and G-d as understood in Jewish tradition; these are followed by many examples of the prophets denouncing Jewish involvement in other religions.

Certainly no Israelite of ancient times intended to offend G-d by having a comforting little amulet of a goddess in her home, or participating in a seasonal ritual of a Canaanite god. But all such practices were consistently weeded out, as much as possible, by those clear-sighted leaders of biblical times whom scholars call the Yahwists (and sometimes refer to, less objectively, as the zealous fanatics). These prophets and

---

[1] For readers familiar with studies in comparative religion, I am referring to what are known as archetypes—a word one finds used, with different nuances, in the work of psychologist Carl Jung, comparativist Joseph Campbell (whose thought largely follows Jung) and historian of religions Mircea Eliade. Whether one regards archetypes as part of the psychological collective unconscious, as does Jung, or as transcendental in their referent, like Eliade, they remain common structures in all thought. Examples: associations of the moon with the feminine, sun with the masculine; themes of death and rebirth; rituals of immersion in water, rituals of sacrifice; stories of the hero who conquers a monster and wins the princess.

sages recognized how easily alien practices diluted the reality of the historic Jewish experience of G-d: the G-d who transcended nature. Other religions tended to return the mind to the easier, more comfortable affirmation of god in nature, god in the forces around us. Judaism affirmed a G-d who was beyond all this, beyond all of reality as we know it.

Today, even the most innocuous-sounding statements about religion can lead in the same direction, toward a kind of nature-religion and away from the distinctive impulses of Jewish thought. We can see this, for example, in the work of Joseph Campbell, the well-known popularizer of comparative religion whose interviews with Bill Moyers on PBS attracted thousands of viewers. Campbell promoted the view that the many religions are similar paths to the same goal (except for Judaism!—his anti-Semitic views were well known to his acquaintances). He emphasized the personal spiritual quest over the communal dimension of religion, thus tuning his ideas to American individualism. At the same time he presented his views, ambitiously enough, as a foretaste of the planetary religion of the future.

But what was the goal of this religion? Not G-d in our sense—or what he disparagingly called the supernatural—but rather oneness with all life, the universal will in nature. This is a form of the same essentially pagan approach that Judaism has always challenged—the affirmation that nature is the ultimate. It is really an affirmation that I am the ultimate (hence, "Follow your bliss" was Campbell's motto), and a refusal to recognize G-d's transcendence over all the created world.

Our tradition, in short, is right to be suspicious of comparative religion. There are many genuinely spiritual dangers lurking down those attractive paths. It is true that one can find similarities among religions, but there are quite obvious reasons for that. All religions, even those which are based on a divine revelation, have some elements that are humanly constructed (in Judaism, an outstanding example is the prayer book). Since all human minds have certain patterns of imagery and understanding, we will find similar structures. Even in the category of what religious people regard as direct revelations, G-d certainly intended them for human minds, so one might find similarities even there.

For me, the examples of similarity became less and less important, because it became increasingly clear that Judaism's own strengths were so great, intellectually, communally, and in the daily life of observance, that there was virtually nothing to compete with it. The issue was not occasional striking parallels, or structural similarities between religions, but the comprehensive way in which these were interpreted, the coherent view of the world that had evolved, and most of all the effects on one's life.

I recall hearing a rabbi at a lecture, responding to a young man in the audience who had taken the opportunity of the question period to detail his wondrous mystical experiences. He asked if the rabbi would consider them authentic. The rabbi asked simply: have these brought you to do more mitzvot? Have they brought you to lead a better life? For me, the same was true of my ventures into comparative religion. If they helped me to deepen my belief in the wonder's of G-d's universe, or to have greater purpose in my performance of mitzvot, then they were fruitful. Otherwise, they were of academic interest only.

But, I am often asked, hasn't comparative religion undermined belief in the Divine revelation of Torah? As I mentioned above, all religions have some human elements. But the tendency of scholarship since the Enlightenment is to regard all of religion as humanly invented; in other words, to regard Divine revelation as impossible—or at least impossible to discover by rational means.

For a long time this assumption prevented me from appreciating even the written Torah itself. After all, I had been receiving strong doses of biblical criticism since I took my first course in Old Testament, as it was called, when I was sixteen-years-old. For years I had to struggle just to read the text of the Pentateuch straight, let alone understand what Rashi or the Midrash were trying to communicate. Gradually I began to realize that my difficulties were related to the fact that I had been taught that there was really no such thing as communication from G-d to human beings. Religious experience was some sort of emotional fluke, and anything that claimed to come from religious experience was really a fake. The guy's followers made it up later.

The main target of this argument in the college courses I had taken was Christianity; and indeed, it has been proven to be true, beyond the shadow of a reasonable doubt, that most of what was attributed to Christianity's founder (who in any case never claimed to be a prophet like Moses) was reconstructed later by the early church. But the assumption that people make things up after the fact and then persuade, delude, or force others to believe them ran through almost all of the scholarship on Western religions.

But, I realized, each case had to be understood on its own terms. I discovered that recent research done on the books of the Bible was finding more historical reliability than scholars had previously thought. As far as revelation was concerned, scholars had been unable to call the Biblical Prophets into question in the same way as they had the New Testament; these men and women we call the *neviim* apparently did receive messages while in an unusual state of consciousness. I knew, too, that parallels are found universally of individuals undergoing unusual experiences and then bringing a message—usually a vision, sometimes a verbal message—to their people. Often the ability, or susceptibility, for such experiences is inherited.

Scholars were claiming that religion was a human invention, but now I realized that scholarship had presented me with its own invented story, one with little believability. The story went something like this: A group of priests and scribes who have inherited powerful positions decide to rewrite all the traditional narratives to favor themselves. They invent laws which keep them in power, and attribute them to ancient authorities. They create (or borrow from other tribes) rituals which keep money coming into their temples. Power is kept in the hands of an elite, and the common people believe because they have no way of questioning what they are taught.

This pseudo-Marxist version of religion is, of course, beyond the pale of credibility. No one would believe a sudden, new rewriting of tradition. It would be as if someone came and told me that, contrary to everything I knew, I was really adopted and belonged to an ancient race from Atlantis. Theories about a small elite holding onto power and forcing others to accept their version of history are equally implausible. In the complex society of ancient Israel, prophets, priests, tribal and national dignitaries, traders, and agriculturalists all coexisted, none of them necessarily common, i.e. ignorant, people. One could say there was a natural system of checks and balances that kept any one group from pulling the wool over the others eyes (indeed, this was true of many traditional societies).

We have our own confirmation of this in the remarkable tradition that all the people heard the revelation at Sinai. This is unique in the history of religions. Often a group makes a claim that its leader is specially endowed, that s/he is enlightened or has contact with the Divine. But in no other case (except Christianity's Pentecost, which is clearly a copy of Judaism's Shavuot) do we have the claim that the whole group received a revelation. In addition, we have stories of the elders receiving part of Moses' prophetic spirit, and of people prophesying in the camp, suggesting that many had additional experiences of revelation. Indeed, in such a situation it was difficult for Moses to hold onto his leadership position—we are told that many people, including even Miriam and Aaron, expressed jealousy of him.

If you were making up a religion, you wouldn't claim that everyone had a revelation. On the contrary, you would try to prove that the privilege was very limited. Otherwise you would be opening yourself to all sorts of challenges, as indeed Moses experienced. The result was that Judaism, while acknowledging the primacy of the revelations to Moses, became a very open religion. Prophets, priests, scribes, and people of various lineages all made their contribution to the biblical dialogue; all had their distinct claims to authority and understanding. Later, with the development of the academies of the sages, Judaism continued to be open to discussion, to different opinions (three Jews, four opinions).

What this meant for my understanding of our written and oral tradition was even more mind-boggling. It became pointless to ask whether a section of the Torah was written by J, E, P, or D. I might as well ask whether Moses was writing with his right or his left hand. Instead, I had to be convinced—and I was becoming convinced—that the tradition as a whole was authentic. After all, even the most divine document could have been distorted if its transmission was controlled by people of evil character.

I recognized that those who wrote down, selected, and copied the books of the Bible had to be committed, as fully as humanly possible, to the faithful transmission of the Divine word. So did the teachers who passed down the oral Torah. I had to believe that each link in the chain was faithful, down to the present day, down to my rabbi and my teachers; that none of them would knowingly deviate from the Word that had come down at Mount Sinai and the teachings that had been passed down for generations after.

A tall order? Yes—but not as difficult as it might seem. I had been learning with men and women of incredible dedication, of personal integrity and devotion such as I had never known before. They were also intelligent, inquiring, critical in their thinking. They told me that they were but midgets standing on the shoulders of giants: the generations that came before. They told me inspiring stories of their fathers and mothers, grandmothers and grandfathers, on back to the great scholars and great *tzaddikim* of earlier times.[2] At the same time, the tradition was not merely a series of eulogies. The stories of even the greatest men and women showed their faults as well as their strengths, and this made them believable. I came to understand that this was an incredibly strong chain of human faithfulness, to one another, to Torah, and to G-d.

I realized that G-d had taught our people, through Torah, how to create human bonds of love and learning, compassion and wisdom, which could in turn sustain faith in G-d and in the Torah. The centrality of those bonds reminded me of the story of Ruth which we read at Shavuot. Ruth was the first convert, symbol of the whole Jewish people at Mount Sinai, the great event when we all accepted G-d, when we all converted. Yet Ruth's story

_____

[2] I am often asked whether there really are *tzaddikim*, people of such a high degree of righteous behavior that they stand out as perfect or nearly so. There are. What is difficult is to find unambiguous statements about who they are. Interestingly, however, those who stand out as great Jewish sages seem to have received fewer personal criticisms (i.e. on moral as distinct from intellectual issues) from opponents than is usually the case in other religious traditions. Even the rabid anti-Semites, who invented many attacks on Jews as a group, seldom found anything to say against the impeccable character of the individuals who were the guardians of tradition—the Rabbi Akivas and Rashis and Maimonides. They were essentially beyond suspicion.

tells of a human bond that cements her to the Jewish people, namely, her relation to Naomi. Ruth tells Naomi: Where you go, I will go; where you die, I will be buried; your people are my people, and your G-d, my G-d. Naomi, her mother-in-law, had been an example of faith, honor, and integrity during all the difficulties they had encountered in Moab. Her character impressed Ruth so much that she said, "This is the way I want to live."

Ruth is not only the first convert; she also shows us the human chain of faithfulness on which our lives depend. It is people of faith, dedication, and good character who guarantee the Torah itself, and connect us through more than thirty centuries to the word of G-d.

As I came to understand the nature of the Jewish people and Jewish tradition, I understood better the nature of Torah itself. Slowly, then, the conflicts between my intellectual training and my Jewish life had begun to resolve themselves. I had peace of mind. I no longer felt brainwashed. I had discovered that Torah ways of thought were deeply connected to a Torah life. Both were not only rich sources of inspiration and challenge, but also an intricate melody that resonates in the mind, finally creating its own space for itself.

Then I began to understand at another level the statement that everything is in Torah: Torah is the space in which everything else comes to be thought. As we all live and breathe in G-d, so we understand our existence in Torah. This does not mean that we must be exclusive, or that there is no room for anything non-Jewish. But everything is filtered through our understanding of the purpose of life, how we and others play our part in G-d's plan for all humankind.

Other religions, then, serve a purpose, and not just the negative one of warning us about idol-worship. They remind us of our common humanity, the world we share on this planet, and the search of all human beings for G-d. We can appreciate the spiritual achievements of non-Jews as well as Jews, just as we can appreciate achievements in art, music, or science. We can acknowledge the moral leadership of a Gandhi, the grace of a Japanese tea ceremony, or the inner discipline taught by a master of meditation. These should inspire us to seek higher levels in our own practice. For Torah outlines

the structure of our practice; but the human side of our religion, the way we respond to G-d, is not just to do the mitzvot in robot-like fashion. We should beautify the mitzvah, as it is said, externally by adding to its aesthetic quality, internally by increasing our level of devotion. In these respects, we can learn from others—as the sages said in *Ethics of the Fathers*, "Who is wise? He who learns from everyone."

We will do this wisely, however, only if we are continually enriching our personal relation to G-d, our Torah learning, and our sense of ourselves as part of a people. The Sages said that G-d, Torah, and Israel are one. These three are the mutually interdependent conditions of our existence. To be fully and vitally alive, we must connect ourselves to these—and each will lead us more deeply into the others. Through prayer, through the study of Halachah and Bible and Talmud, through extending our knowledge of our history and our exemplary leaders, and by becoming more involved in community life, we are inscribing a circle within which we can live consistently, richly, faithfully. Everything significant to life can be encompassed within this circle; nothing we deeply care about, nothing that nourishes us need be left out. We need not fear that we are missing anything out there in the world. As we deepen our practice and our learning, all that we need will come to us, as it is written: "You open your hand and fulfill the desire of every living thing" (Psalm 145).

Reprinted with permission from chabad.org.

Book Review:
Hitler's Justice: The Courts of the Third Reich

By **Rabbi Dr. Yitzchok A. Breitowitz**

Since the end of World War II, many have wondered about the roles of lawyers, judges, and law professors in Hitler's rise to power and the role they continued to play for the duration of the Third Reich. How could persons committed to the rule of law and steeped in fundamental notions of due process and respect for individual dignity become active participants in a regime of lawlessness and unparalleled brutality? In the aftermath of the war, there were a number of attempts made to justify or at least excuse the conduct of the legal profession, the most prominent of which was the work authored by Hubert Schorn, a former County Judge. Schorn argued that: (1) judicial resistance to the arbitrary edicts of the Reich was in fact widespread; (2) judges were "victims" of their legal training which stressed "positivism," a definition of law that was divorced from any moral vision and which must be automatically obeyed and mechanically applied; (3) judges were legitimately fearful of losing not only their jobs but their lives and thus acted under duress; (4) judges retained their position in the honest belief that they would be better than any successors the Nazis would have chosen. Many have noted the inconsistent strands of Schorn's argument (akin to the criminal defendant who asserts both that he didn't commit the crime and that he was forced into doing it through duress) but his work provided virtually every jurist of the Nazi era with a panoply of excuses to choose from. Still others maintain that the Nazi regime was *sui generic*—a temporary aberration that is disconnected from either the German past or its present.

In 1987, Ingo Muller, an official in the Justice Department of Bremen and a former law professor, published a meticulously documented work in German which sought to demolish the widely held Schorn thesis. In *Hitler's Justice*—which became a best-seller in Germany—Muller convincingly argues that the extent of active resistance was dismally small, that many jurists were active collaborators in the worst excesses of the Nazi regime beyond the call of duty or the limits of positivistic thinking, and most shocking of all, many of the offenders successfully reintegrated themselves into the judicial system of West Germany. He also argues that far from being an aberration, Nazi attitudes were rooted in Weimar jurisprudence and to a large extent, survive intact in the law today. Muller's book has now appeared in English, lucidly translated by Deborah Lucas Schneider.

Coming on the heels of German reunification and shortly before the formal reunification of Europe in 1992, it is perhaps not the most auspicious time to reopen the painful old wounds of World War II and the Holocaust, yet Muller's work contains important lessons and as George Santayana reminds us, those who don't learn from history may be condemned to repeat it.

The book is divided into three parts. The first and shortest portion of the book describes the judicial system that existed under the Weimar Republic and demonstrates that, rather than being an aberration, much of the jurisprudence of the Nazi era stemmed directly from authoritarian attitudes prevalent among the educated middle class in Weimar Germany and that were enthusiastically embraced by its jurists and legal scholars.

The longest portion of the book describes the operation of the German legal system from 1933 to the unconditional surrender to the allied powers in 1945. In eighteen well-documented chapters, Muller paints a terrifying portrait of a judicial and administrative system where legal niceties are at least occasionally observed but where decency and justice have ceased to exist—a nightmarish caricature of law without moral value. Legalization of euthanasia and sterilization, the creation of concentration camps, the ruthless crushing of political opposition, the cancerous growth of racist and anti-Semitic laws labeling Jews as civilly—dead are introduced in rapid succession with nary a word of protest from the lawyers and judges who then proceed to apply the laws as routinely as one would apply some technical provision of the Internal Revenue Code. The death penalty was meted out for even trivial offenses if the State (read: judge, read: the Nazi party) regarded the offense as "undermining the security of the state" or the purity of the Aryan race. Thus, Leo Katzenberger was executed for merely maintaining a friendship with a German female tenant (pp. 113-115). Nor was this persecution limited to Jews. Two Greeks, one 19 and the other 20, were shot for removing a pair of discarded shoes from an abandoned bombed-out building (p. 169).

Where the Nazi regime could not obtain its desired results through the official judicial system, it simply created special courts not subject even on paper to the minimal constraints of due process. The most infamous of these was the People's Court specializing in expeditious justice against those who questioned the wisdom of the Fuehrer (even if the "attack" was nothing more than a casual comment made over the dinner table). When all else failed and for some reason an accused was acquitted, the doctrine of preventive detention allowed for his immediate re-arrest by the Gestapo on no legal grounds at all. We read in astonishment that the Gestapo would often arrest a person in the very courtroom in which he had just been acquitted. To the extent this practice elicited protest, the Gestapo was merely requested to wait until the defendant left the room in order not to assault the dignity of the court (pp. 175-176). In a sense, being acquitted was even worse than a conviction; while prison sentences had fixed terms, preventive detention was functionally equivalent to a death sentence following torture. Under the infamous "night and fog" decrees, persons simply vanished without a trace and even their families were not notified (pp. 170-173).

Basic notions of fundamental fairness in the enactment of criminal legislation simply didn't exist. Ex post-facto laws were common; people could be punished for acts that were not even criminal when they were committed. Indeed, people could be punished even for acts that were never made expressly criminal if such acts were "similar" to those that were (doctrine of analogy in criminal law). The state had the right to appeal an acquittal or what it regarded as a lenient sentence, or it could simply forego the appeals route altogether and invoke preventive detention. Contrary to the central idea that conduct proscribed as criminal should be identified with specificity, criminal statutes were often phrased in vague, general terms that could, and often did, apply to virtually anything giving defendants no advance warning that their conduct could be prosecutable. Rules of

evidence (at least on the prosecution side) were nil; defendants were routinely convicted and even sentenced to death through uncorroborated hearsay or guilt by association. (In one case, a defendant was sentenced on the basis of out-of-court growling of a dog (p. 166).) Nor was there any notion of a meaningful right to counsel. Attorneys for the defense were regarded, and regarded themselves, as agents of the state and would have no hesitation to turn against their "client." Nor were these miscarriages of justice limited to the sphere of criminal prosecution. Even routine cases of contract, labor law, the issuance of drivers' licenses, and child custody were permeated with the racist hatreds that were at the core of National Socialist ideology.

Stories of Nazi brutality are of course nothing new. Indeed, one might say that whatever perversions of justice occurred in the operation of the courts pale into insignificance when compared to the lawless brutality of the ghettos and concentration camps. Yet there is a special significance and dimension to vignettes of systemic judicial terror. First, we learn that the brutalistic Nazi regime implemented its "crimes" not through sheer force alone but through a patina of legality; statutes were duly enacted, regulations drafted by competent and often talented legal technicians, judicial opinions were carefully crafted all to explain and justify what would otherwise be nothing more than state-sponsored terrorism. Utilization of at least the rhetoric of the "rule of law"—in spite of Hitler's own personal contempt for the concept and it practitioners—served a vital legitimizing function for the Reich. Legalism lent the Reich's excesses the appearance of respectability and legality, a sense of continuity with the Weimar traditions of the past, a sense of false comfort and security to the citizenry that the reality of barbaric terror was in fact cabined by civilized traditions and orderly procedures which at least externally bore superficial resemblances to comparable institutions in other countries and those that had previously existed in Germany itself. This legitimization could well have been a potent psychological factor in deluding the German people into accepting what was going on. It was also an important first step; had Hitler been unable to operate through the established legal institutions of the country in all likelihood much of his program would have been nipped in the bud. It was only by wresting control of the legal structure that the Third Reich was ultimately able to ignore it. In short, it may be surmised that without the cooperation and cooption of the legal system, and its abrogation of individual rights under the guise of law, none of the later brutalities could ever have been tolerated or accepted. (Moreover, couching political and religious persecution in "laws" and having those laws enforced through judicial proceedings create a sense of bloodless abstraction—where the application of a given statute becomes an exercise in technical skill rather than the imposition of unjust suffering on a human being—and this in turn could be partial explanation why so many judges just did their job without ever considering just what it was they were doing.)

Second, we like to think that civilization, a sophisticated legal system and respect for the rule of law stand as firm bulwarks for the protection of individual liberties against infringement by the state. Yet Muller's book reminds us of the disheartening truth—the fragility of even long-standing legal systems and the fact that not only will they crack under stress but may in fact be enlisted as a potent tool in the legitimization of oppression and the powers of evil. Remember: the Nazis did what they did not by ignoring law but by manipulating it.

Third, the book reminds us that contrary to the self-serving assertions of postwar jurists, the extent of resistance to the Nazi terror on the part of the legal profession was minuscule. While many jurists were removed and executed because they were Jewish and other judges resigned in protest over attacks on their pension rights, Muller claims that only one jurist officially protested Nazi injustices and was forced to take early retirement (pp. 193-197). Nor is it wholly true that jurists were simply "victims" of their "positivistic" orientation to mechanically follow and apply the law. While legal positivism may well have contributed to a psychological detachment from the antisocial consequences of their rulings and in an emotional sense may have made it easier for judges to live with their consciences, their creative and enthusiastic application of Nazi doctrine was closer in many cases to active and coequal collaboration than to passive acquiescence. It is also argued that jurists had no meaningful choice; resisting National Socialism would not only have cost them their careers but their lives as well. It is significant, however, that in the one case of recorded

resistance, that of Kreyssig's early retirement was all that was required and if many more judges had truly protested the tenets of Nazism, one wonders whether Hitler, at least in the early years of the Reich, would have had the effrontery to even dismiss them.

Undoubtedly, Muller paints with a fairly broad brush. Certainly, there were many judges who openly and enthusiastically embraced the racist tenets of National Socialism. Witness the performance of Roland Freisler, the President of the People's Court, whose rantings were so offensive that the Nazis themselves refused to release a film of his proceedings originally made for public relations purposes (p. 150). Others, equally if not more culpable, were rank opportunists willing to jump on any bandwagon to advance their careers (pp. 41-45). Others may indeed have adopted a stance of relative passivity out of sheer fear and yet a final group went around their business in corporate and commercial law with little or no daily involvement in racist/Aryan policies. While members of the legal profession are not all equally culpable, the message that emerges from Muller's book is crystal-clear. Neither the bar nor the judiciary made any organized attempts to oppose *any* aspects of Hitler's regime; the bar and judiciary as bodies heartily endorsed racial exclusionary policies; the number of individual resisters was extremely small. The very best that can be said for the legal profession is that they had no impact in stopping Nazism and in all likelihood, had complicity in its growth. The choice is between impotence and culpability—they were certainly *not* an active force for good.

The question that Muller does not answer, and on which we can only speculate, is whether widespread legal resistance would have made a difference. On one level, of course, the answer may be irrelevant. The duty to oppose evil does not depend on any calculus of success. On another level, I would submit that resistance may very well have been effective. Particularly in the early years of the Reich, the 1935-1936 period when Hitler was still consolidating his power, the legitimization of his decrees by the courts and the legal profession was a crucial element in extending the government's authority. Each small victory, each incursion into personal liberties without protest enabled Nazism to extend its insidious tentacles further. The policy of appeasement in domestic affairs worked as effectively as it later did in the area of foreign policy with the same disastrous results. Perhaps more so than for any other segment of German society, the judiciary's abdication of responsibility was not only a personal moral failure but a catastrophe for the world at large. (Again, however, I speak from hindsight—if anything, this should teach us to be vigilant about our own liberties).

The third part of the book focuses on the aftermath and here, the author presents us with a number of shocking conclusions. Despite the wavering, half-hearted attempts at the de-Nazification that the allied powers sought to impose on post-war Germany, many jurists with strong affiliations to Nazism were reinstated and in many cases promoted. Initial postwar appointments of opponents of the Reich were later rescinded on the grounds of disloyalty to the state while faithful civil servants of the 1933-1945 period were given priority in hiring. To take one extreme example, an S.S. trooper involved in atrocities against the Jews in the Ukraine turns up again 25 years later issuing rulings against Communists and student protestors (p. 217). A former Nazi winds up as head of the Central Office of State Administration for the Prosecution of National Socialist Crimes and served in that capacity for six years (p. 215).

Perhaps even more disturbing than continuity of personnel—which due to the numbers of Germans pledging allegiance to Nazism was essentially an administrative necessity—are the strong undercurrents of hostility found in many judicial decisions against opponents of the Reich; the continuing insistence of the courts that actions taken pursuant to the laws of the Reich were "legal" in accepting the defense of legal necessity; and in the refusal of the Bundestag to this very day to set aside the judicial decisions of the Nazi era, even those of the infamous People's Court. Muller also demonstrates how postwar courts have shown remarkable solicitude and forgiveness for the administrators of Nazi justice while taking an unusually hard-line on other radical groups. Victims received little or nothing through the postwar judicial system while perpetrators continued unscathed through retirement or natural death. Finally, much of the legislation currently on the books embodies racial concepts drawn directly from National Socialist policy with only cosmetic changes.

In short, Muller has presented us with a profoundly troubling book, but an important one—a work that invites pensive reflection on what might have been; a work that reminds us how fragile a legal system is against the powers of darkness; a work that teaches us that civilization, culture, and an ostensible commitment to and tradition of the rule of law are at best frail barriers against the onslaught of tyranny and how moral courage is a rare commodity in any age. He also reminds us that Nazism was not an anomalous virus coming down from outer space but was part and parcel of the German legal culture that preceded 1933 and continues to have echoes that reverberate in 1991, echoes that have not yet been dissipated or erased.

The author has taken well-defined positions on a sharply debated and controversial period of modern history and indeed, as previously noted sometimes overstates his case. He fails to acknowledge, for example, the West German reparations policy nor does he mention East Germany's fairly radical purging of Nazi elements from *its* government. Some of his readings of current West German legislation seem unduly condemnatory, particularly in view of West German's strong rules against Neo-Nazi propaganda and its renewed commitment to human rights. The book preceded such recent conciliatory (although largely symbolic) gestures as the formal apologies by East Germany and Austria for atrocities committed during the Holocaust (though technically these do not involve West Germany). On balance, however, Muller's points are well-documented and worthy of our careful consideration and scrutiny.

Note should also be taken of the very helpful introduction and bibliography authored by Detlev Vagts who, although unidentified in the book, is a Professor of Law at Harvard University and a well-known expert in comparative law. Vagts lays out the precise areas of historical debate, qualifies some of Muller's generalizations, and provides suggestions for further reading.

Reprinted with permission from jlaw.com.

Epilogue

Our course has ended, yet it has just begun. Opening up a window into the complexity of the Holocaust experience means that we discovered questions for which there are no answers, and answers for questions that we have not yet discovered.

Judaism can maintain the reality of G-d while not denying the reality of suffering; life becomes filled with meaning and sensitivity as a result of such tension. As Jews, we live with paradox, but also with hope.

It is fitting, therefore, to end the course with a selection from an inspiring address by the chief rabbi of the United Kingdom, Jonathan Sacks:

All the key words of Judaism—*emunah,* faith; *bitachon,* trust; even the concept of *brit,* of covenant itself— are essentially linked to the idea of linear time . . . .

Until Judaism, God had been seen in nature. With Judaism, for the first time, God is seen as above, or beyond, nature. If God is above nature, then God is not bound by nature. In other words,

God is free. In other words, what is interesting about God and important about Him, is His choice, His will, His creativity. God chooses—*asher bachar bonu mekol ho'amim* etc. etc.—God wills. *Vayomer Elokim yehi*—God said, "Let there be." God creates. *Bereishit bara*. Those are the key things about Judaism and you cannot find them in the universe of myth because choice, creativity, and will are aspects of a Being that is somehow above nature, not determined by natural laws.

It therefore follows that if human beings are *betzelem Elokim*—they share the image and the nature of God—then we too, for the first time, were able to see ourselves as beings with the capacity to choose, to will, and to create. And that remains the single most important responsibility. A failure to understand that what makes us human is that we have will, we have choice, we have creativity. . . . Because human beings are free—therefore we are not condemned to eternal recurrence. We can act differently today from the way we did yesterday—in small ways individually, in very big ways collectively. Because we can change ourselves, we can change the world. …

That is where linear time is born. That is where hope is born and that is the incredible concept, the Jewish drama of redemption.

Now, I just want to give you a "for instance" of the difference that makes, and here it is. If I were to ask you: What is the greatest contribution of the Greeks to literature? What genre? What would you say? Tragedy? Yes. Exactly. That is the unsurpassed achievement of Sophocles, Aeschylus, and the rest. Tragedy. Now tragedy belongs to cyclical time. It takes a very specific view of the world, which is that the world is fated more or less to remain the same. That is called *moyra*. That is called fate. And every belief that we have that we can somehow resist fate is what the Greeks called hubris and is punished by nemesis. All our dreams of changing the world are destined to be shipwrecked on the hard rocks of reality.

What is the Hebrew word for tragedy? There isn't one, actually....

What is the [modern] Hebrew word for tragedy? Exactly! *Tragedia*! They couldn't find a word for it. There is no Jewish word for tragedy because Judaism is the principled rejection of tragedy in the name of hope. And I find this extraordinary, that despite the many tragedies of Jewish history, there is no word. There are words for catastrophe. There's a word like *asson*. There's a word like *churban*. We have even borrowed a word from sacrificial stuff and use the word *shoah*. But not one of those words means what the Greek tragedy is about, namely bad things that happen because of the innate structure of reality which is fundamentally blind and deaf to human hopes and aspirations. There cannot be a Jewish tragedy. You can't write it. It doesn't translate.

In other words, at the heart of linear time is:

Human free will because we can change ourselves, we can change the world.

The very structure of reality. Reality is not blind. It is not indifferent to us. It is that at the very heart of it there is a Presence, a Being, a Thou Who cares, Who wants us to be here, Who assures us that our aspirations are not destined to fail....

So, as a result, the most striking thing Judaism ever taught the world was a concept of time which gave rise to the possibility of hope and thereby gave the West an alternative to Greek culture, namely to tragedy. An alternative to tragedy as the meta-narrative of the human condition....

And that, of course, constitutes the third great belief of Judaism: creation, revelation. This is the belief in redemption....

So you understand that when we are on this journey, it takes a long time but we never have any doubt as to where we should be going because those ideals were already set out in the beginning and we know where we should be going to. However, we know that the Jewish journey, the journey to redemption which we see as the human journey, is a journey that is painfully slow. It is full of digressions, setbacks, and wrong-turnings. And the eternal metaphor for that is the journey of the Israelites through the wilderness that should have taken a few weeks and instead took forty years, and essentially, and this is the crucial fact, took more than one generation. Redemption is the work of many generations.

However, the outcome is never in doubt. Moses knew that the Israelites would eventually get to the Land even though he didn't live to see it. . . .

The essential feature of Jewish life, the first command to Adam and Eve: Have children. The first statement, the only statement, in the whole of Torah as to why God chose Abraham, *ki yedativ lema'an asher yetzaveh et banav ve'et beito acharav veshamru derech Hashem*, so that he will instruct his children and the household after him that they will keep the way of the Lord. Abraham was chosen in order to be a parent. Moses keeps telling you: Be parents. *Veshinantom levanecha*: education is the conversation between the generations. We now understand why. Because Jewish redemption, because Jewish time, is a story and it is a story that takes many generations and therefore, essential to it, is a covenant extended through time in which we hand on our ideals to our children and they to theirs and that is why to be a Jew is to be a link in the chain of generations.

And that is why Judaism is essentially a religion of history, a religion of linear time.

Now the closing chapter of that story is of course *yemot hamashiach*, the Messianic Age. . . .

This is what Paul Johnson says in the beginning of his book on Jewish history, and it is so true and so beautiful and here it is.

> No people has ever insisted more firmly than the Jews that history has a purpose and humanity a destiny. The Jews, therefore, stand right at the centre of the perennial attempt to give human life the dignity of a purpose. . . .
>
> Let me just say this: I love Judaism. I love its courage. I love its boldness. I love its humanity. I love its refusal to bow down to the idols of the age, including the politically correct idols of our age. I love the Jewish vision of redemption; its extraordinary, unique, and still hardly understood ideals of covenantal politics, of a free society in which my liberty respects yours, of the dignity of the human person, of the sanctity of human life. I love the Jewish passion for education and the life of the mind. I love its burning sense of justice which leads us to argue with God Himself, the way Moses and Abraham and Job argued with God. . . .
>
> Above all, I love the way Judaism mediates between universalism and particularism, in which it asks us to be true to ourselves and, at the same time, to be a blessing to others. . . .

Our task, to repeat, is to be true to ourselves and to be a blessing to others, to bring forward the Messianic Age, the narrative of redemption, to do so by the example of our lives and, through our lives, to reduce that dissonance . . . which Judaism is borne between the world that is and the world that we know and God has told us ought to be.

We bring *Moshiach*, we bring redemption, one day at a time, one act at a time, one life at a time, respecting the faiths of others because we are confident in our own, inviting others to join with us in building a world worthy of being a home for the divine presence. I have to tell you that although that is a lofty goal, there is not one of us here in this room, there is not one member of the Jewish world today, that does not have an important and unique task in that process. . . .

Jewish tradition views history as linear, moving in a particular direction. In this view, we *are* heading toward a better world; we are not endlessly doomed to repeat history. When we remember the past, we can change our present and ultimately our future.

As we conclude this course, let us resolve to go *"Beyond* Never Again." We must be certain that genocide will never be permitted to happen again. But we set our goals beyond that. Our world must be brought to its ultimate state, which is a time of peace, a time of joy, and a time of tranquility.

Acknowledgments

The Holocaust is often described as the most documented event in the history of the world. The vast amount of material already published about the Holocaust and range of Holocaust course offerings can make it a daunting task to author a curriculum that offers a unique contribution to the field. I am therefore indebted to all of those who participated in the fashioning of this course. In a sense, my role was not so much to author a course, but to compile a curriculum that included the ideas, wisdom, and insight that have been shared by some of Judaism's most profound thinkers in their search for the meaning of Jewish life in a post-Holocaust age.

The curriculum was enriched by the comments and critiques of the editorial review board; **Rabbi Shmuel Klatzkin**, **Rabbi Shlomo Yaffe**, **Rabbi Chaim Block**, **Rabbi Nochum Schapiro**, and **Rabbi Dovid Eliezrie** all helped to guide the flow and structure of each individual lesson. I especially appreciated the input of **Rabbi Hesh Epstein**, who provided valuable advice about each lesson and insured that the course kept its focus.

A very special thank you is due to my editor, **Dr. Chana Silberstein**, for her assistance in every aspect of the course, both content and presentation. I am grateful for her patience and assistance, and for skillfully illuminating topics that often appeared overwhelmingly complex. I also enjoyed working with the associate editor of JLI, **Rabbi Mordechai Dinerman**, who improved each lesson by providing scholarly analysis and helpful suggestions, and played a critical role in the preparation of the final manuscript as well.

A number of people assisted with the book production. Thanks to **Mrs. Reuvena Leah Grodnitzky** for proofing the text; to **Mrs. Chana Lightstone** for technical and research assistance; to **Nachman Levine** for layout of the book; to **Mr. Shimon Leib Jacobs** for publication; and to **Rabbi Mendel Sirota** for production assistance.

Appreciation is due to the administrative staff. Thanks to **Mrs. Rivka Sternberg**, flagship administrator, who ensures that the many details of the department are well-coordinated, and who spearheaded the initiative to contact over one hundred Holocaust centers across the country to encourage collaborative endeavors with local JLI chapters; to **Rabbi Mendel Sirota**, who always goes the extra mile in providing JLI affiliates with exemplary support; to **Mrs. Musie Keselman**, who holds down the "front-lines" with grace and good humor; to **Mrs. Mindy Wallach**, who "manages the connections;" and to **Rabbi Mendel Bell**, who oversees JLI's web presence. Thanks also to the accounting staff: **Mrs. Shaina Basha Mintz**, **Mrs. Nechama Shmotkin**, and **Mrs. Shainy Weinberg**. Together, you make a vast operation appear almost effortless!

The course has been substantially enhanced by the creative efforts of **Rabbi Zalman Moshe Abraham**, director of marketing and public relations, **Rabbi Benny Rapoport**, who created the Powerpoint slides that accompany each lesson, and **Rabbi Levi Teldon**, who created the weekly videos. Special thanks to **Mrs. Chana Lightstone** for her assistance in multi-media production.

Various scholars at the **Holocaust Museum** in Washington, D.C. and at **Yad Vashem** in Israel gave generously of their time and scholarship to clarify issues of a historical and factual nature. Any errors that remain are the sole responsibility of the author.

Special thanks to **Chabad.org,** an invaluable online resource of Jewish learning and information, for providing many of the articles for our additional readings.

Course instructors may notice that a particular comment or suggestion that they provided via the JLI Instructors Message Board (when the course ran originally in 2005) has been incorporated in the newly revised edition. As a result of space constraints, I will refrain from individually naming the contributions of individual instructors. Please know that this is not meant to diminish my appreciation for their input and involvement.

Deep gratitude is due to **Rabbi Efraim S. Mintz**, JLI director, who had the vision and dedication to personally shepherd this course from its conception, and succeeded in bringing it to fruition.

Thanks are especially due to our chairman, vice chairman of Merkos L'Inyonei Chinuch—Lubavitch World Headquarters, **Rabbi Moshe Kotlarsky**, as well as to our primary benefactors, **George** and **Pamela Rohr**, who are dedicated to JLI and its mission of providing quality adult education to all.

Finally, I would like to dedicate this course to the Lubavitcher Rebbe, who responded to the darkness of the post-Holocaust era by spreading the light of Torah throughout the world, restoring faith in the power of our individual actions to create a home for the Divine within our world and within our souls.

Rabbi Aaron Herman
Course author

Cary, North Carolina
Nissan 1, 5770

The **Rohr Jewish Learning Institute**

An affiliate of
Merkos L'Inyonei Chinuch
The Educational Arm of
The Chabad Lubavitch Movement
822 Eastern Parkway, Brooklyn, NY 11213

Rohr JLI Affiliates

Share the **Rohr JLI** experience with friends and relatives worldwide

ALABAMA
BIRMINGHAM
Rabbi Yossi Friedman
205.970.0100

ARIZONA
CHANDLER
Rabbi Mendel Deitsch
480.855.4333

FLAGSTAFF
Rabbi Dovie Shapiro
928.255.5756

GLENDALE
Rabbi Sholom Lew
602.375.2422

PHOENIX
Rabbi Zalman Levertov
Rabbi Yossi Friedman
602.944.2753

SCOTTSDALE
Rabbi Yossi Levertov
Rabbi Yossi Bryski
480.998.1410

ARKANSAS
LITTLE ROCK
Rabbi Pinchus Ciment
501.217.0053

CALIFORNIA
AGOURA HILLS
Rabbi Moshe Bryski
Rabbi Yisroel Levin
Rabbi Shlomo Bistritzky
818.991.0991

BAKERSFIELD
Rabbi Shmuel Schlanger
661.835.8381

BEL AIR
Rabbi Chaim Mentz
310.475.5311

BRENTWOOD
Rabbi Boruch Hecht
Rabbi Mordechai Zaetz
310.826.4453

BURBANK
Rabbi Shmuly Kornfeld
818.954.0070

CALABASAS
Rabbi Eliyahu Friedman
818.585.1888

CARLSBAD
Rabbi Yeruchem Eilfort
Rabbi Michoel Shapiro
760.943.8891

CENTURY CITY
Rabbi Tzemach Cunin
310.859.6060

CHATSWORTH
Rabbi Yossi Spritzer
818.718.0777

GLENDALE
Rabbi Simcha Backman
818.240.2750

HUNTINGTON BEACH
Rabbi Aron Berkowitz
714.846.2285

IRVINE
Rabbi Alter Tenenbaum
Rabbi Elly Andrusier
949.786.5000

LAGUNA BEACH
Rabbi Elimelech Gurevitch
949.499.0770

LOMITA
Rabbi Eli Hecht
Rabbi Sholom Pinson
310.326.8234

LONG BEACH
Rabbi Abba Perelmuter
562.621.9828

LOS FELIZ
Rabbi Leibel Korf
323.660.5177

MALIBU
Rabbi Levi Cunin
310.456.6588

MARINA DEL REY
Rabbi Danny Yiftach
Rabbi Mendy Avtzon
310.859.0770

MILL VALLEY
Rabbi Hillel Scop
415.381.3794

MISSION VIEJO
Rabbi Zalman Aron Kantor
949.770.1270

MONTEREY
Rabbi Dovid Holtzberg
831.643.2770

MT. OLYMPUS
Rabbi Sholom Ber Rodal
323.650.1444

NEWHALL
Rabbi Elchonon Marosov
661.254.3434

NEWPORT BEACH
Rabbi Reuven Mintz
949.721.9800

NORTH HOLLYWOOD
Rabbi Nachman Abend
818.989.9539

NORTHRIDGE
Rabbi Eli Rivkin
818.368.3937

PACIFIC PALISADES
Rabbi Zushe Cunin
310.454.7783

PASADENA
Rabbi Chaim Hanoka
626.564.8820

RANCHO CUCAMONGA
Rabbi Sholom B. Harlig
909.949.4553

RANCHO PALOS VERDES
Rabbi Yitzchok Magalnic
310.544.5544

REDONDO BEACH
Rabbi Dovid Lisbon
310.214.4999

ROSEVILLE
Rabbi Yossi Korik
916.677.9960

SACRAMENTO
Rabbi Mendy Cohen
916.455.1400

S. BARBARA
Rabbi Yosef Loschak
805.683.1544

S. CLEMENTE
Rabbi Menachem M. Slavin
949.489.0723

S. CRUZ
Rabbi Yochanan Friedman
831.454.0101

S. DIEGO
Rabbi Motte Fradkin
858.547.0076

S. FRANCISCO
Rabbi Peretz Mochkin
415.571.8770

S. MONICA
Rabbi Boruch Rabinowitz
310.394.5699

S. RAFAEL
Rabbi Yisrael Rice
415.492.1666

S. ROSA
Rabbi Mendel Wolvovsky
707.577.0277

SIMI VALLEY
Rabbi Nosson Gurary
805.577.0573

STOCKTON
Rabbi Avremel Brod
209.952.2081

STUDIO CITY
Rabbi Yossi Baitelman
818.508.6633

TEMECULA
Rabbi Yitzchok Hurwitz
951.303.9576

THOUSAND OAKS
Rabbi Chaim Bryski
805.493.7776

TUSTIN
Rabbi Yehoshua Eliezrie
714.508.2150

VENTURA
Rabbi Yakov Latowicz
Mrs. Sarah Latowicz
805.658.7441

WEST HILLS
Rabbi Avrahom Yitzchak Rabin
818.337.4544

YORBA LINDA
Rabbi Dovid Eliezrie
714.693.0770

COLORADO
ASPEN
Rabbi Mendel Mintz
970.544.3770

BOULDER
Rabbi Pesach Scheiner
303.494.1638

COLORADO SPRINGS
Rabbi Moshe Liberow
719.634.2345

DENVER
Rabbi Yossi Serebryanski
303.744.9699

HIGHLANDS RANCH
Rabbi Avraham Mintz
303.694.9119

LONGMONT
Rabbi Yaakov Dovid Borenstein
303.678.7595

VAIL
Rabbi Dovid Mintz
970.476.7887

WESTMINSTER
Rabbi Benjy Brackman
303.429.5177

CONNECTICUT
BRANFORD
Rabbi Yossi Yaffe
203.488.2263

GLASTONBURY
Rabbi Yosef Wolvovsky
860.659.2422

GREENWICH
Rabbi Yossi Deren
Rabbi Menachem Feldman
203.629.9059

LITCHFIELD
Rabbi Yoseph Eisenbach
860.567.3609

NEW LONDON
Rabbi Avrohom Sternberg
860.437.8000

ORANGE
Rabbi Sheya Hecht
Rabbi Adam Haston
203.795.5261

RIDGEFIELD
Rabbi Sholom Y. Deitsch
203.748.4421

SIMSBURY
Rabbi Mendel Samuels
860.658.4903

STAMFORD
Rabbi Yisrael Deren
Rabbi Levi Mendelow
203.3.CHABAD

WESTPORT
Rabbi Yehuda L. Kantor
Mrs. Dina Kantor
203.226.8584

WEST HARTFORD
Rabbi Yosef Gopin
Rabbi Shaya Gopin
860.659.2422

DELAWARE
WILMINGTON
Rabbi Chuni Vogel
302.529.9900

FLORIDA
AVENTURA
Rabbi Laivi Forta
305.933.0770

BAL HARBOUR
Rabbi Mendy Levy
305.868.1411

BOCA RATON
Rabbi Moishe Denberg
Rabbi Zalman Bukiet
561.417.7797

EAST BOCA RATON
Rabbi Ruvi New
561.417.7797

BOYNTON BEACH
Rabbi Yosef Yitzchok Raichik
561.732.4633

BRADENTON
Rabbi Menachem Bukiet
941.388.9656

BRANDON
Rabbi Mendel Rubashkin
813.657.9393

COCONUT CREEK
Rabbi Yossi Gansburg
954.422.1987

CORAL GABLES
Rabbi Avrohom Stolik
305.490.7572

DEERFIELD BEACH
Rabbi Yossi Goldblatt
954.422.1735

DELRAY BEACH
Rabbi Sholom Ber Korf
561.496.6228

FORT LAUDERDALE
Rabbi Yitzchok Naparstek
954.568.1190

FORT MYERS
Rabbi Yitzchok Minkowicz
Mrs. Nechama Minkowicz
239.433.7708

HOLLYWOOD
Rabbi Leizer Barash
954.965.9933

Rabbi Zalman Korf
Rabbi Yakov Garfinkel
954.374.8370

KENDALL
Rabbi Yossi Harlig
305.234.5654

KEY BISCAYNE
Rabbi Yoel Caroline
305.365.6744

KEY WEST
Rabbi Yaakov Zucker
305.295.0013

MIAMI BEACH
Rabbi Zev Katz
305.672.6613

Rabbi Aron Rabin
Rabbi Mendy Halberstam
305.535.0094

NAPLES
Rabbi Fishel Zaklos
239.262.4474

NORTH MIAMI BEACH
Rabbi Moishe Kievman
305.770.1919

ORLANDO
Rabbi Yosef Konikov
407.354.3660

PALM BEACH GARDENS
Rabbi Dovid Vigler
561.215.0404

PARKLAND
Rabbi Mendy Gutnik
954.796.7330

PINELLAS COUNTY
Rabbi Shalom Adler
727.789.0408

S. PETERSBURG
Rabbi Alter Korf
727.344.4900

SARASOTA
Rabbi Chaim Shaul Steinmetz
941.925.0770

SOUTH PALM BEACH
Rabbi Leibel Stolik
561.889.3499

SUNNY ISLES BEACH
Rabbi Alexander Kaller
CLASSES IN RUSSIAN
305.803.5315

TALLAHASSEE
Rabbi Schneur Zalmen Oirechman
850.523.9294

VENICE
Rabbi Sholom Ber Schmerling
941.493.2770

WALNUT CREEK
Rabbi Zalman Korf
954.374.8370

WESTON
Rabbi Yisroel Spalter
954.349.6565

West Palm Beach
Rabbi Yoel Gancz
561.659.7770

GEORGIA
Alpharetta
Rabbi Hirshy Minkowicz
770.410.9000

Atlanta
Rabbi Yossi New
Rabbi Isser New
404.843.2464

Atlanta: Intown
Rabbi Eliyahu Schusterman
Rabbi Ari Sollish
404.898.0434

Gwinnett
Rabbi Yossi Lerman
678.595.0196

Marietta
Rabbi Ephraim Silverman
Rabbi Zalman Charytan
770.565.4412

IDAHO
Boise
Rabbi Mendel Lifshitz
208.853.9200

ILLINOIS
Chicago
Rabbi Meir Hecht
312.714.4655

Gurnee
Rabbi Sholom Ber Tenenbaum
847.782.1800

Glenview
Rabbi Yishaya Benjaminson
847.998.9896

Highland Park
Mrs. Michla Schanowitz
847.266.0770

Naperville
Rabbi Mendy Goldstein
630.778.9770

Northbrook
Rabbi Meir Moscowitz
847.564.8770

Peoria
Rabbi Eli Langsam
309.692.2250

Skokie
Rabbi Yochanan Posner
847.677.1770

Wilmette
Rabbi Dovid Flinkenstein
847.251.7707

INDIANA
Indianapolis
Rabbi Mendel Schusterman
317.251.5573

KANSAS
Overland Park
Rabbi Mendy Wineberg
913.649.4852

LOUISIANA
Metairie
Rabbi Yossi Nemes
504.454.2910

MARYLAND
Bethesda
Rabbi Bentzion Geisinsky
Rabbi Sender Geisinsky
301.913.9777

Baltimore
Rabbi Elchonon Lisbon
410.358.4787

Rabbi Velvel Belinsky
Classes in Russian
410.764.5000

Columbia
Rabbi Hillel Baron
410.740.2424

Gaithersburg
Rabbi Sholom Raichik
301.926.3632

Potomac
Rabbi Mendel Bluming
301.983.4200

Silver Spring
Rabbi Berel Wolvovsky
301.593.1117

MASSACHUSETTS
Hyannis
Rabbi Yekusiel Alperowitz
508.775.2324

Longmeadow
Rabbi Yakov Wolff
413.567.8665

Natick
Rabbi Levi Fogelman
508.650.1499

Sharon
Rabbi Chaim Wolosow
Rabbi Ilan Meyers
781.784.4269

Sudbury
Rabbi Yisroel Freeman
978.443.3691

Swampscott
Mrs. Layah Lipsker
781.581.3833

MICHIGAN
Ann Arbor
Rabbi Aharon Goldstein
734.995.3276

Novi
Rabbi Avrohom Susskind
248.790.6075

West Bloomfield
Rabbi Kasriel Shemtov
248.788.4000

Rabbi Elimelech Silberberg
Rabbi Avrohom Wineberg
248.855.6170

MINNESOTA
Minnetonka
Rabbi Mordechai Grossbaum
952.929.9922

Rochester
Rabbi Dovid Greene
507.288.7500

MISSOURI
S. Louis
Rabbi Yosef Landa
314.725.0400

MONTANA
Bozeman
Rabbi Chaim Shaul Bruk
406.585.8770

NEBRASKA
Omaha
Rabbi Mendel Katzman
402.330.1800

NEVADA
Henderson
Rabbi Mendy Harlig
Rabbi Tzvi Bronstein
702.617.0770

Summerlin
Rabbi Yisroel Schanowitz
Rabbi Tzvi Bronstein
702.855.0770

NEW JERSEY
Basking Ridge
Rabbi Mendy Herson
908.604.8844

Cherry Hill
Rabbi Mendy Mangel
856.874.1500

Clinton
Rabbi Eli Kornfeld
908.623.7000

Fort Lee
Rabbi Meir Konikov
201.886.1238

Franklin Lakes
Rabbi Chanoch Kaplan
201.848.0449

Hillsborough
Rabbi Shmaya Krinsky
908.874.0444

Hoboken
Rabbi Moshe Shapiro
201.386.5222

MADISON
Rabbi Shalom Lubin
973.377.0707

MANALAPAN
Rabbi Boruch Chazanow
732.972.3687

MEDFORD
Rabbi Yitzchok Kahan
609.953.3150

Mountain Lakes
Rabbi Levi Dubinsky
973.551.1898

NORTH BRUNSWICK
Rabbi Levi Azimov
732.398.9492

RANDOLPH
Rabbi Avraham Bechor
973.895.3070

ROCKAWAY
Rabbi Asher Herson
Rabbi Mordechai Baumgarten
973.625.1525

TEANECK
Rabbi Ephraim Simon
201.907.0686

TENAFLY
Rabbi Mordechai Shain
Rabbi Yitzchak Gershovitz
201.871.1152

TOMS RIVER
Rabbi Moshe Gourarie
732.349.4199

WAYNE
Rabbi Michel Gurkov
973.694.6274

WEST ORANGE
Rabbi Efraim Mintz
Rabbi Mendy Kasowitz
973.731.0770

WOODCLIFF LAKE
Rabbi Dov Drizin
201.476.0157

NEW MEXICO
S. FE
Rabbi Berel Levertov
505.983.2000

NEW YORK
ALBANY
Rabbi Yossi Rubin
518.482.5781

BEDFORD
Rabbi Arik Wolf
914.666.6065

BINGHAMTON
Mrs. Rivkah Slonim
607.797.0015

BRIGHTON BEACH
Rabbi Zushe Winner
Rabbi Avrohom Winner
718.946.9833

CEDARHURST
Rabbi Shneur Zalman Wolowik
516.295.2478

DIX HILLS
Rabbi Yaakov Saacks
631.351.8672

DOBBS FERRY
Rabbi Benjy Silverman
914.693.6100

EAST HAMPTON
Rabbi Leibel Baumgarten
631.329.5800

FOREST HILLS
Rabbi Eli Blokh
Rabbi Yossi Mendelson
718.459.8432 ext.17

GREAT NECK
Rabbi Yoseph Geisinsky
516.487.4554

ITHACA
Rabbi Eli Silberstein
607.257.7379

KINGSTON
Rabbi Yitzchok Hecht
845.334.9044

LARCHMONT
Rabbi Mendel Silberstein
914.834.4321

NYC GRAMERCY PARK
Rabbi Naftali Rotenstreich
212.924.3200

NYC KEHILATH JESHURUN
Rabbi Elie Weinstock
212.774.5636

OSSINING
Rabbi Dovid Labkowski
914.923.2522

PORT WASHINGTON
Rabbi Shalom Paltiel
516.767.8672

RIVERDALE
Rabbi Levi Shemtov
718.549.1100

ROCHESTER
Rabbi Nechemia Vogel
585.271.0330

ROSLYN
Rabbi Yaakov Reiter
516.484.8185

SEA GATE
Rabbi Chaim Brikman
Mrs. Rivka Brikman
718.266.1736

STATEN ISLAND
Rabbi Moshe Katzman
Rabbi Shmuel Bendet
718.370.8953

STONY BROOK
Rabbi Shalom Ber Cohen
631.585.0521

SUFFERN
Rabbi Isaac Lefkowitz
Rabbi Shmuel Gancz
845.368.1889

WOODBURY
Rabbi Shmuel Lipszyc
516.682.0404

NORTH CAROLINA
ASHEVILLE
Rabbi Shaya Susskind
828.505.0746

CHARLOTTE
Rabbi Yossi Groner
Rabbi Shlomo Cohen
704.366.3984

RALEIGH
Rabbi Aaron Herman
919.637.6950

Rabbi Pinchas Herman
Rabbi Sholom Ber Estrin
919.847.8986

OHIO
BEACHWOOD
Rabbi Yossi Marosov
216.381.4736

BLUE ASH
Rabbi Yisroel Mangel
513.793.5200

COLUMBUS
Rabbi Areyah Kaltmann
Rabbi Levi Andrusier
614.294.3296

DAYTON
Rabbi Nochum Mangel
Rabbi Dr. Shmuel Klatzkin
937.643.0770

TOLEDO
Rabbi Yossi Shemtov
419.843.9393

OKLAHOMA
OKLAHOMA CITY
Rabbi Ovadia Goldman
405.524.4800

TULSA
Rabbi Yehuda Weg
918.492.4499

OREGON
PORTLAND
Rabbi Moshe Wilhelm
Rabbi Mordechai Wilhelm
503.977.9947

PENNSYLVANIA
AMBLER
Rabbi Shaya Deitsch
215.591.9310

BALA CYNWYD
Rabbi Shraga Sherman
610.660.9192

CLARKS SUMMIT
Rabbi Benny Rapoport
570.587.3300

DEVON
Rabbi Yossi Kaplan
610.971.9977

DOYLESTOWN
Rabbi Mendel Prus
215.340.1303

Newtown
Rabbi Aryeh Weinstein
215.497.9925

Philadelphia: Center City
Rabbi Yochonon Goldman
215.238.2100

Pittsburgh
Rabbi Yisroel Altein
412.422.7300 ext. 269

Pittsburgh: South Hills
Rabbi Mendy Rosenblum
412.278.3693

Reading
Rabbi Yosef Lipsker
610.921.2805

Rydal
Rabbi Zushe Gurevitz
215.572.1511

SOUTH CAROLINA
Columbia
Rabbi Hesh Epstein
803.782.1831

TENNESSEE
Bellevue
Rabbi Yitzchok Tiechtel
615.646.5750

Chattanooga
Rabbi Shaul Perlstein
423.490.1106

Memphis
Rabbi Levi Klein
901.766.1800

Knoxville
Rabbi Yossi Wilhelm
865.588.8584

TEXAS
Houston
Rabbi Moishe Traxler
713.774.0300

Houston: Rice University Area
Rabbi Eliezer Lazaroff
Rabbi Yitzchok Schmukler
713.522.2004

Plano
Rabbi Mendel Block
Rabbi Yehudah Horowitz
972.596.8270

S. Antonio
Rabbi Chaim Block
Rabbi Yossi Marrus
210.492.1085

UTAH
Salt Lake City
Rabbi Benny Zippel
801.467.7777

VERMONT
Burlington
Rabbi Yitzchok Raskin
802.658.5770

VIRGINIA
Alexandria/Arlington
Rabbi Mordechai Newman
703.370.2774

Fairfax
Rabbi Leibel Fajnland
703.426.1980

Norfolk
Rabbi Aaron Margolin
Rabbi Levi Brashevitzky
757.616.0770

Richmond
Rabbi Dr. Shlomo Pereira
804.740.2000

Tysons Corner
Rabbi Levi Deitsch
Rabbi Chezzy Deitsch
703.356.3451

WASHINGTON
Bellevue
Rabbi Mordechai Farkash
Rabbi Sholom Elishevitz
425.957.7860

Olympia
Rabbi Cheski Edelman
360.584-4306

Seattle
Rabbi Elazar Bogomilsky
206.527.1411

Spokane County
Rabbi Yisroel Hahn
509.443.0770

WISCONSIN
Mequon
Rabbi Menachem Rapoport
262.242.2235

Milwaukee
Rabbi Mendel Shmotkin
414.961.6100

PUERTO RICO
Carolina
Rabbi Mendel Zarchi
787.253.0894

ARGENTINA
Buenos Aires
Rabbi Hirshel Hendel
5411 4807 7073

AUSTRALIA
Brisbane
Rabbi Chanoch Sufrin
617.3843.6770

Melbourne
Rabbi Schneier Lange
613.9522.8222

Rabbi Shimshon Yurkowicz
613.9822.3600

Sydney
Bondi
Rabbi Pinchas Feldman
612.9387.3822

Double Bay
Rabbi Yanky Berger
612.9327.1644

Dover Heights
Rabbi Benzion Milecki
612.9337.6775

North Shore
Rabbi Nochum Schapiro
Mrs. Fruma Schapiro
Rabbi Shmuly Kopel
612.9488.9548

AUSTRIA
Vienna
Rabbi Shaya Boas
431.369.1818 ext. 123

BELGIUM
Antwerp
Rabbi Mendy Gurary
32.3.239.6212

BRAZIL
Rio de Janeiro
Rabbi Yehoshua Goldman
Rabbi Avraham Steinmetz
21.3543.3770

S. Paulo
Rabbi Avraham Steinmetz
55.11.3081.3081

CANADA
ALBERTA
Calgary
Rabbi Mordechai Groner
403.238.4880

BRITISH COLUMBIA
Richmond
Rabbi Yechiel Baitelman
604.277.6427

Victoria
Rabbi Meir Kaplan
250.595.7656

MANITOBA
WINNIPEG
Rabbi Avrohom Altein
Rabbi Shmuel Altein
204.339.8737

ONTARIO
LONDON
Rabbi Eliezer Gurkow
519.434.3962

NIAGARA FALLS
Rabbi Zalman Zaltzman

OTTAWA
Rabbi Menachem M. Blum
613.823.0866

GREATER TORONTO
REGIONAL OFFICE & THORNHILL
Rabbi Yossi Gansburg
905.731.7000

LAWRENCE/EGLINTON
Rabbi Menachem Gansburg
416.546.8770

MISSISSAUGA
Rabbi Yitzchok Slavin
905.820.4432

RICHMOND HILL
Rabbi Mendel Bernstein
905.770.7700

BJL
Rabbi Leib Chaiken
416.916.7202

YORK UNIVERSITY
Rabbi Vidal Bekerman
416.856.4575

QUEBEC
MONTREAL
Rabbi Ronnie Fine
Rabbi Leibel Fine
514.342.3.JLI

TOWN OF MOUNT ROYAL
Rabbi Moshe Krasnanski
514.739.0770

COLOMBIA
BOGOTA
Rabbi Yehoshua B. Rosenfeld
Rabbi Chanoch Piekarski
571.635.8251

DENMARK
COPENHAGEN
Rabbi Yitzchok Lowenthal
45.3316.1850

GREECE
ATHENS
Rabbi Mendel Hendel
30.210.520.2880

GUATEMALA
GUATEMALA CITY
Rabbi Shalom Pelman
502.2485.0770

NETHERLANDS
DEN HAAG
Rabbi Shmuel Katzman
31.70.347.0222

ROTTERDAM
Rabbi Yehuda Vorst
31.10.466.9481

RUSSIA
MOSCOW
Rabbi Shneor Leider
Rabbi Yanky Klein
749.5783.8479

SINGAPORE
SINGAPORE
Rabbi Mordechai Abergel
656.337.2189

SOUTH AFRICA
CAPE TOWN
Rabbi Mendel Popack
Rabbi Pinchas Hecht
27.21.434.3740

JOHANNESBURG
Rabbi Dovid Masinter
Rabbi Yossi Hecht
Rabbi Dovi Rabin
27.11.440.6600

SWEDEN
STOCKHOLM
Rabbi Chaim Greisman
468.679.7067

SWITZERLAND
LUGANO
Rabbi Yaakov Tzvi Kantor
091.921.3720

UNITED KINGDOM
EDGEWARE
Rabbi Leivi Sudak
Rabbi Yaron Jacobs
44.208.905.4141

LONDON
Rabbi Gershon Overlander
Rabbi Dovid Katz
502.2485.0770

Rabbi Bentzi Sudak
020.8800.0022 ext. 103

LEEDS
Rabbi Eli Pink
44.113.266.3311

URUGUAY
MONTEVIDEO
Rabbi Eliezer Shemtov
5982.709.3444 ext. 109/110

VENEZUELA
CARACAS
Rabbi Yehoshua Rosenblum
58.212.264.7011

NOTES

NOTES

A Time to **Study**

And

A Time to **Act**

BeyondNeverAgain.com

Visit **BeyondNeverAgain.com** and take on a Mitzvah, a good deed of your choice, to perpetuate the memory of a life lost in the Holocaust and to help rebuild the Judaism the Nazis sought to destroy. Your resolution and good deed will add the name of a Holocaust victim to the **Virtual Living Holocaust Memorial** at **www.BeyondNeverAgain.com** and serve as a living, everlasting memorial.

JEWISH LEARNING INSTITUTE

THE JEWISH LEARNING MULTIPLEX

Brought to you by the Rohr Jewish Learning Institute

In fulfillment of the mandate of the Lubavitcher Rebbe, of blessed memory,
whose leadership guides every step of our work,
the mission of the Rohr Jewish Learning Institute is to transform
Jewish life and the greater community through the study of Torah,
connecting each Jew to our shared heritage of Jewish learning.

While our flagship program remains the cornerstone of our organization,
JLI is proud to feature additional divisions catering to specific populations,
in order to meet a wide array of educational needs.

THE ROHR JEWISH LEARNING INSTITUTE
is an affiliate of *Merkos L'Inyonei Chinuch*,
the educational arm of the Chabad-Lubavitch Movement.

Torah Studies provides a rich and nuanced
encounter with the weekly Torah reading.

MyShiur courses are designed to assist students in developing
the skills needed to study Talmud independently.

IN PARTNERSHIP WITH CHABAD ON CAMPUS

This rigorous fellowship program invites select college
students to explore the fundamentals of Judaism.

IN PARTNERSHIP WITH CTEEN: CHABAD TEEN NETWORK

Jewish teens forge their identity as they engage in
Torah study, social interaction, and serious fun.

IN PARTNERSHIP WITH CHABAD ON CAMPUS

The rigor and excellence of JLI courses,
adapted to the campus environment.

TorahCafe.com provides an exclusive selection
of top-rated Jewish educational videos.

This yearly event rejuvenates mind, body, and spirit with
a powerful synthesis of Jewish learning and community.

The Rosh Chodesh Society gathers Jewish women
together once a month for intensive textual study.

Select affiliates are invited to partner with peers and noted
professionals, as leaders of innovation and excellence.

Mission participants delve into our nation's rich past while
exploring the Holy Land's relevance and meaning today.